IMAGES
of America

HANNIBAL

THE OTIS HOWELL COLLECTION

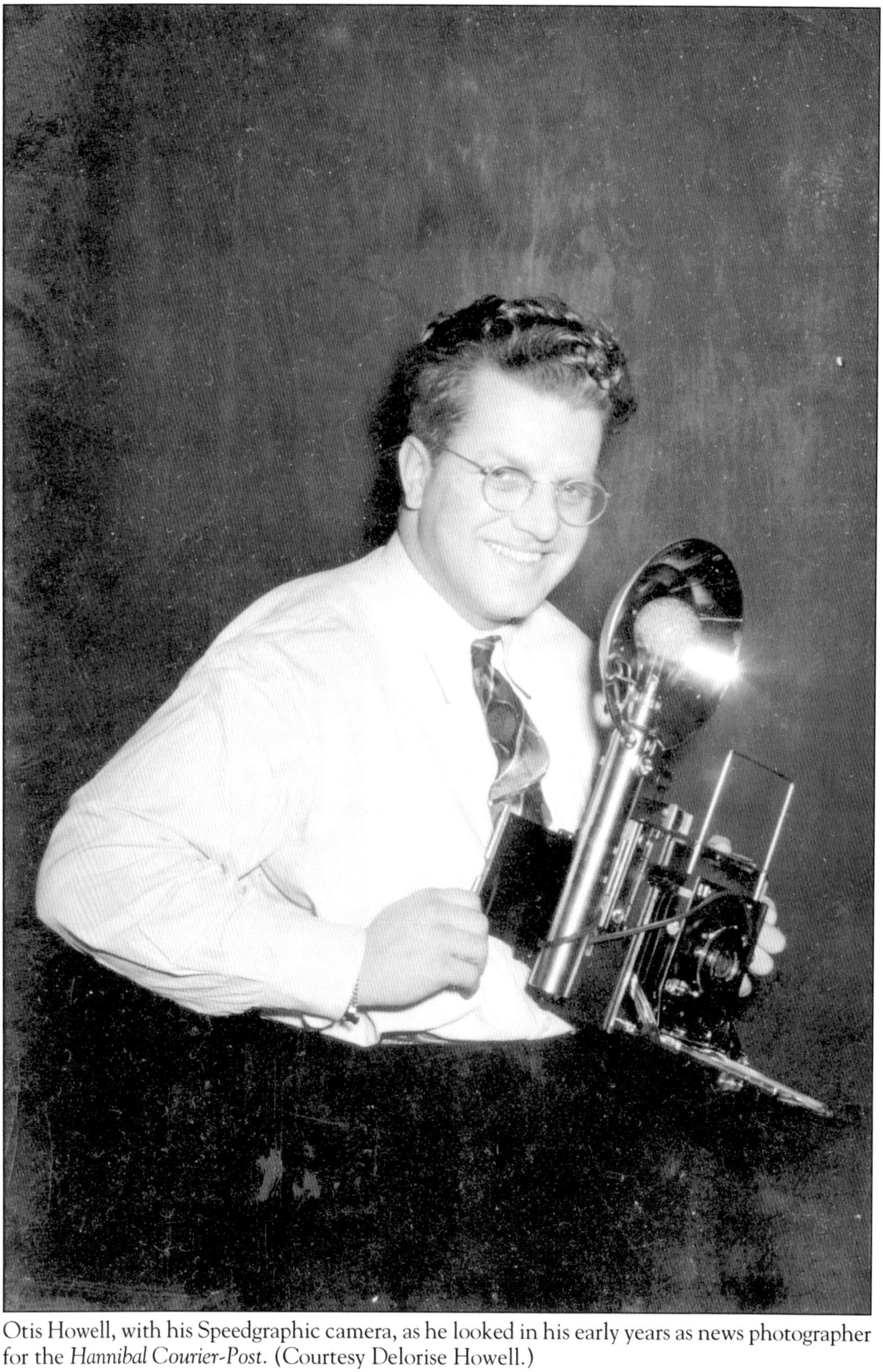

Otis Howell, with his Speedgraphic camera, as he looked in his early years as news photographer for the *Hannibal Courier-Post*. (Courtesy Delorise Howell.)

IMAGES
of America

HANNIBAL
THE OTIS HOWELL COLLECTION

Steve Chou

ARCADIA
PUBLISHING

ISBN 978-0-7385-3242-1

Published by Arcadia Publishing
Charleston, South Carolina

Printed in the United States of America

Library of Congress Catalog Card Number: 2004101207

For all general information contact Arcadia Publishing at:
Telephone 843-853-2070
Fax 843-853-0044
E-mail sales@arcadiapublishing.com
For customer service and orders:
Toll-Free 1-888-313-2665

Visit us on the Internet at www.arcadiapublishing.com

About the cover: View of the west side of the 300 block of North Main Street as it appeared in the early 1950s. Today this is a parking lot.

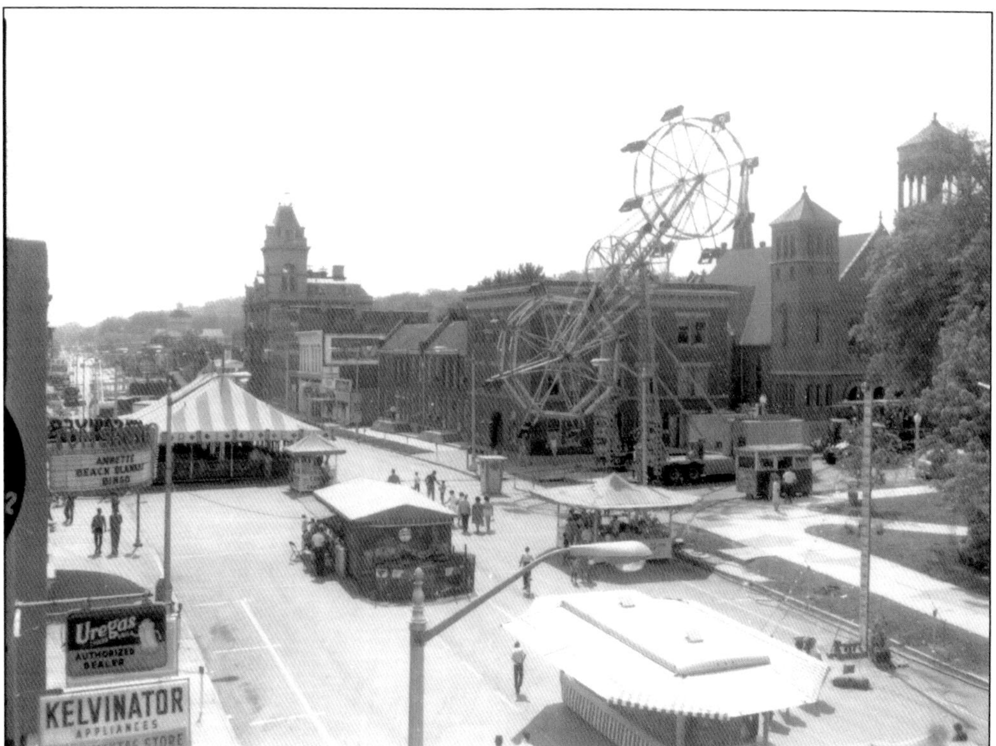

A street carnival is underway in this 1965 photo, which highlights attractions at Broadway at Fifth Street. The towers of Fifth Street Baptist Church, the First Presbyterian Church, and the Federal Building rise in the background. *Beach Blanket Bingo* was showing at the Tom Sawyer Theater.

Contents

ACKNOWLEDGMENTS

I am most grateful to the *Hannibal Courier-Post* for their permission to use these photos, which were taken during Otis Howell's employment as photographer for the paper. To the Hannibal Public Library, as the repository of the Otis Howell negatives, I wish to extend a heartfelt thanks for the part they played in allowing this book to come about. Ann Sundermeyer and her wonderful staff at the library bent over backwards to accomodate this work, allowing me full access to the collection; making many, many trips to have negatives made into prints; and helping to track down needed information. Special thanks to Butch Anderson and Curt Van Winkle at River City Photo for the marvelous work rendered in producing the prints were used in this book. Thanks to those who provided both research and encouragement in this task, including Kathy Threlkeld, Archie Hayden, Jim Mitchell, Martha Adrian, and Roberta Hagood. I wish also to thank Delorise Howell for taking time to reminisce on her late husband, giving me a much better idea of the man behind the pictures celebrated in this volume. And last but not least, a thank you to my proofreader, wife, and encourager (all the same person), Linda Chou.

INTRODUCTION

The year was 1945. War was over and the soldiers were headed home. Among them was a 27-year-old Army medic named Otis Howell who had served in the Pacific Theater of Operations. Arriving back in Hannibal, Missouri, he was immediately hired at the local newspaper, the *Courier-Post*, where he had worked delivering papers before the war. The staff photographer was leaving and a vacancy would be created. Otis had no prior photographic experience save for snapshots taken with a Kodak box camera while in the service.

Thus began a thirty-five-year career in photo journalism. In that time Otis Howell traveled untold thousands of miles with his trusty Speedgraphic, photographing fires, floods, building dedications, demolitions, parades, and graduations throughout the Northeast Missouri area. He was a familiar fixture at high school football games and would often be called in the middle of the night to cover some auto accident or other developing story. Otis rubbed shoulders with all walks and classes of humanity, from the President of the United States to a nine-year-old who had found an early crop of mushrooms.

The man behind the camera was born April 13, 1918 in Frankford, Missouri, the son of Clifton and Dollie (Fisher) Howell. Otis was just nine months old when his father died in the influenza epidemic of 1919. Just before starting school Otis moved to Hannibal with his mother and older sister. Times were tough; Otis left school after the ninth grade in order to help support the family. After Otis returned to Hannibal in 1945, he began courting Delorise Vark, who also worked at the *Courier-Post* as the circulation manager. They were married four years later. The Howells had two daughters, Martha and Mary. Otis retired from the *Courier-Post* in 1980 due to declining health. He passed away on January 24, 1983 just a few months shy of his 65th birthday.

This book is a tribute to a man who preserved a vital slice of local history through the course of his daily occupation, and when wisdom of the day dictated that the vast collection of negatives was needless clutter, he rescued them to be studied and appreciated by future generations. The gift that Otis gave to his beloved town was completed when his widow donated the collection to the Hannibal Public Library.

The collection itself numbers in the tens of thousands of negatives, spanning much of Otis Howell's career with the *Courier-Post*. I have spent more than a year studying these negatives, selecting the material for this book, and cross-referencing pictures with the newspaper editions in which they first appeared. I have sought to give a glimpse of the life and times of Hannibal, Missouri during the years of 1947 to 1967. This book has a lot of streetscape changes, building demolitions, remodelings, and new construction. There are photos of many of the events and happenings, and candid shots of Hannibal at work and at play.

For the person who grew up in Hannibal at that time, this book should bring back many fond memories. For the others, this will give a feel for Hannibal and small-town Midwestern America as a whole during those exciting postwar years.

Those who remember Otis Howell recall a man who was hard-working and dedicated to his profession. He was a man who truly loved what he did. Despite no formal training in photography, Otis became quite proficient at his trade, even winning professional awards for his work. A person of his talent and enthusiasm could have prospered by seeking more prestigious positions with larger papers in larger cities. That he chose not to has made Hannibal a richer community.

Steve Chou
November 2003

One

From VJ to Korea
1947–1953

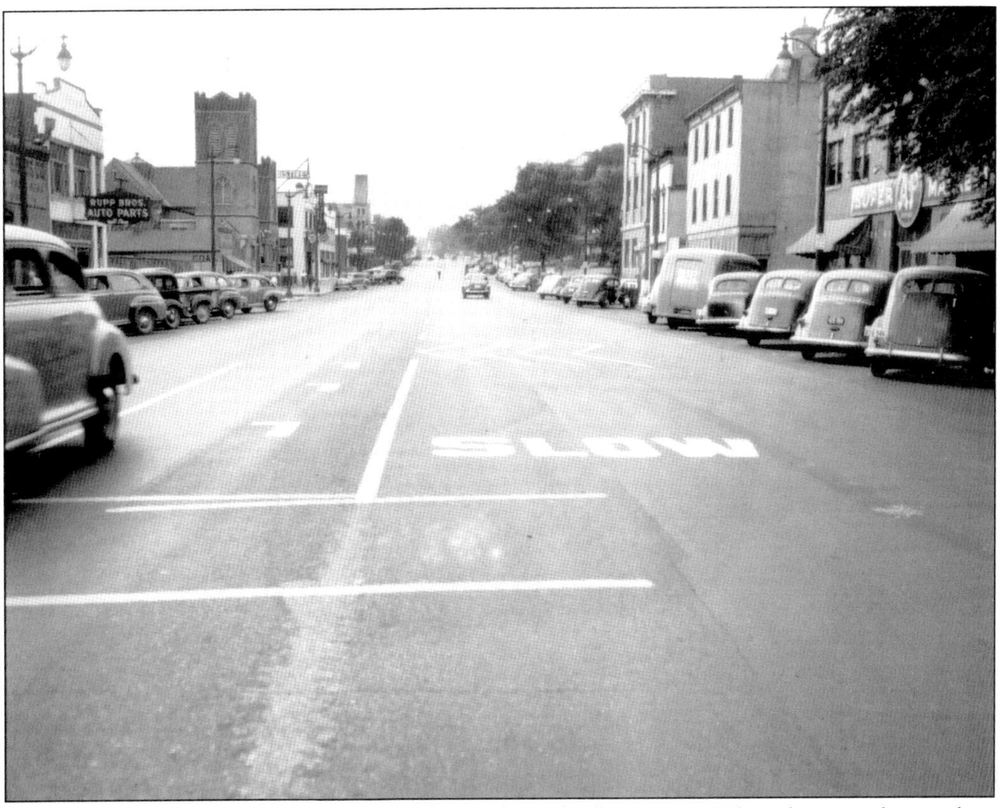

This is a view from the 700 block of Broadway looking west. The photograph is taken from the middle of the street, with the A&P partly visible at right, Kansteiner Hardware in the next block, and then the telephone building. On left is Rupp Bros. Auto Parts, then Conlon Lumber & Coal Co. Just beyond is First Methodist Church. This photo dates from mid-1947.

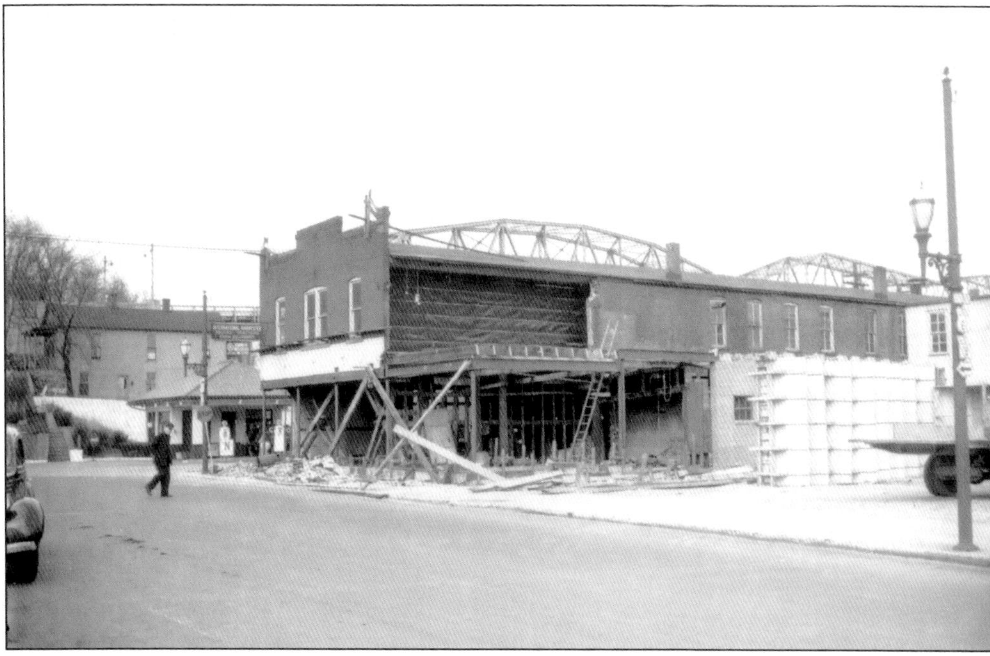

The building at 422 North Main was undergoing a remodeling and expansion in February 1947 when this photo was taken. As of 2004, Murphy Motors occupies this structure.

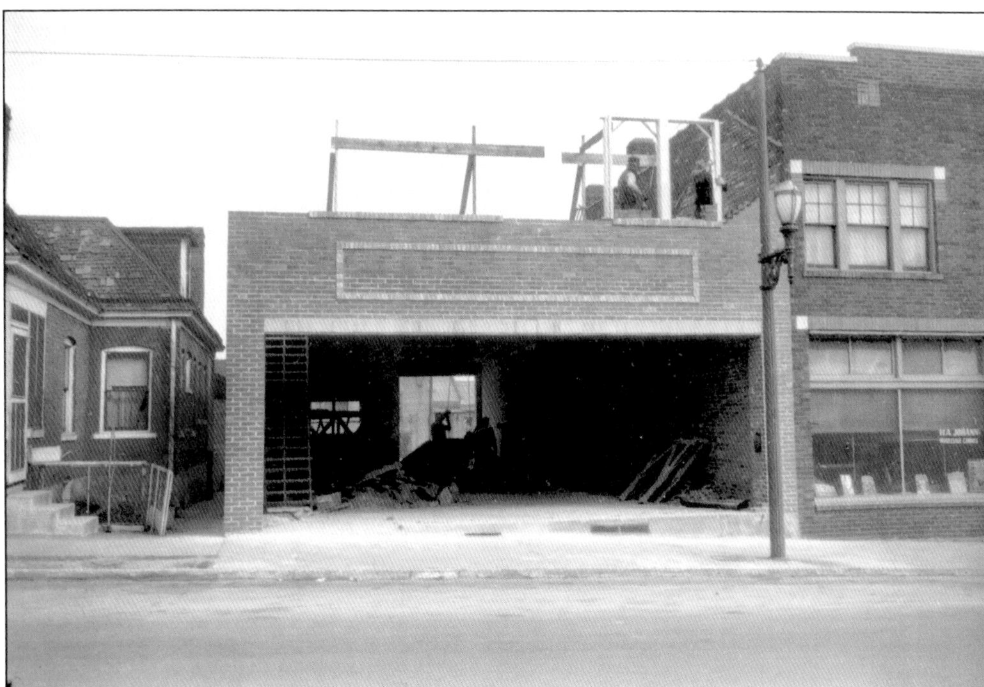

Just a couple of blocks away, Foley Motors, a Packard automobile dealer, was putting up this new building at 308 North Third. It is the current home of Ayers Pottery. (February 1947)

Logan Shoe Store at 123 North Main was another business busily revamping the exterior of their store. Workers on the scaffolding are giving the front a more modern appearance. To the left of Logan's is J.J. Newberry and to the right is Dolly's Hat Shop. (April 1947)

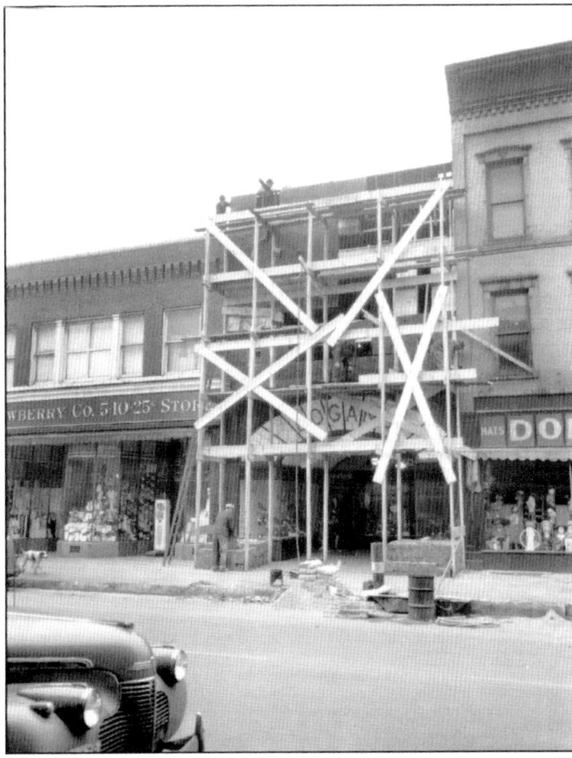

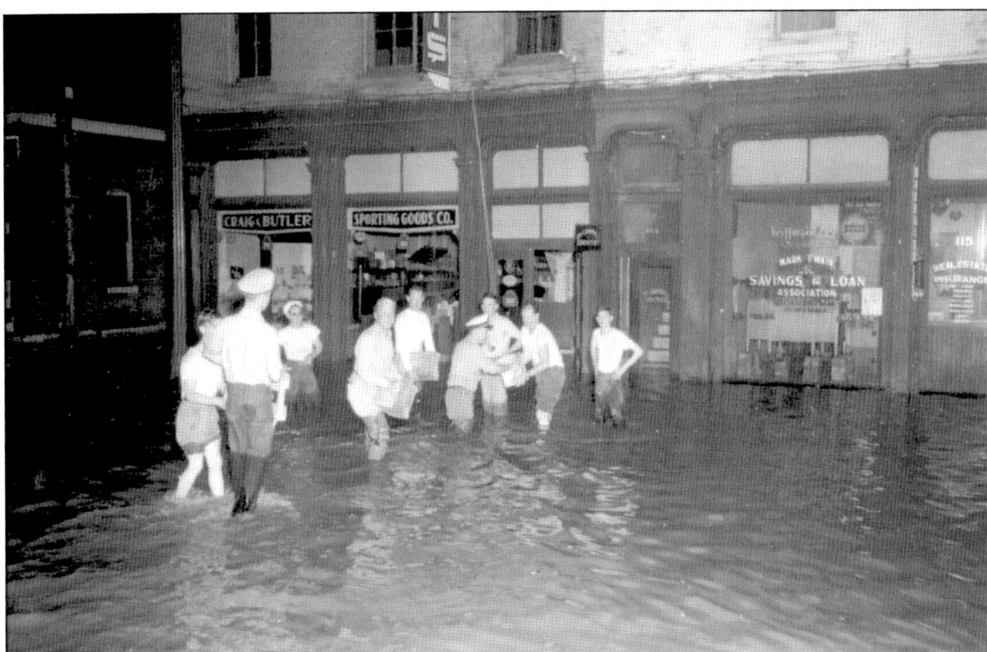

In June 1947, floodwaters rose to a crest of over 24 feet. Many Hannibal merchants saw the river invade their businesses. Here the Naval Reserve is helping Craig & Butler Sporting Goods evacuate their merchandise. Craig & Butler was located at 111 Broadway; the building was demolished in the 1960s.

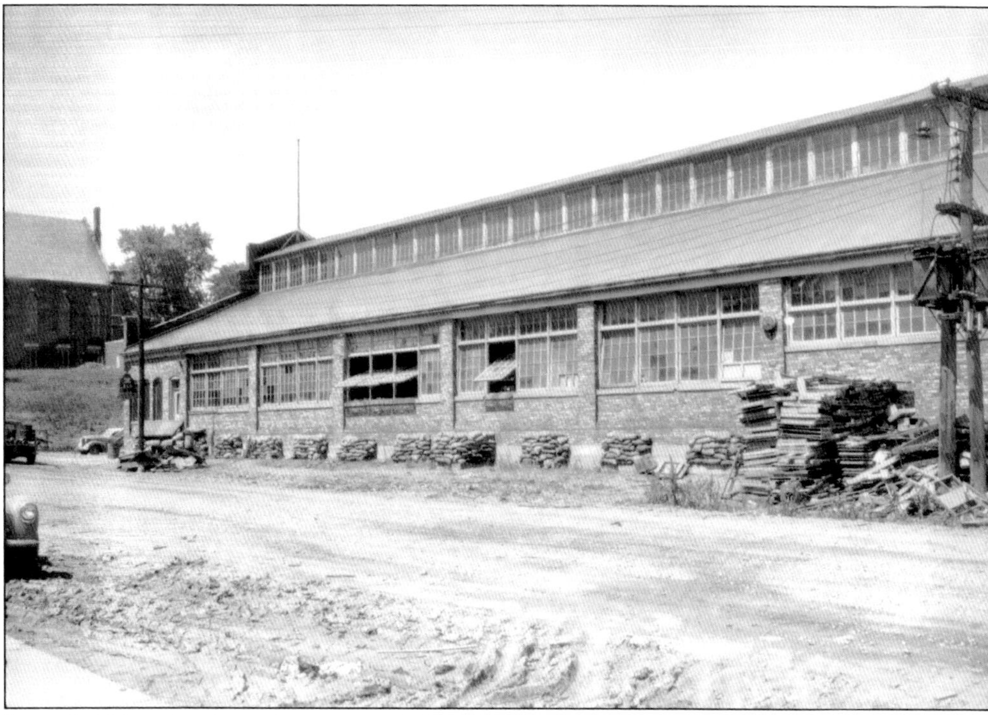

Hannibal Woodworking Company at 523 Collier Street as it appeared in June 1947. Note the sandbags piled along the side of the building as a precaution against flooding.

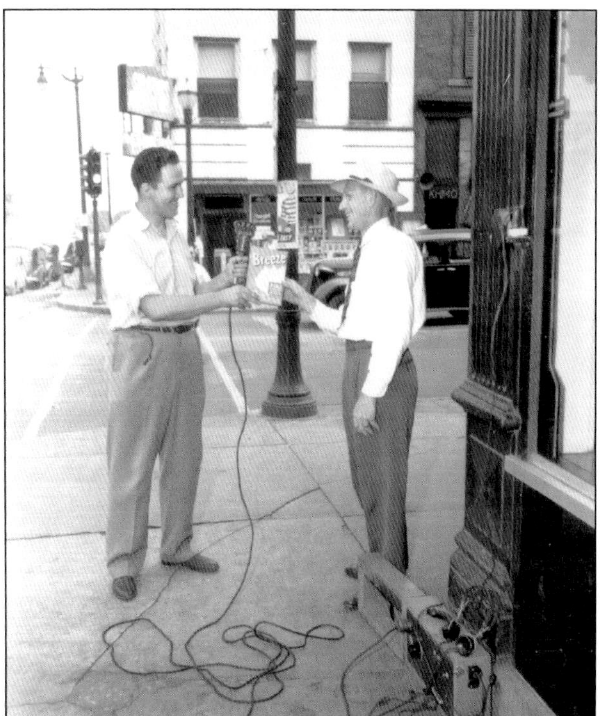

A popular local fixture was KHMO's "Man on the Street" broadcast at Broadway and Main. A question would be posed to a random passerby and if they answered the question correctly they would win a prize, in this case a box of detergent. Visible in the background is KHMO's studio, which at that time was at 102 South Main. (September 1947)

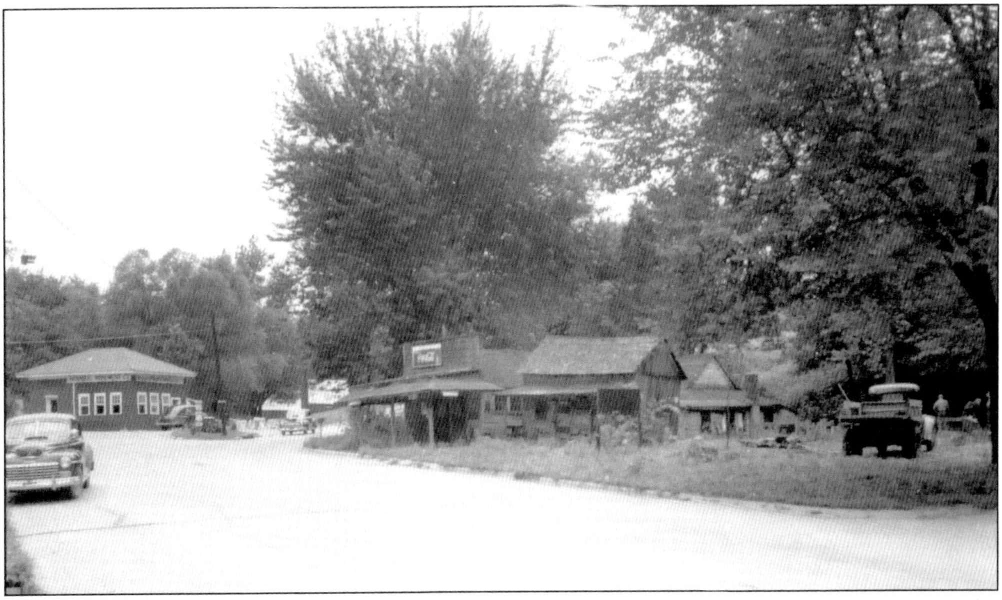

It is hard to imagine the intersection of Mark Twain Avenue and Harrison Hill looking like this at one time. The building at far left is Hannibal Monument Company. The cluster of wood structures at the right, considered by the city to be a traffic hazard, would be removed in 1948. This intersection would disappear entirely when the interchange for the new Mark Twain Bridge would be constructed. (summer of 1947)

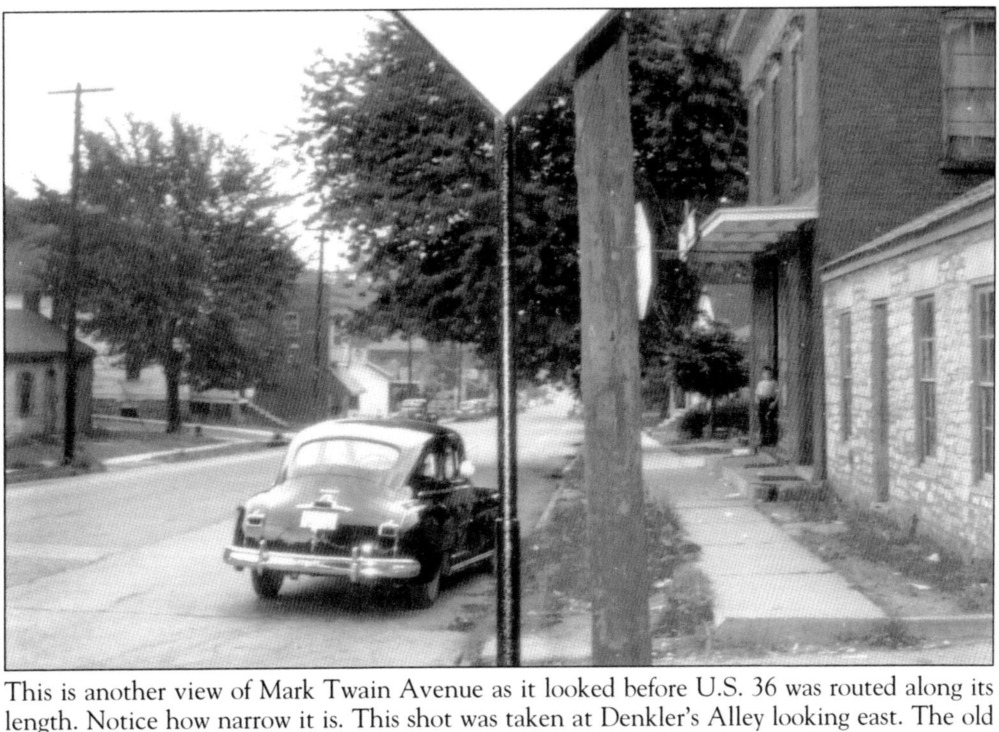

This is another view of Mark Twain Avenue as it looked before U.S. 36 was routed along its length. Notice how narrow it is. This shot was taken at Denkler's Alley looking east. The old Welshman's House at the far right would be moved to its present location at the intersection of Third and Mark Twain Avenue in 1956 (see page 80). (August 1947)

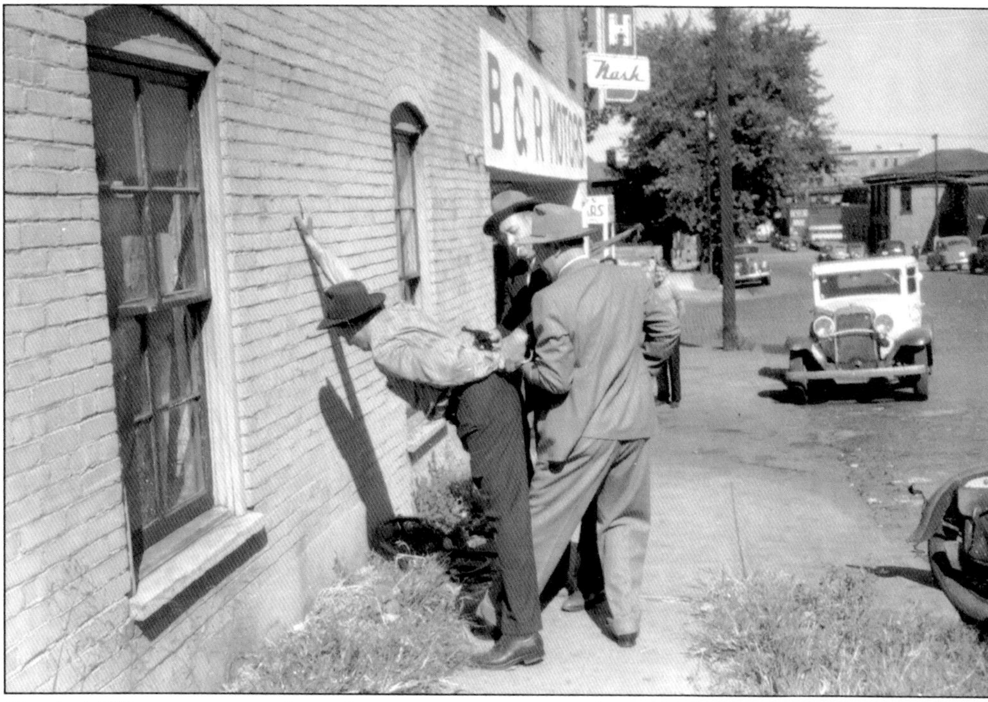

Gotcha! What appears to be a dramatic scene is actually a mock arrest which was part of a police training exercise outside B&R Motors at the intersection of Church and Fourth Streets. (September 1947)

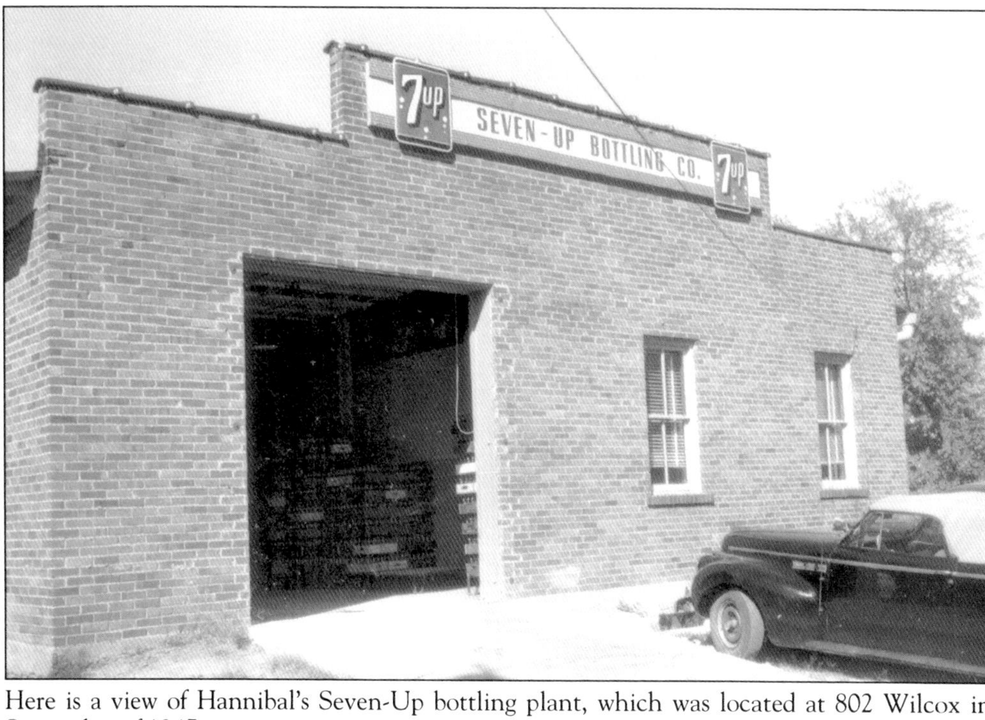

Here is a view of Hannibal's Seven-Up bottling plant, which was located at 802 Wilcox in September of 1947.

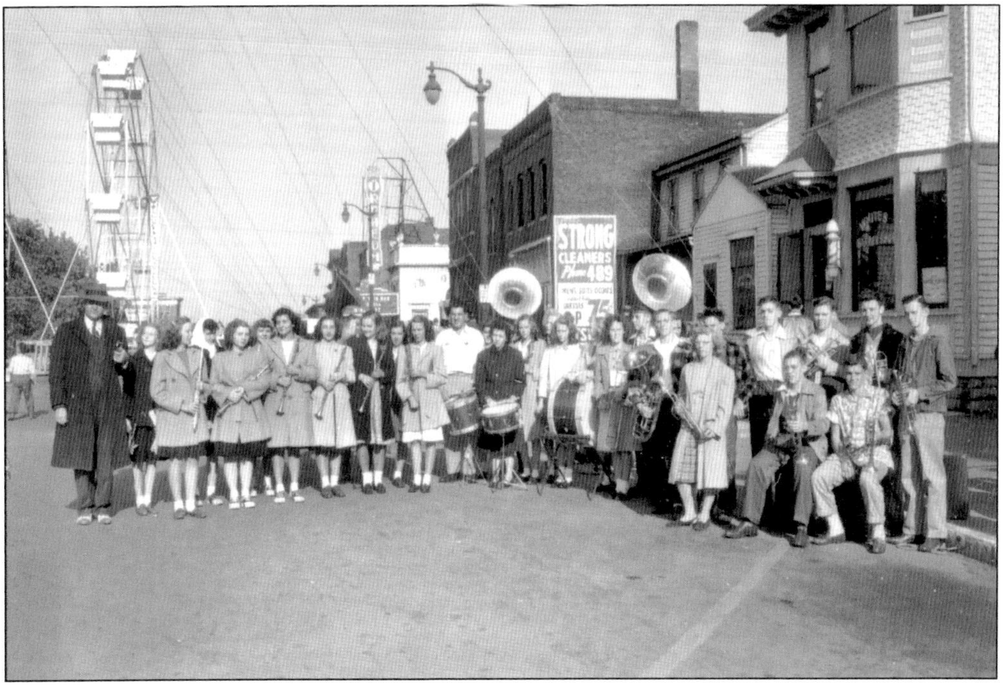

The Hannibal High School band poses for a photo in the 500 block of Broadway during the Fall Festival. Visible in the background from right to left are White's Barbershop, Strong's Cleaners, O'Donnell Drug Store (all since demolished), and the Orpheum Theatre. (October 1947)

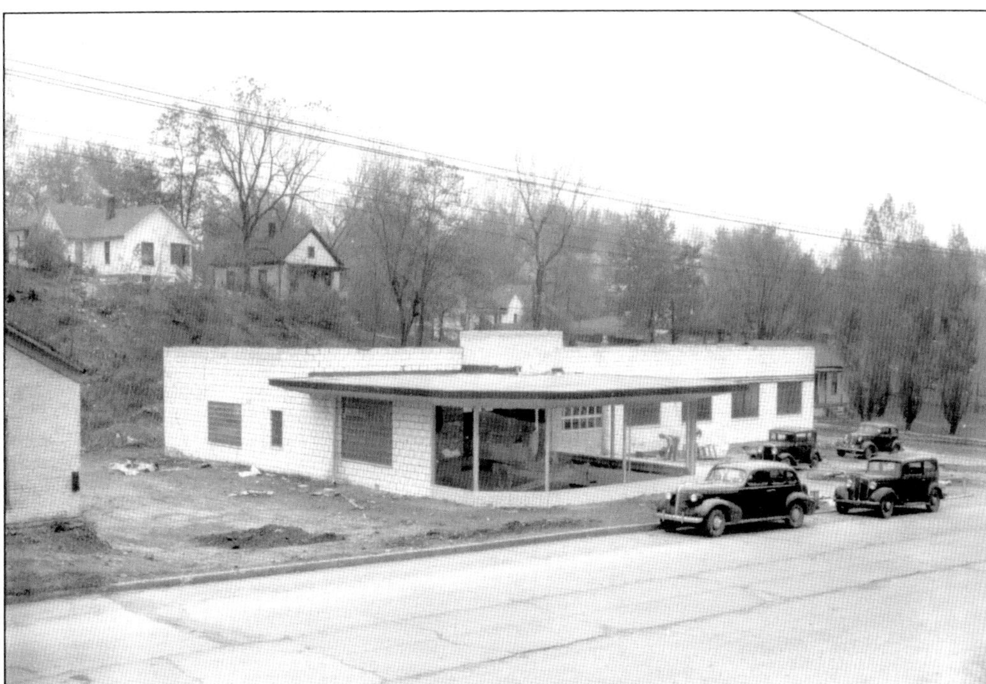

Construction work is underway on Harris Motor Company at 1304 Mark Twain Avenue. As of 2004, the Bakery Thrift Shop is located here. (November 1947)

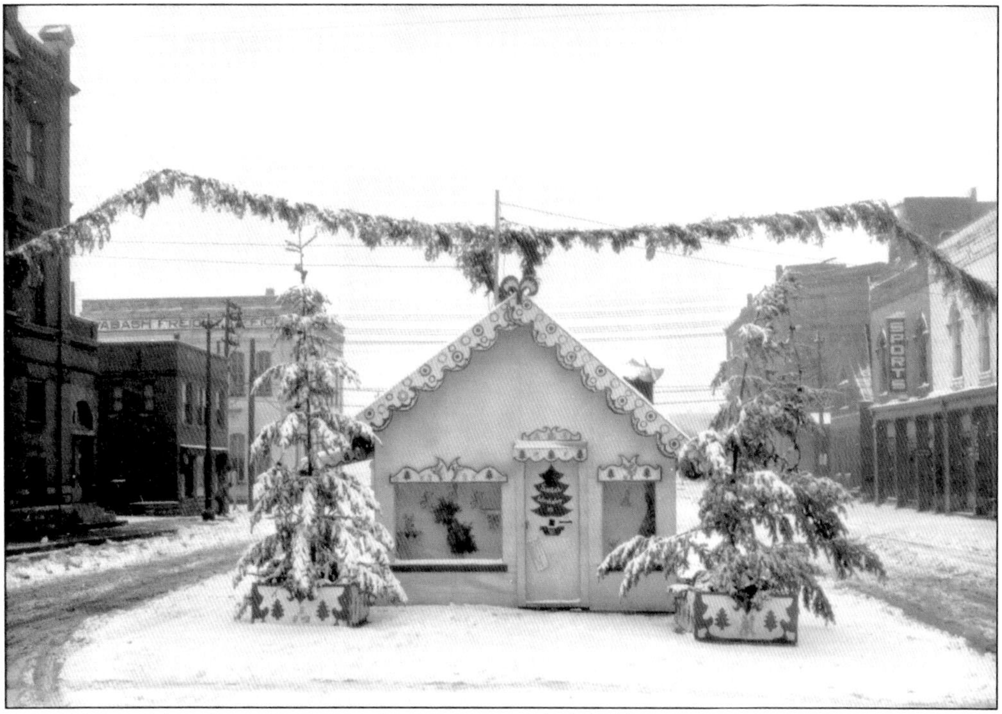

A highlight of the Christmas season for many Hannibal children was a visit to Santa's Workshop at Main and Broadway. The snow adds a festive touch to the scene. Part of Hannibal National Bank is visible at left. (December 1947)

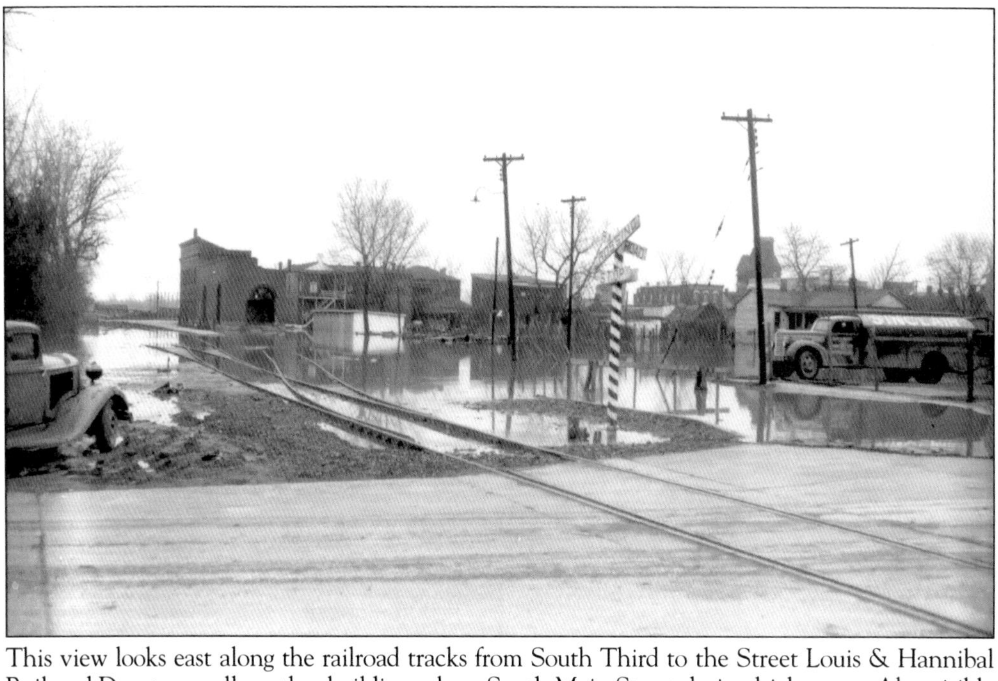

This view looks east along the railroad tracks from South Third to the Street Louis & Hannibal Railroad Depot, as well as other buildings along South Main Street during high water. Also visible in the distance is the old coaling tower in the Railroad yards. (March 1948)

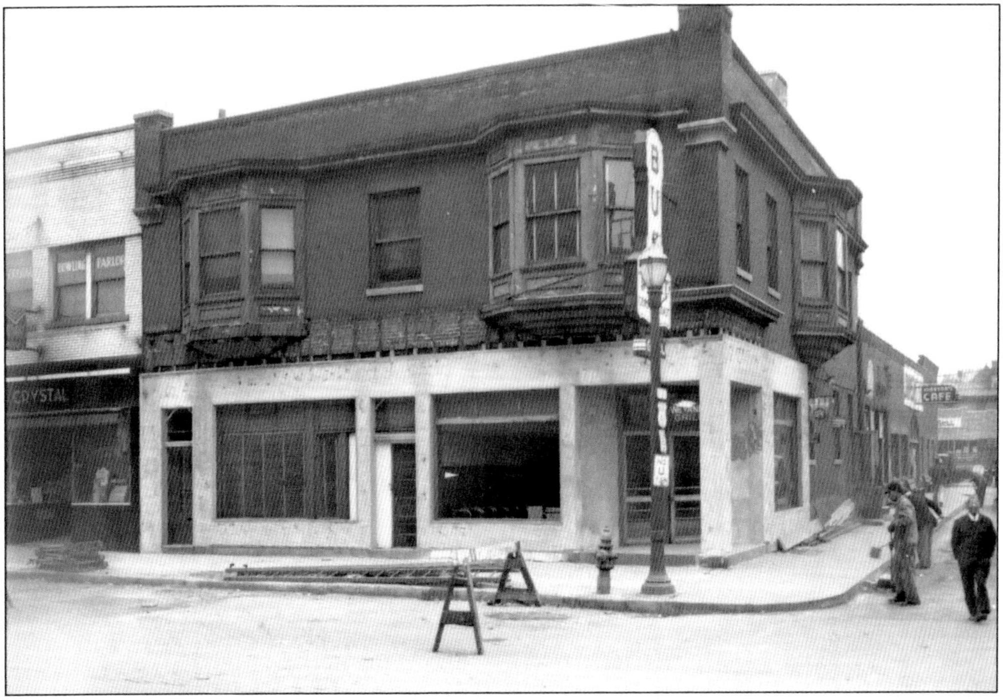

Remodeling of the exterior of the Hannibal Bus Depot at the Southwest corner of Main and Church Streets is in progress in this photo. Some of the later tenants of this building were the Hannibal Appliance Company, H&R Block, and Dee's Cafe. It would be demolished in the 1990s.

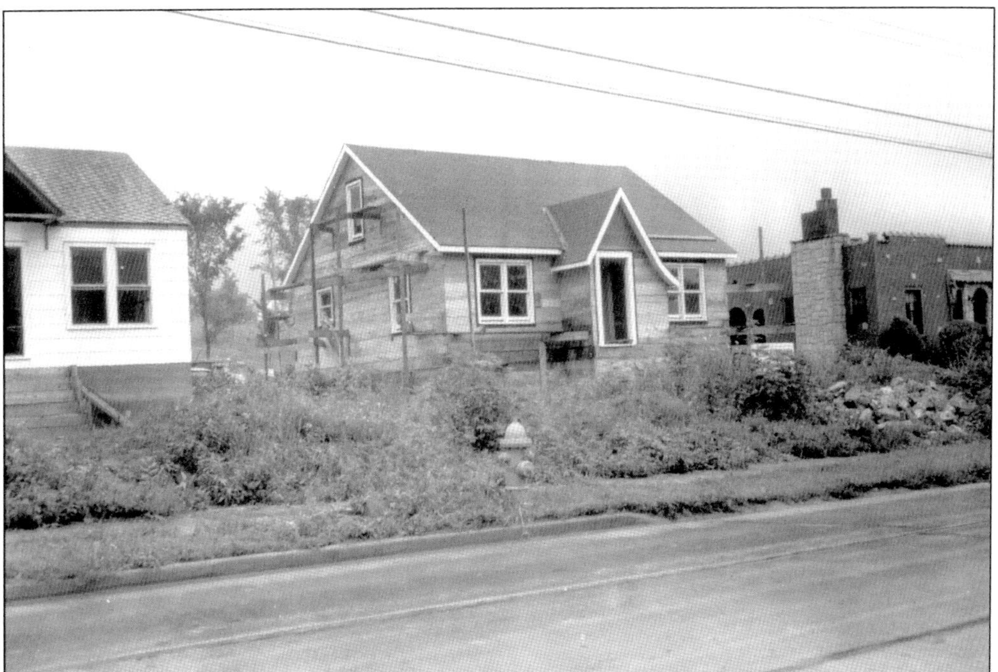

The 4000 block of McMasters was still very rural when these homes were constructed in July 1948.

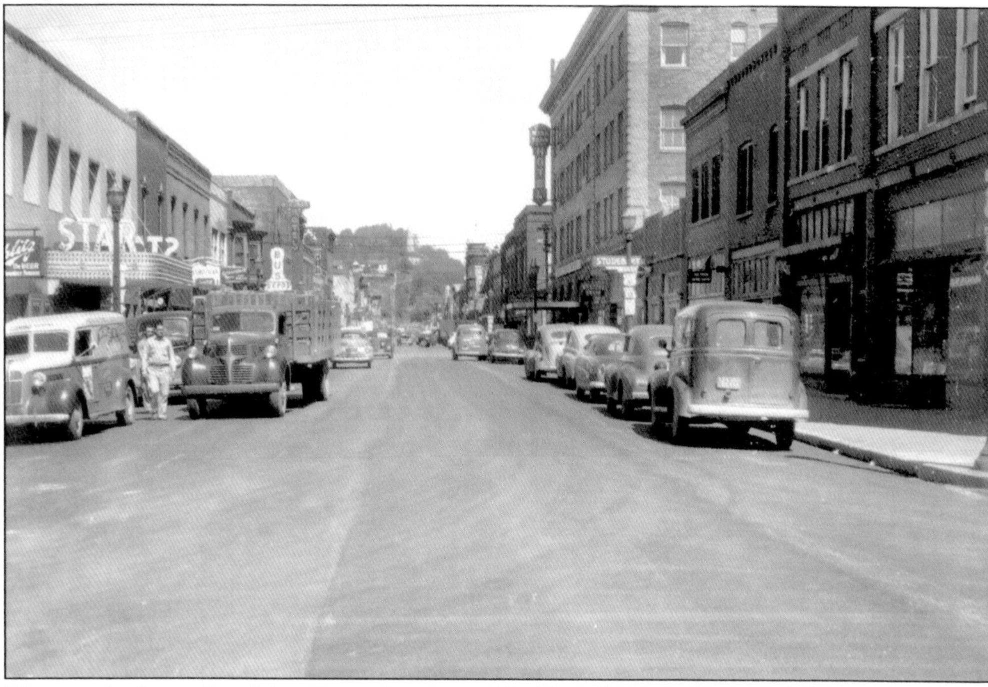

This view looks north up Main Street from Lyon. Visible is the Star Theater at left, the Mark Twain Hotel at right, and the Hannibal National Bank tower can be seen beyond. (July 1948)

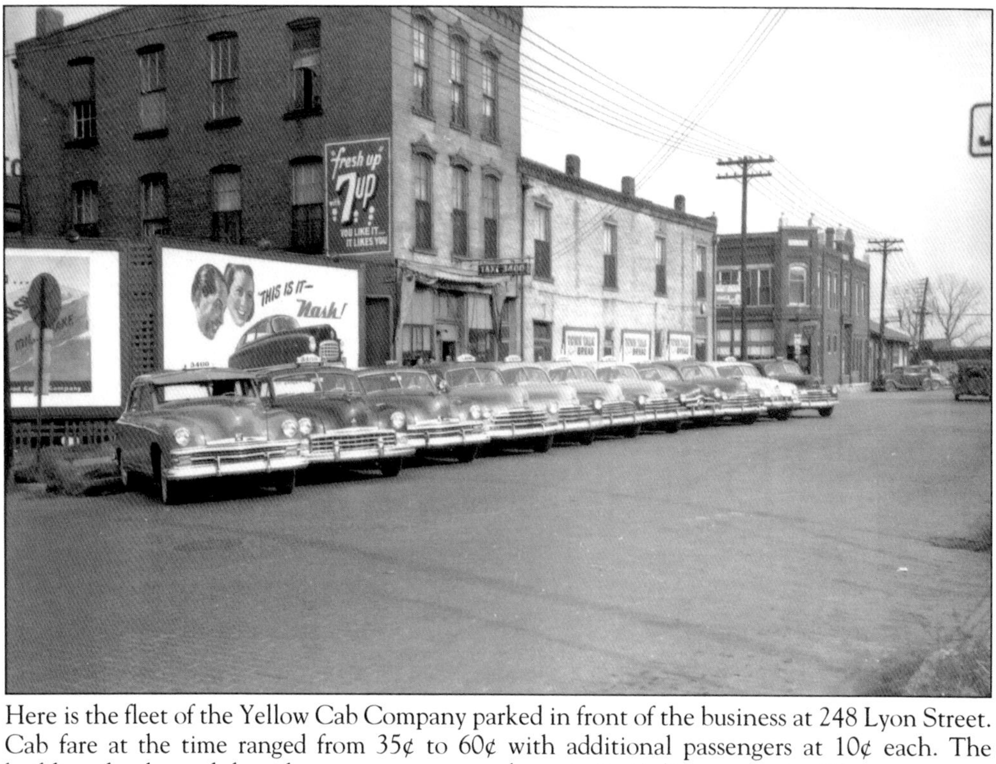

Here is the fleet of the Yellow Cab Company parked in front of the business at 248 Lyon Street. Cab fare at the time ranged from 35¢ to 60¢ with additional passengers at 10¢ each. The building that housed the cab company was torn down in 1985. (November 1948)

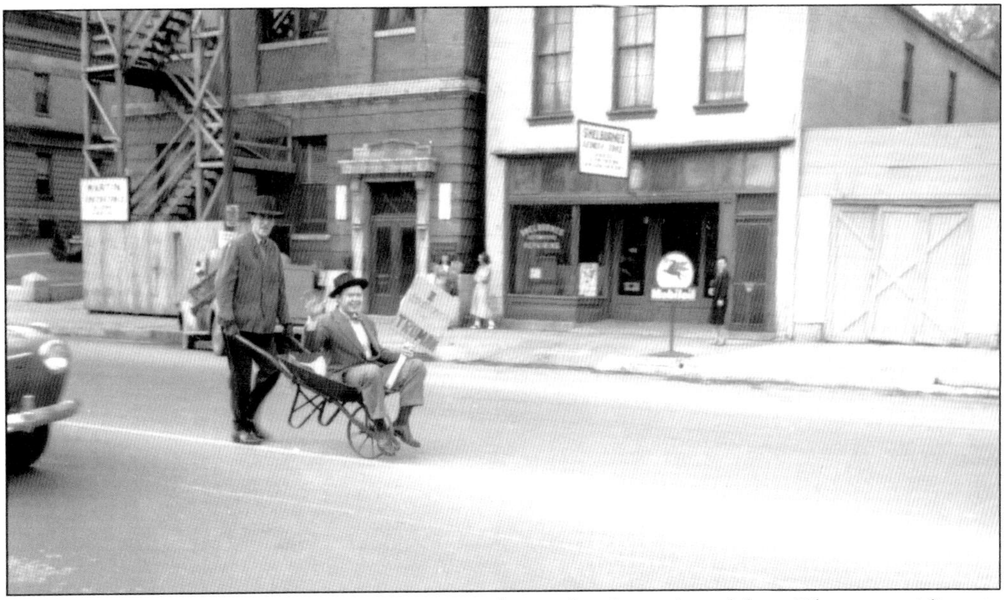

This interesting photo shows the apparent aftermath of a political bet. The man riding in the wheelbarrow holds a sign that says "I Bet on Truman." Harry S. Truman won the 1948 presidential election in a very close race. Presumably the wheelbarrow pusher bet on the loser, Thomas E. Dewey. The photo was taken in the 800 block of Broadway. The Telephone Building, visible in the background, was undergoing a remodeling at the time. (November 1948)

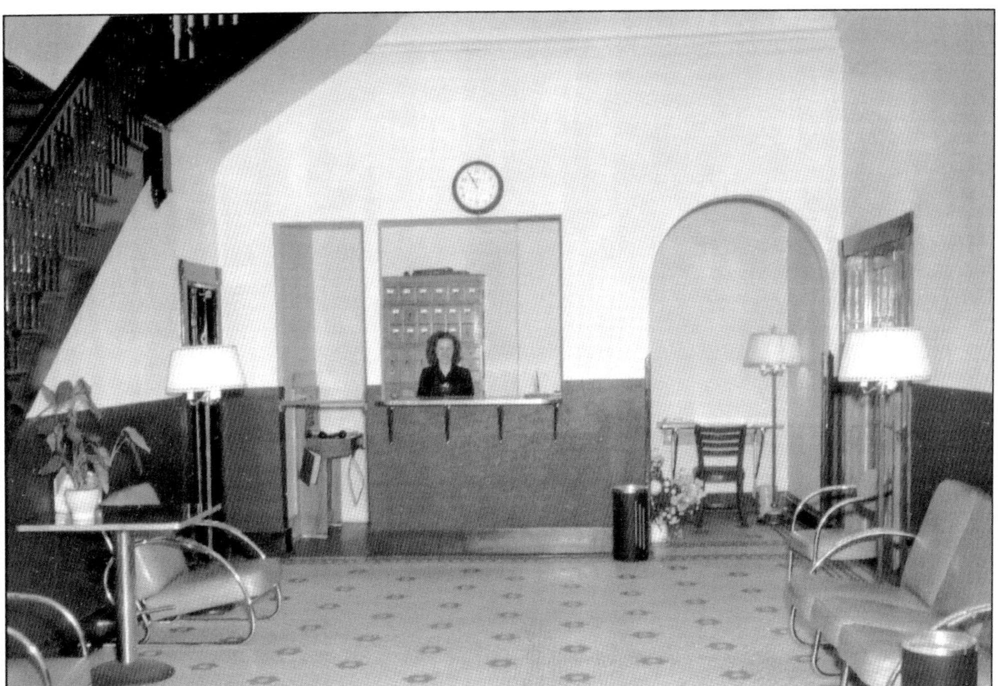

This is the lobby of the newly-renovated Maryland Hotel at 316 Broadway. To the left of the clerk the telephone switchboard can be seen. The Maryland was formerly known as the Conklin Hotel. (November 1948)

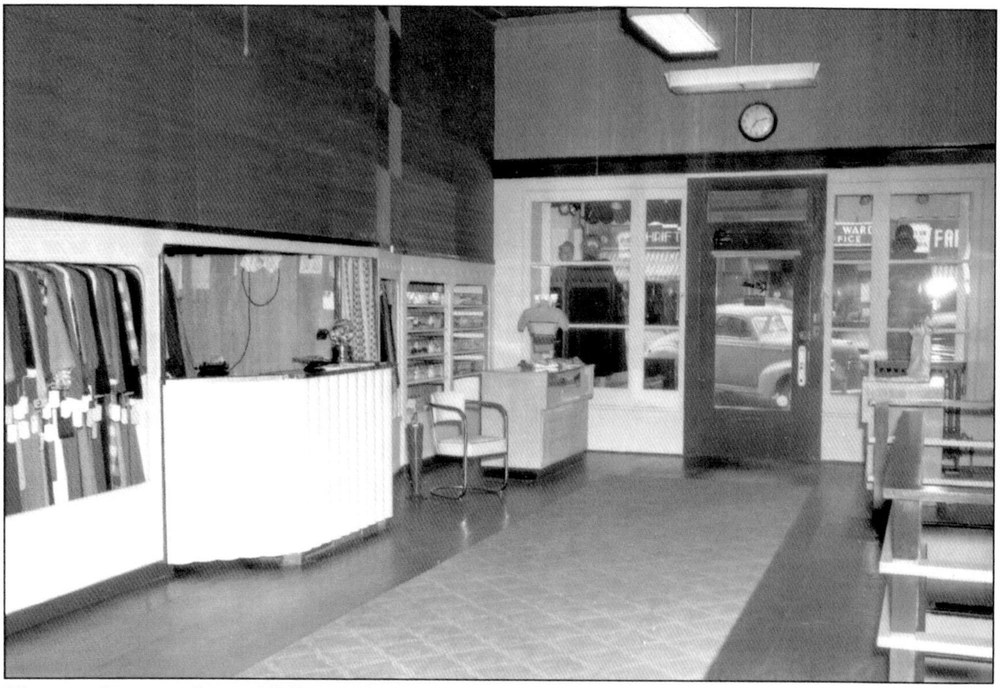

This was the main floor of Kilham's Store at 223 Broadway. Kilham's was a woman's clothing store. Their motto was "Ready to Wear Style Distinction." (November 1948)

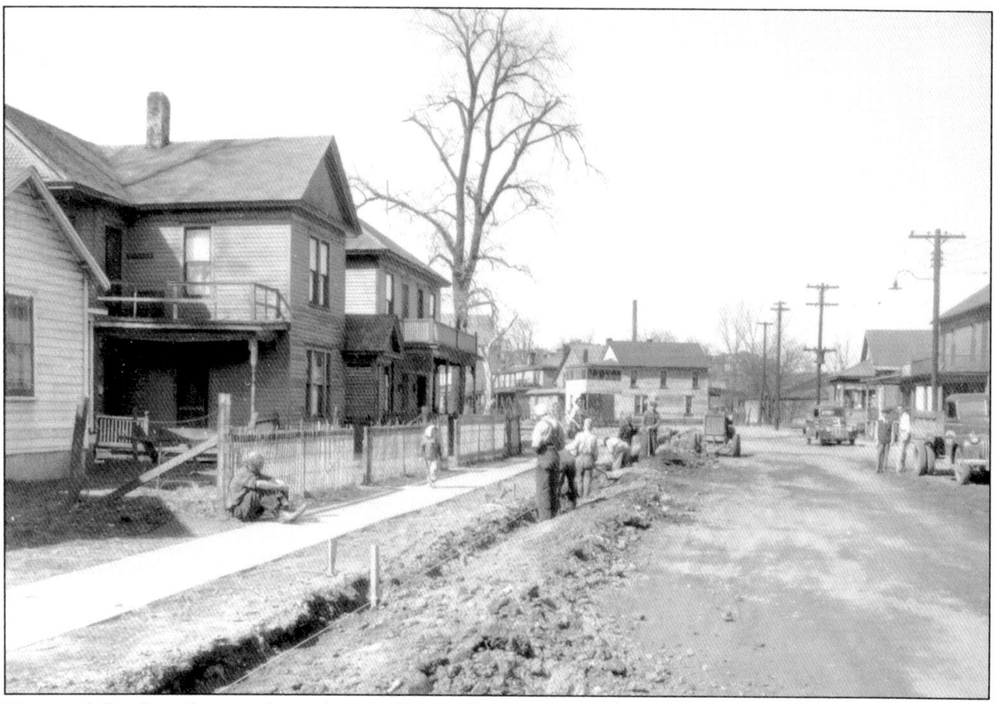

Years of flooding have taken their toll on Ely Street—today all of the houses visible in this March 1949 photo are long gone, with only weedy vacant lots left behind. This view looks north towards Bear Creek. This photo documents city workers installing new sidewalks and curbing.

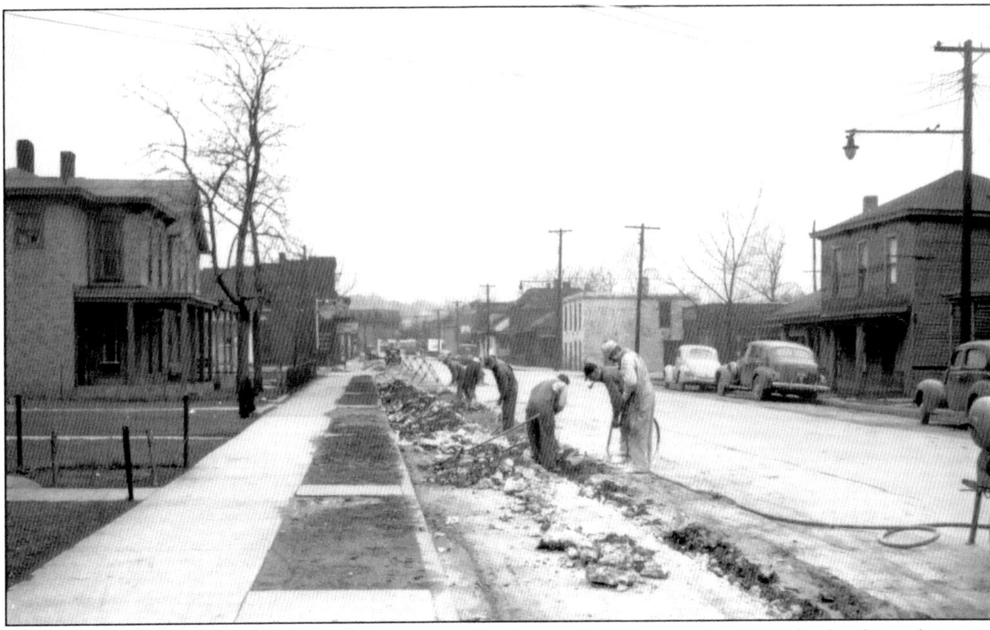

Here is another photo of a street that has greatly changed. Taken in the 700 block of South Main, looking north towards downtown, this photo also shows a streetscape full of buildings, which for the most part are only memories today. Many of the residences in this picture were homes of railroad workers. If you look closely you will notice that one of the street department workers is smoking a pipe. (April 1949)

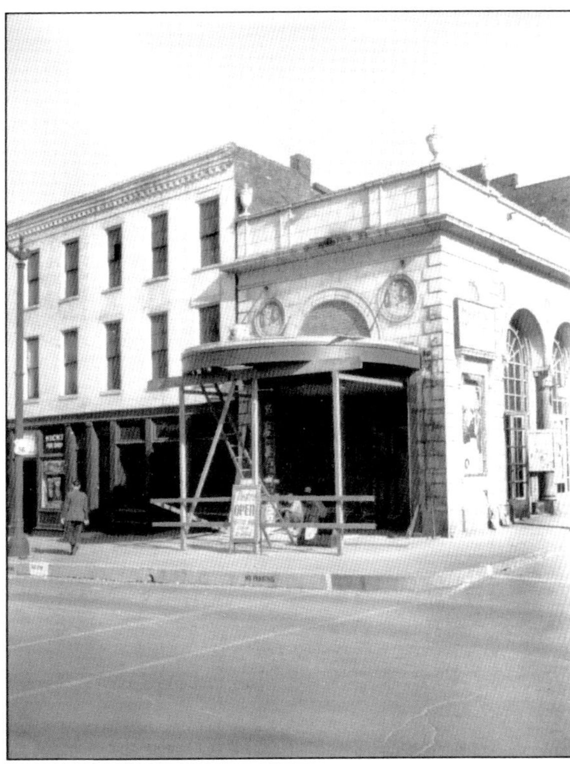

The old Orpheum Theatre at Fifth and Broadway is being remodeled and modernized. The theater had just been purchased by Frisina Entertainment Company and renamed the Tom Sawyer. This photo shows the installation of the new marquee. The French doors on the Fifth Street side have been removed and the entryways have been bricked up. (April 1949)

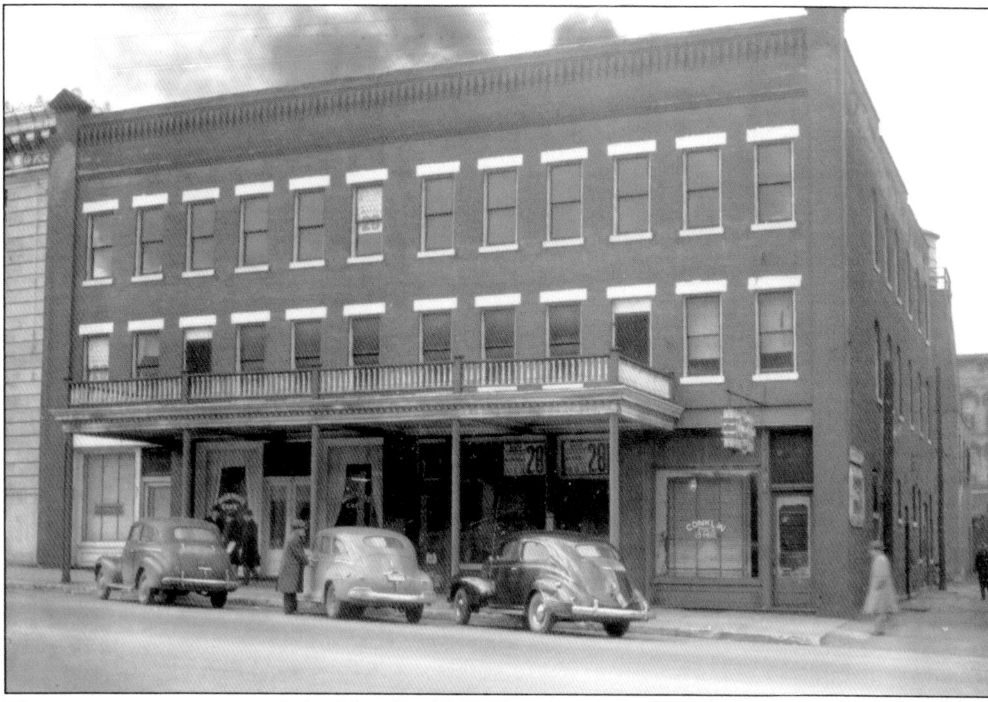

This is an exterior view of the Maryland Hotel at 316 Broadway. This photo was taken just prior to the removal of the large front porch. The hotel also housed Wiseman's Cafe and the Conklin Bar. (June 1949)

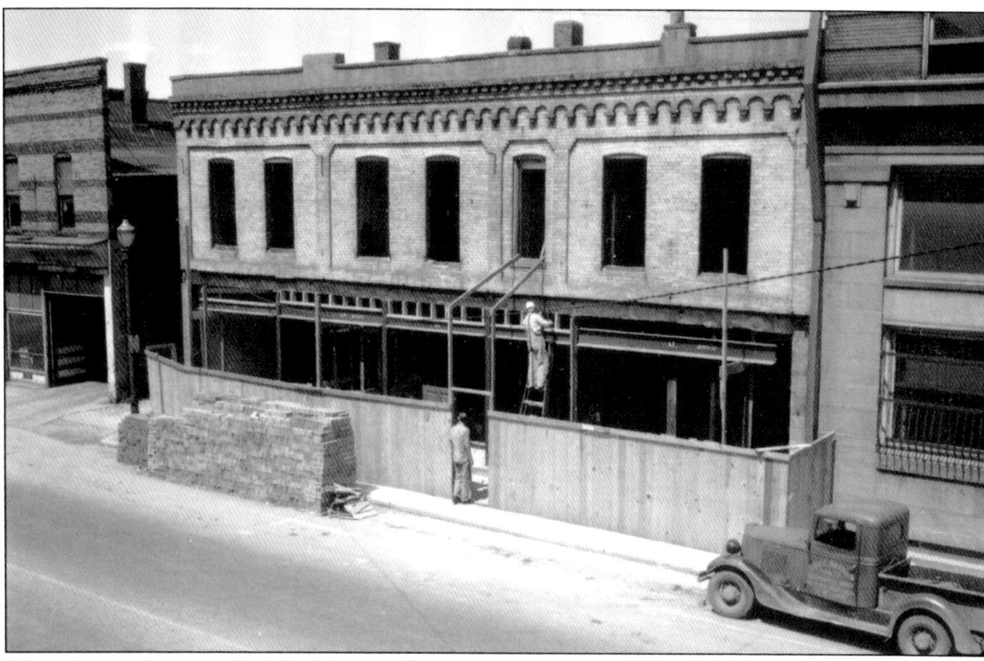

This photo shows 108–110 North Third in the process of an exterior facelift by owner Charles E. Rendlen Sr. in order to accommodate his law firm. The building to the left would be razed for a parking lot in 1956. (June 1949)

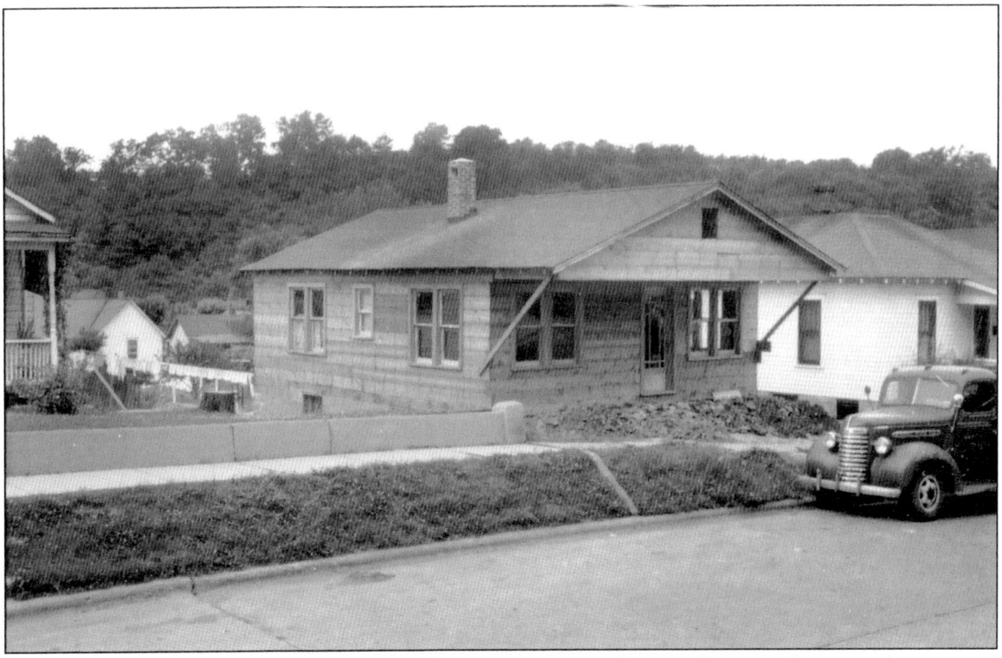

As new homes were built throughout the city, Otis made an effort to photograph many of them for insertion in the newspaper. Here a new 5-room home rises at 2211 Hope for Mr. and Mrs. R.E. Shutze. This house still stands as of 2004. (June 1949)

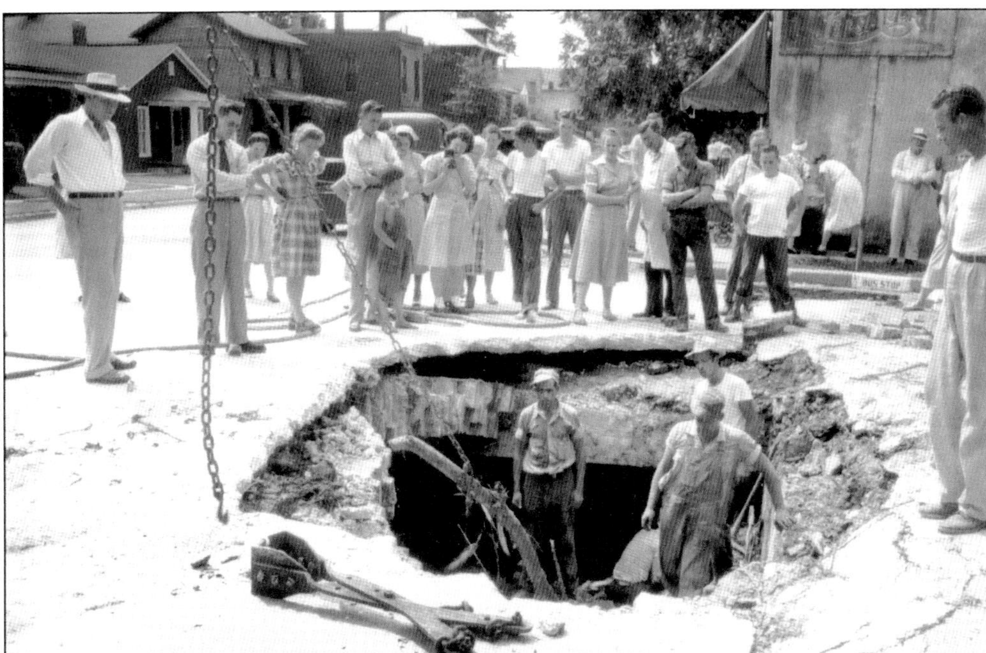

A crowd of curious gathers around a gaping hole in the street at Union and Sycamore, where the roof of an old tunnel collapsed. Spooner Creek flowed through this tunnel, and excess pressure from flash flooding had caused the roof, and the pavement above, to cave in. Newman's Grocery is visible in the background at right. (July 1949)

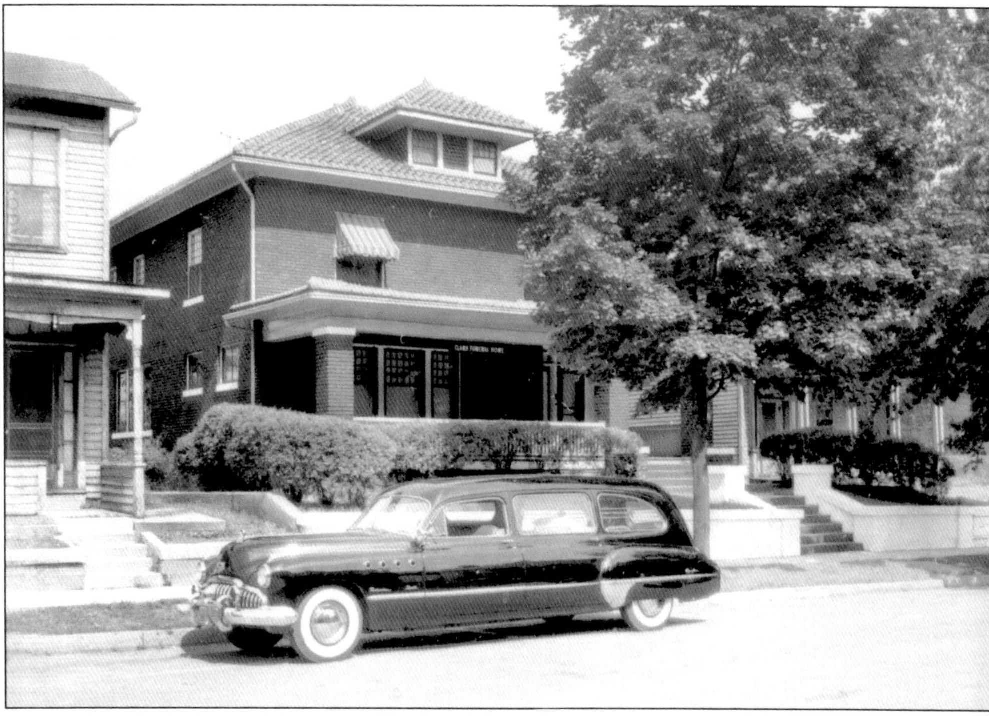

This is the Clark Funeral Home at 208 South Fourth, with their shiny black hearse parked out in front. (August 1949)

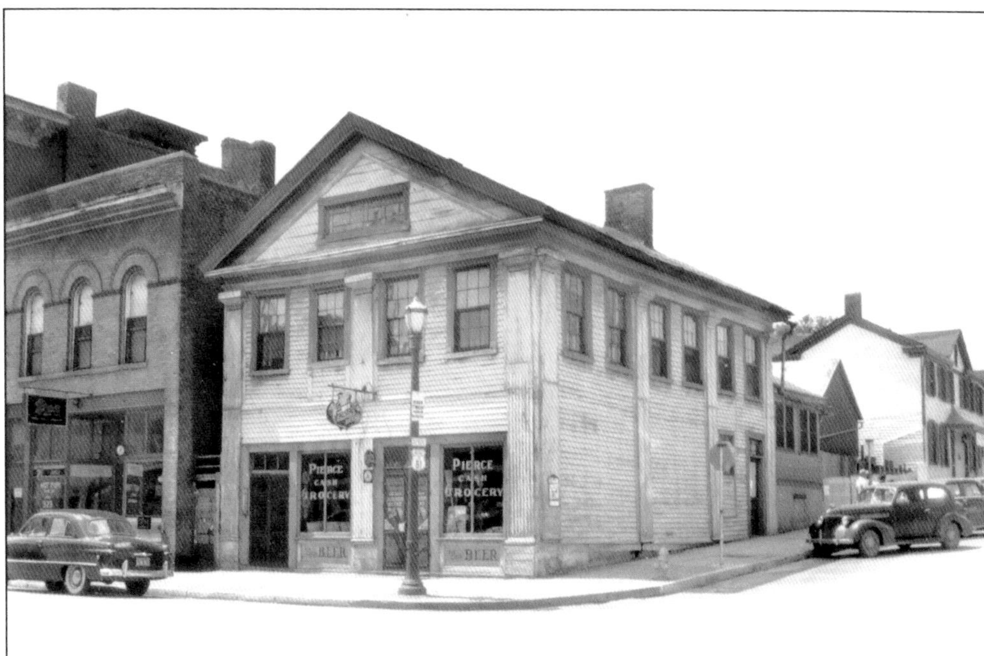

Hannibal's historic Pilaster House looks as if it could use a coat of paint in this August 1949 photo. Missing is the old balcony which was replaced when the building was restored. The beer sign hanging from the front looks sadly out of place. Pierce's Cash Grocery was located there at the time.

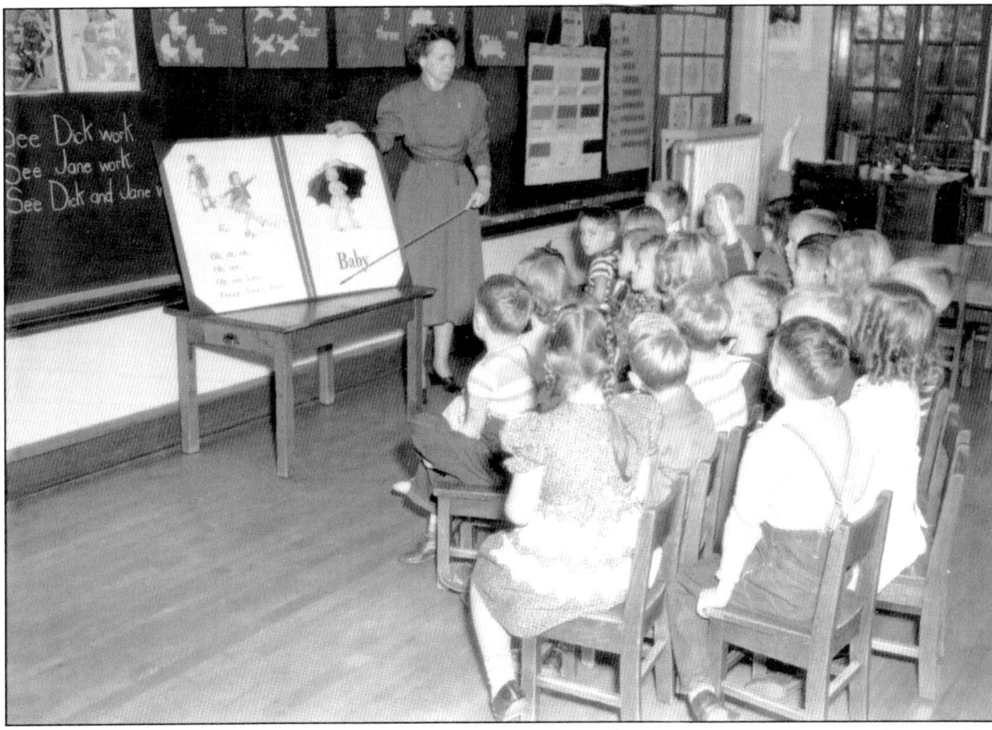

Did you learn to read with Dick and Jane? These first-graders in Miss Frances Swarthout's class at Pettibone School did. Don't those chairs look uncomfortable? (October 1949)

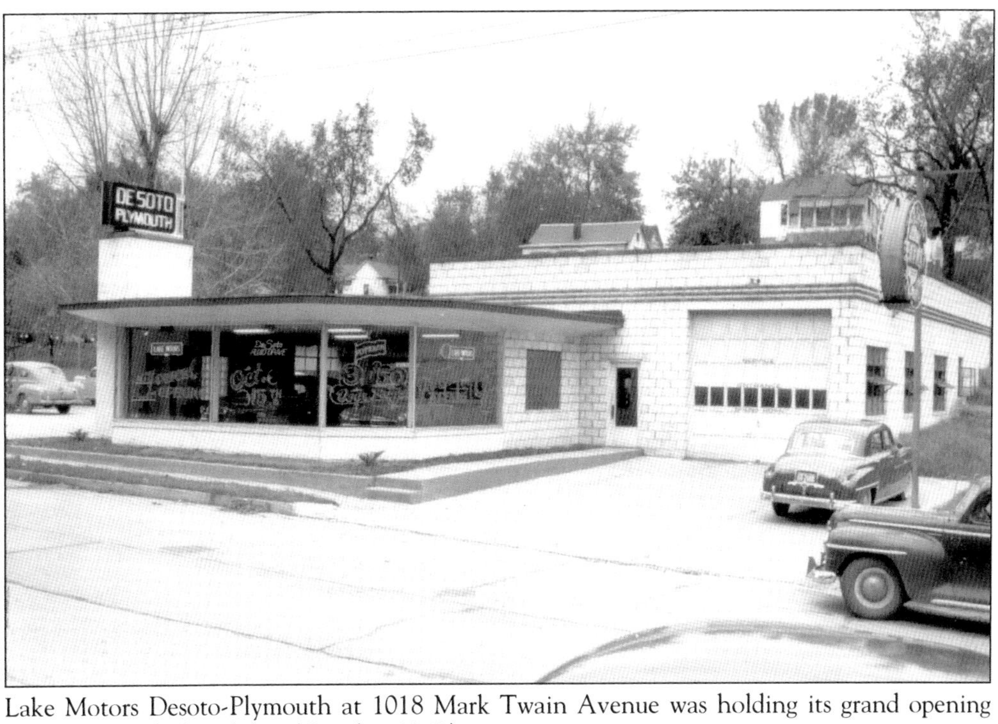

Lake Motors Desoto-Plymouth at 1018 Mark Twain Avenue was holding its grand opening when Otis took this photo. (October 1949)

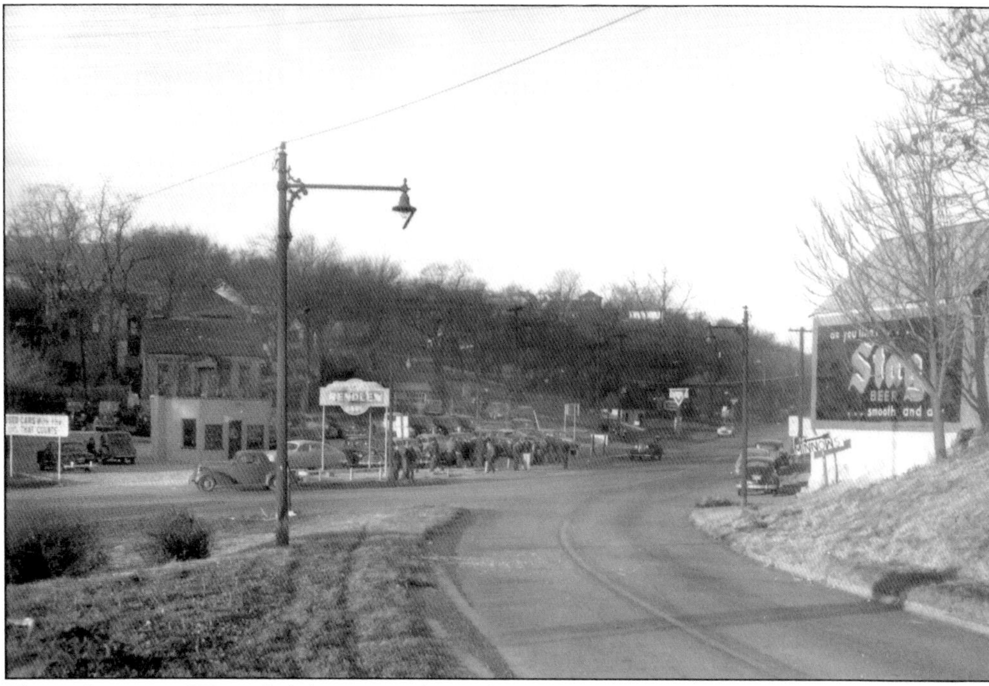

This is the view of Hannibal that greeted travelers coming off the Mark Twain Memorial Bridge and heading out on Mark Twain Avenue in November 1949. To the right is Picadilly's and Rendlen's Used Cars is visible in the center of the photo. Beyond is the Rock Street intersection with Mark Twain Avenue and Norman's Conoco filling station.

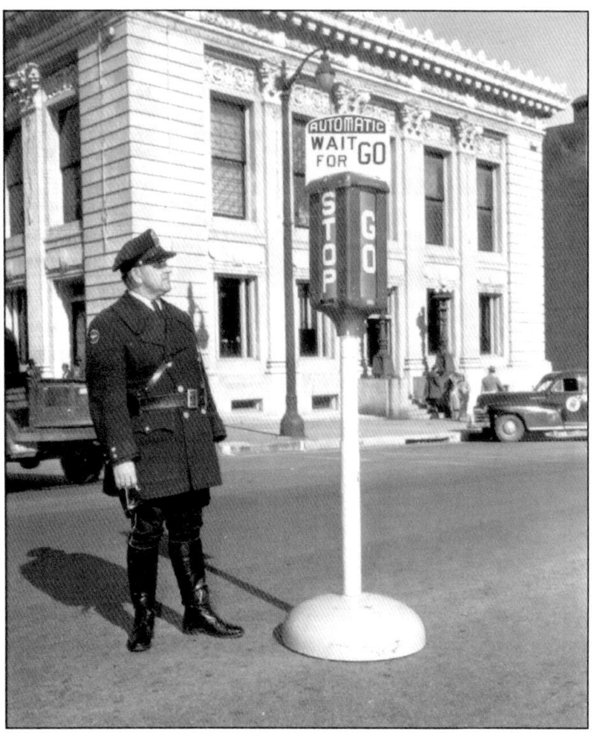

Hannibal policeman Floyd Capps stands beside an automated stop and go signal, which had been placed at the intersection of Broadway and Fourth in November 1949. Note the fancy cornice work on Hannibal's City Hall, which was removed years ago because it was considered a safety hazard.

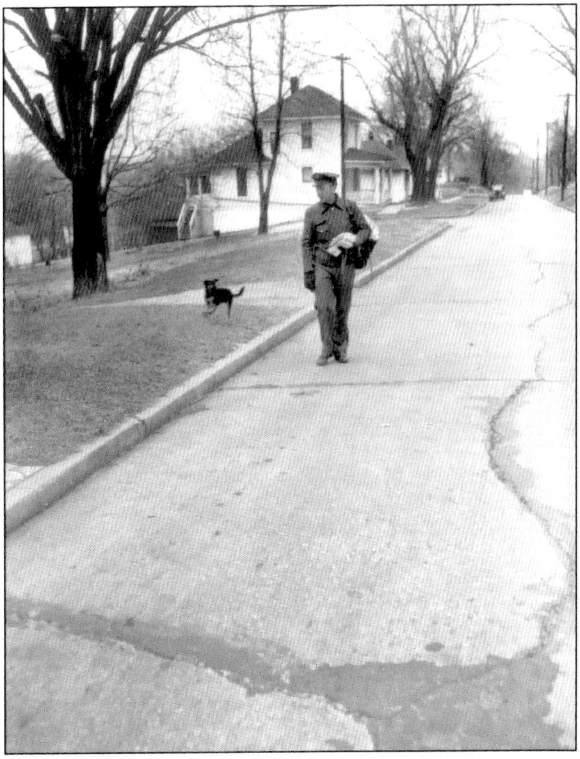

Otis Howell delighted in photographing everyday people in everyday situations. This photo, which appeared in the *Courier-Post* in December 1949, showed mailman Fred Herrin on his mail route near Seventh and Paris Avenue. A little terrier named Bebe waited for him every day to accompany him on that part of his rounds. Twenty years later Fred Herrin would serve as mayor of Hannibal.

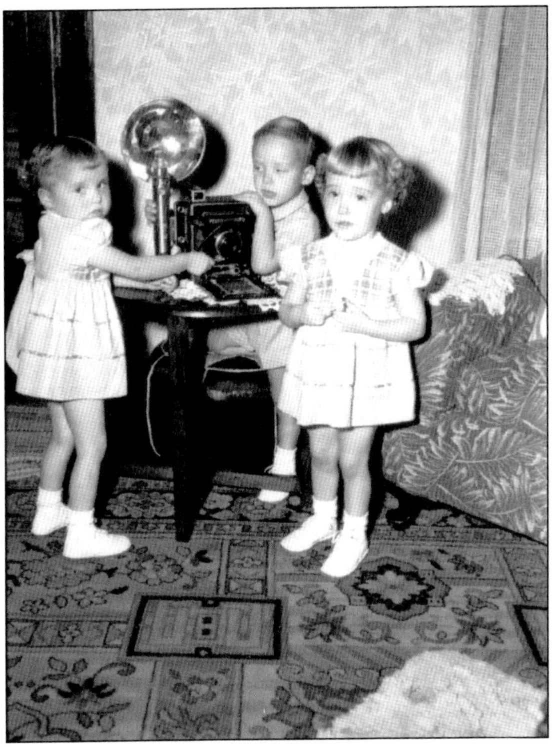

On December 1, 1946, Mr. and Mrs. Gustav Weiss became the parents of triplets, born at Levering Hospital. Larry Lyn, Cheryl Lou, and Sharon Lee often had their pictures printed in the paper on their birthdays. In this December 1949 photo the three pose with one of the photographer's cameras. Pictured left to right are Sharon, Larry, and Cheryl.

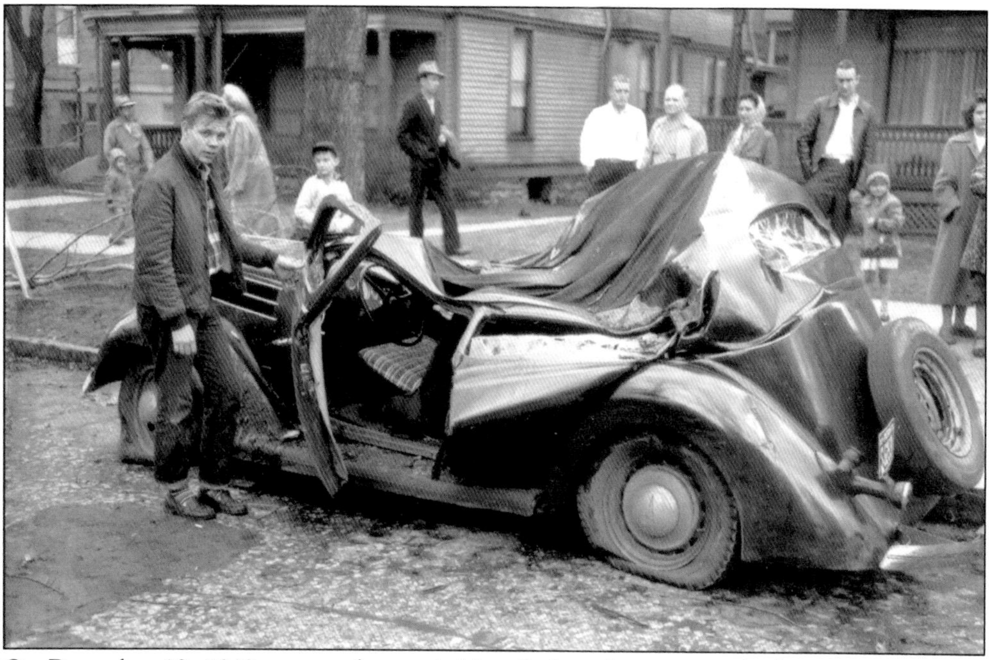

On December 12, 1949, a tornado struck Hannibal resulting in much damage. Among the casualties was a Ford sedan belonging to Bob Blanton, shown here on Center near Maple. A large tree fell, crushing the car.

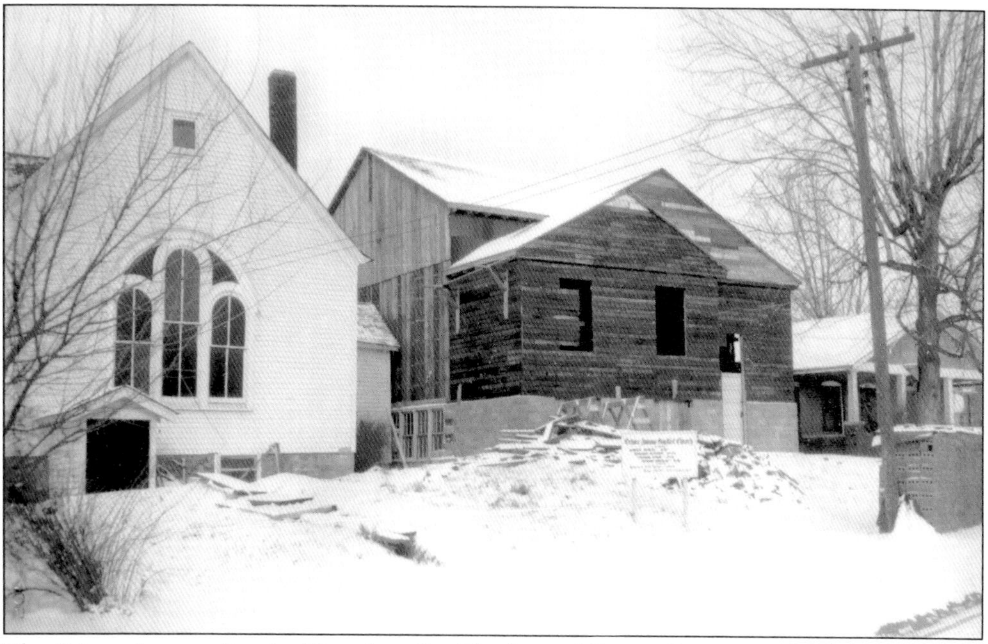

The Prince Avenue Baptist Church at St. Charles and Prince Streets was in the middle of a building program when this photo was taken. At left is the old church building which was built in the 1890s. To the right is the new educational building that would be temporarily used as a sanctuary while the old building was torn down and replaced. The pastor at the time was Rev. E.M. Turner. (January 1950)

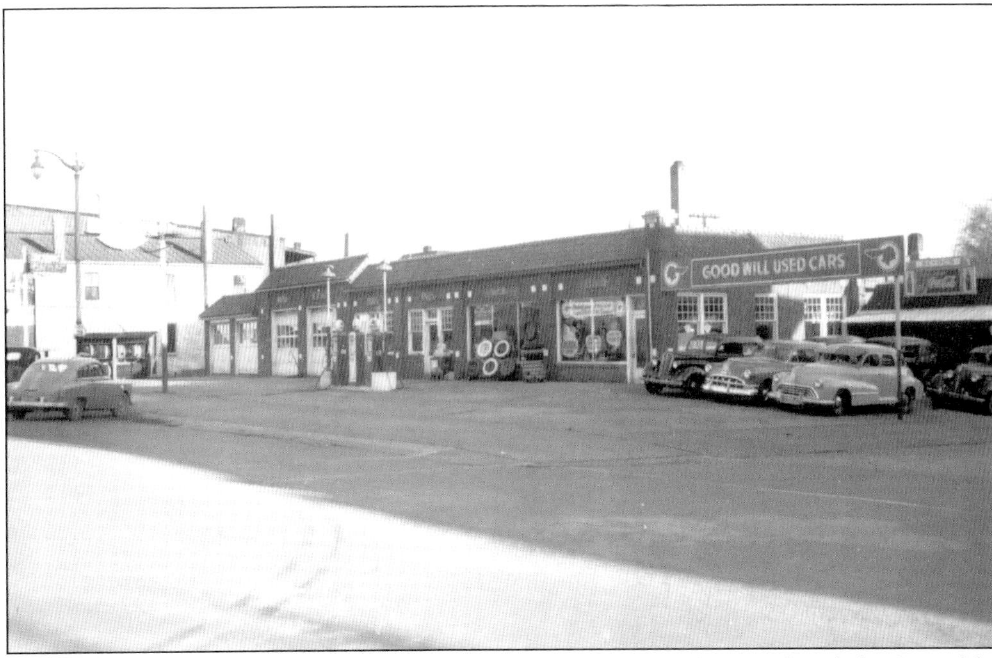

Scyoc Tire and Battery stood at the Southeast corner of Broadway and Eighth. Owned by John Scyoc, the business opened in 1923. Scyoc also sold Pontiac automobiles. Today the Hannibal Police Station stands on the site of the old business. (January 1950)

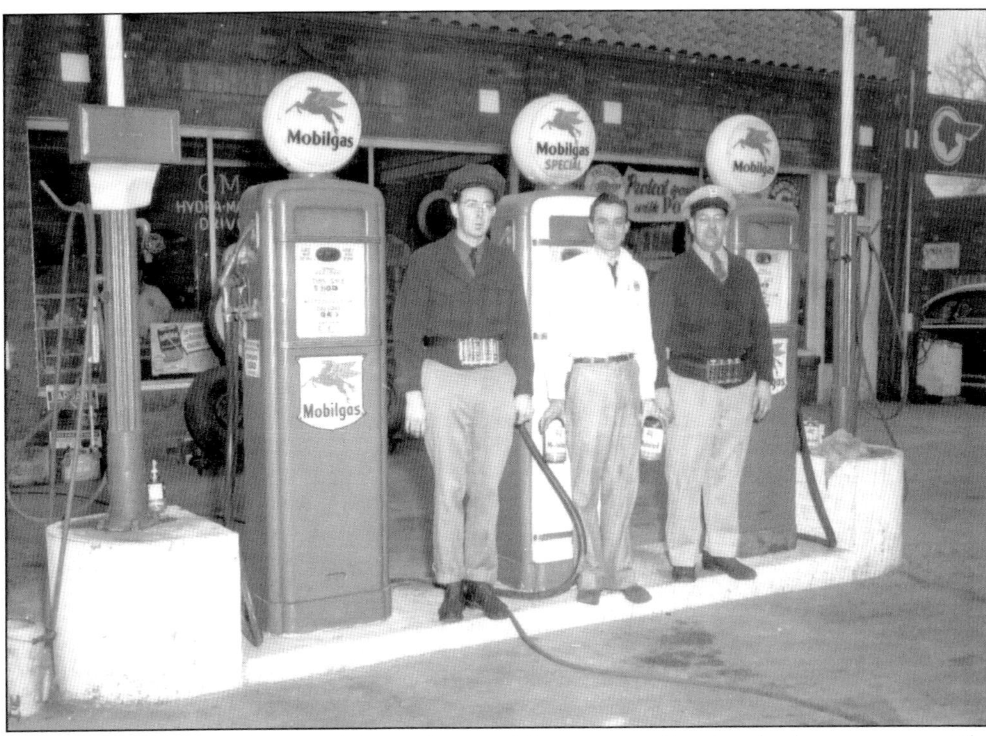

This photo shows employees of Scyoc Tire and Battery standing beside the gas pumps. The price of a gallon of regular gas was 24¢! (January 1950)

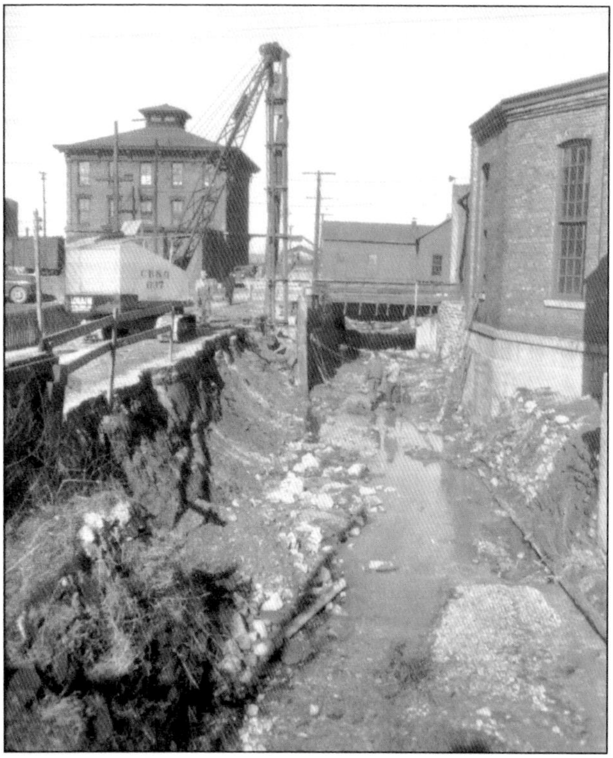

Work is being done along Spooner Creek in the railroad yards. The old Hannibal & St. Joseph Railroad office building is in the background and part of the roundhouse is visible at right. (February 1950)

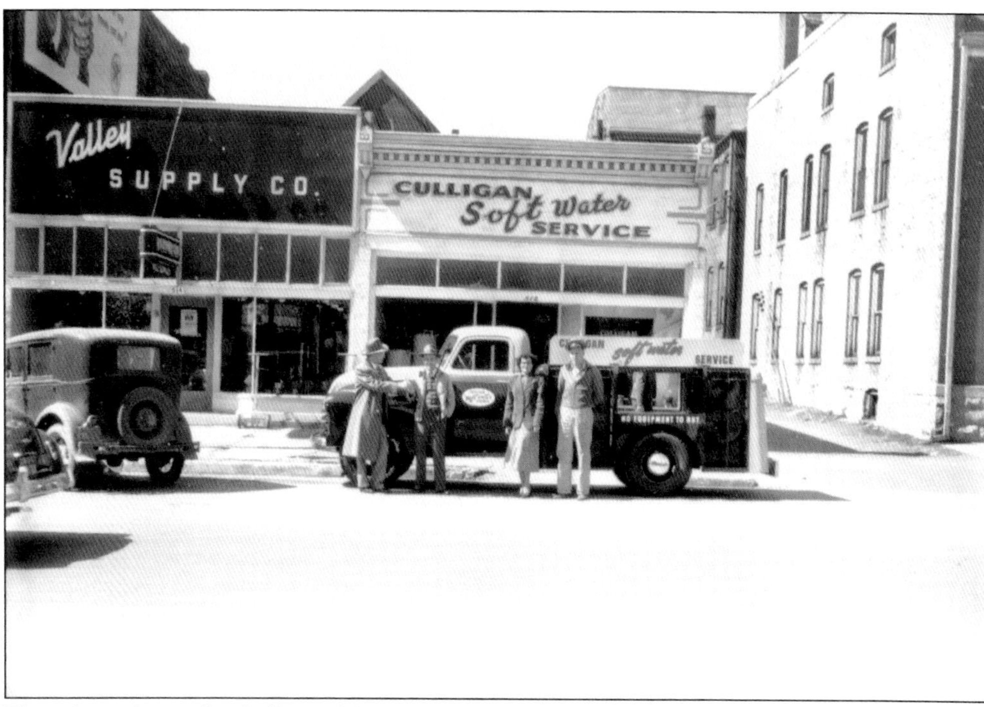

This photo shows the Culligan Water Company, at 512 Broadway, with their truck parked in front. Valley Supply, at 514 Broadway, is to the left. Both buildings have since been demolished. (April 1950)

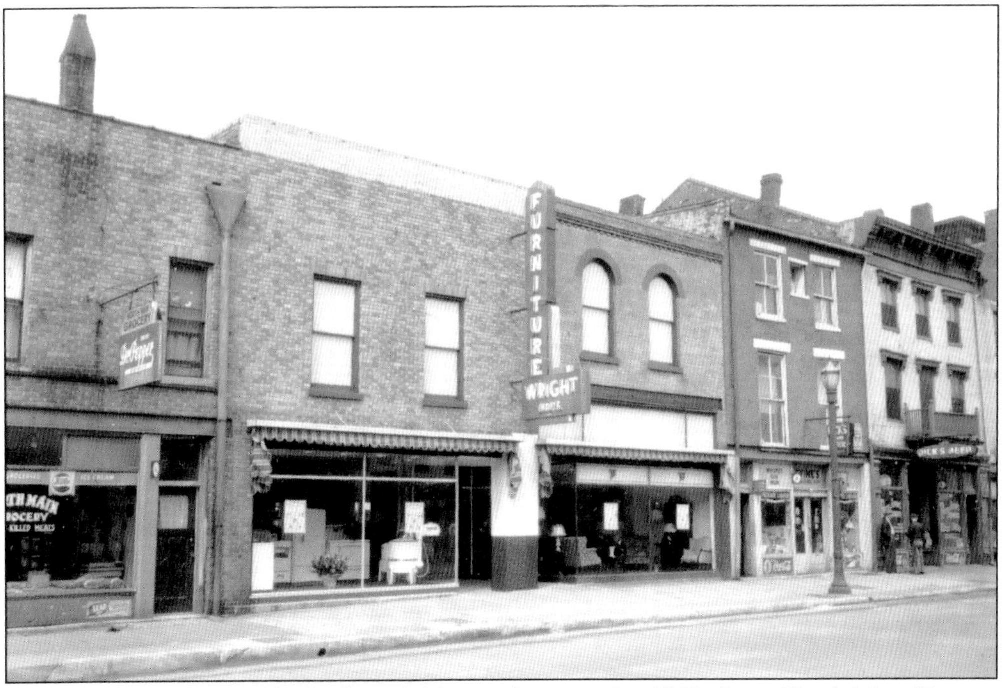

The west side of the 300 block of North Main is shown in this 1950 photo. North Main Grocery is at right and Wright Furniture is in the center.

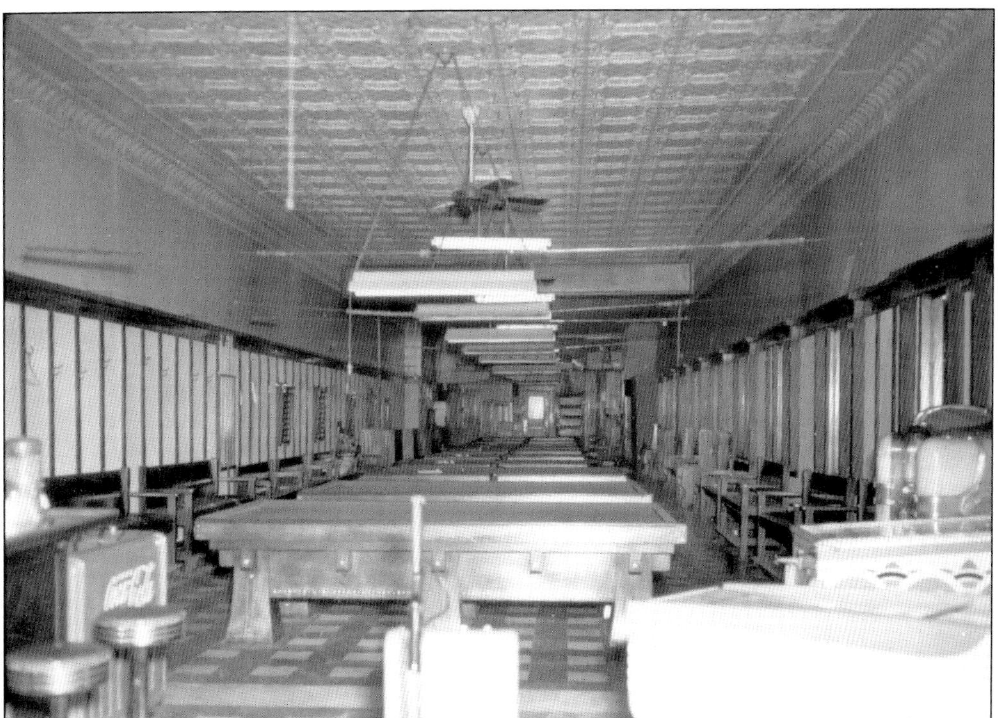

Before video game arcades there were pool halls. Here is the interior of the Crystal Billiard Parlor at 205 South Main. (June 1950)

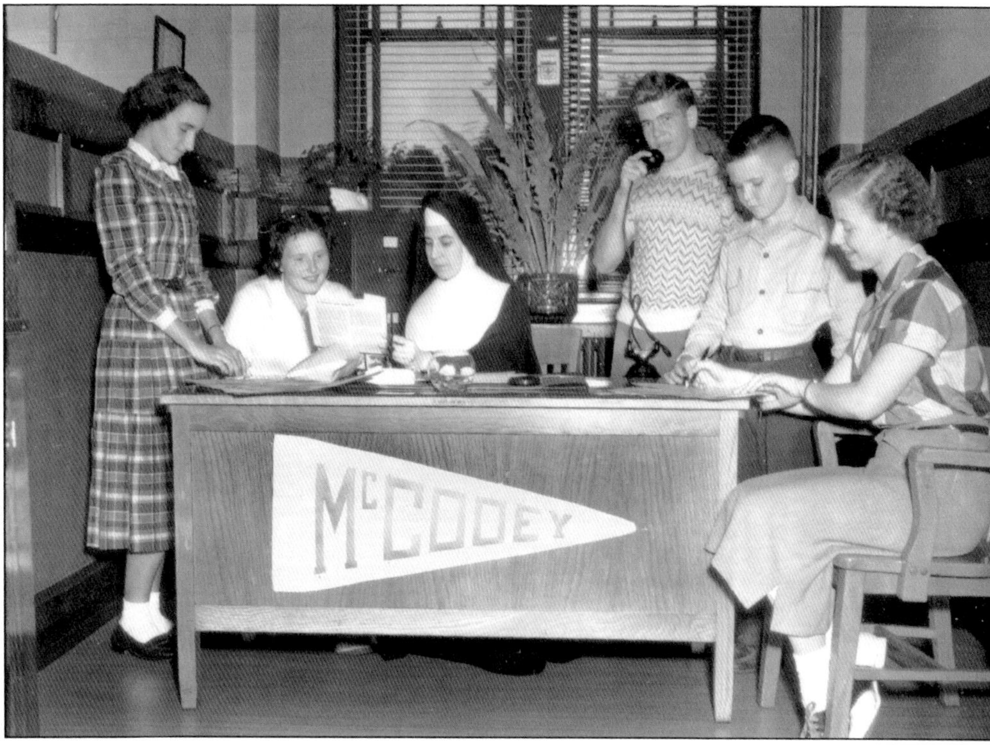

This is a scene at McCooey School, showing the students and teacher at their desks. The girl at far right has been identified as Lois Hirner. (September 1950)

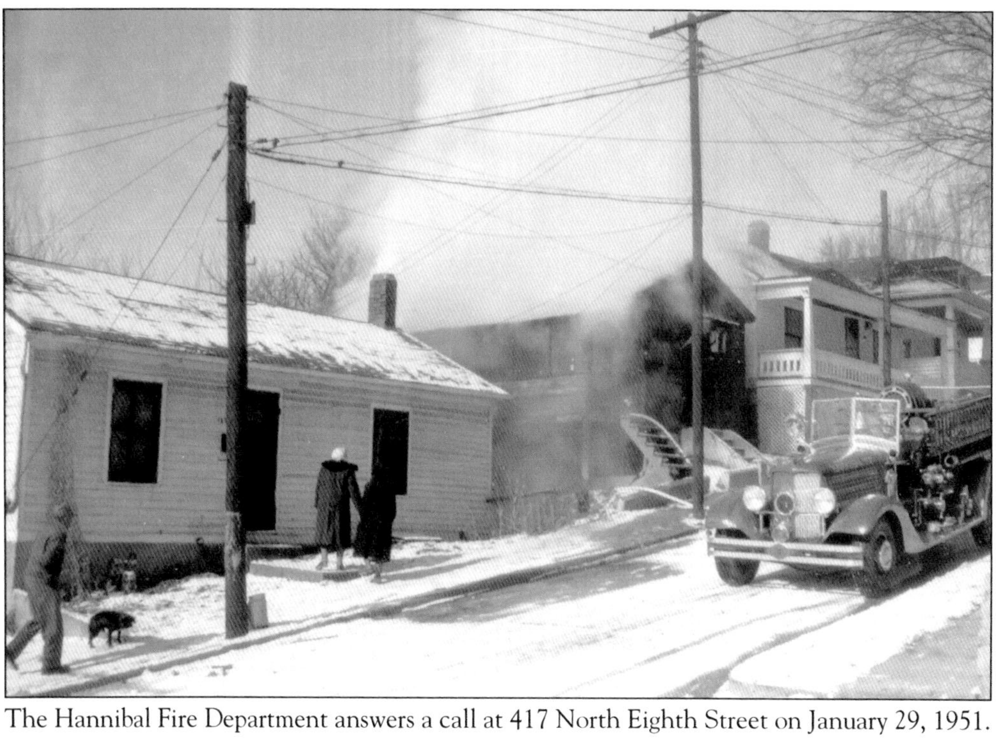
The Hannibal Fire Department answers a call at 417 North Eighth Street on January 29, 1951.

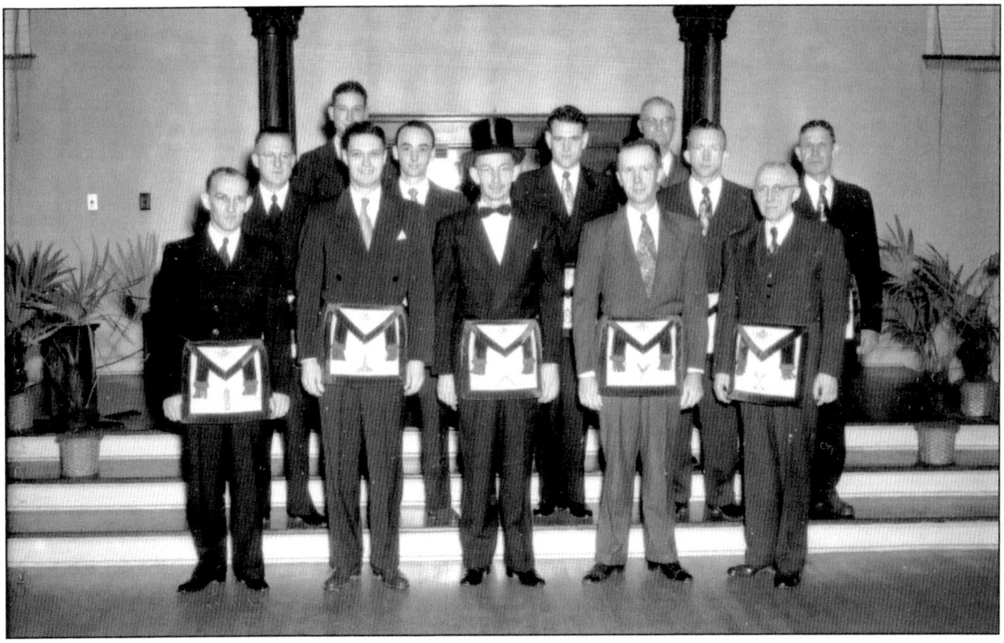

This photo shows the installation of officers of the Hannibal Masonic Lodge on January 8, 1951. Pictured, from left to right, are: (front row) Lee B. Turner, junior warden; Virgil P. Caulk, senior warden; John T. Kretzer, worshipful master; Frederick E. Herrin, secretary; J.A. Ihrig, treasurer; (second row) Marshall Walley, junior steward; James R. Ryan, senior steward; Robert Laswell, senior deacon; Ward Thompson, junior deacon; William C. Rhodes, chaplain, (third row) Kenneth Locke, marshall; Joseph B. Cornelius, tiler. Photo taken in the old Masonic Temple at Fifth and Center.

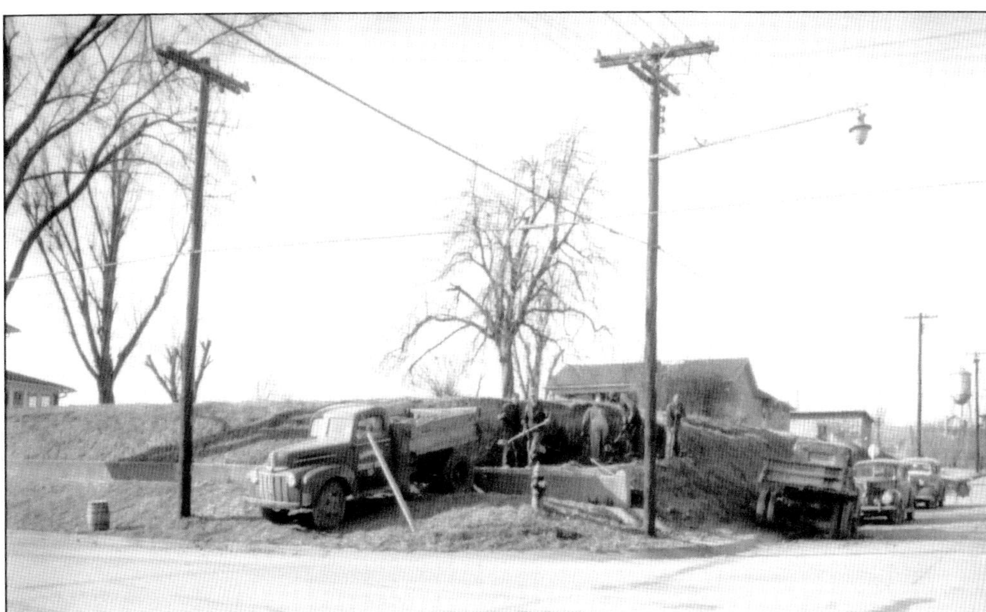

City workers remove a visibility obstruction at the intersection of Grand and Pleasant Streets in January 1951.

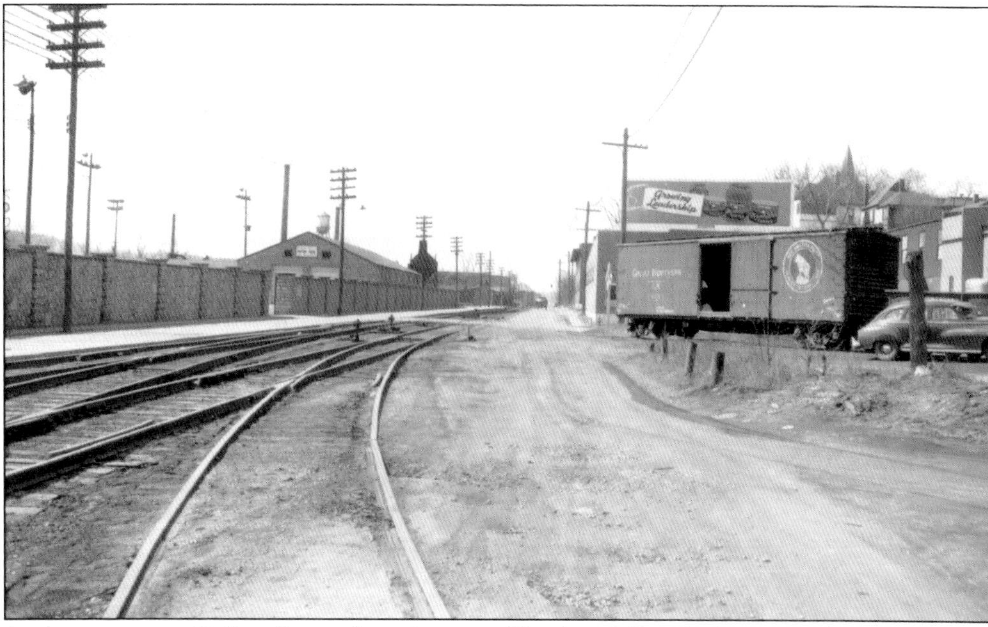

Looking west on Collier Street from between Third and Fourth Streets, railroad tracks are visible along the street and wall of Clemens Field at right. Today the tracks are gone, and where the boxcar sits in this picture, part of Hannibal's flood wall now stands. (February 1951)

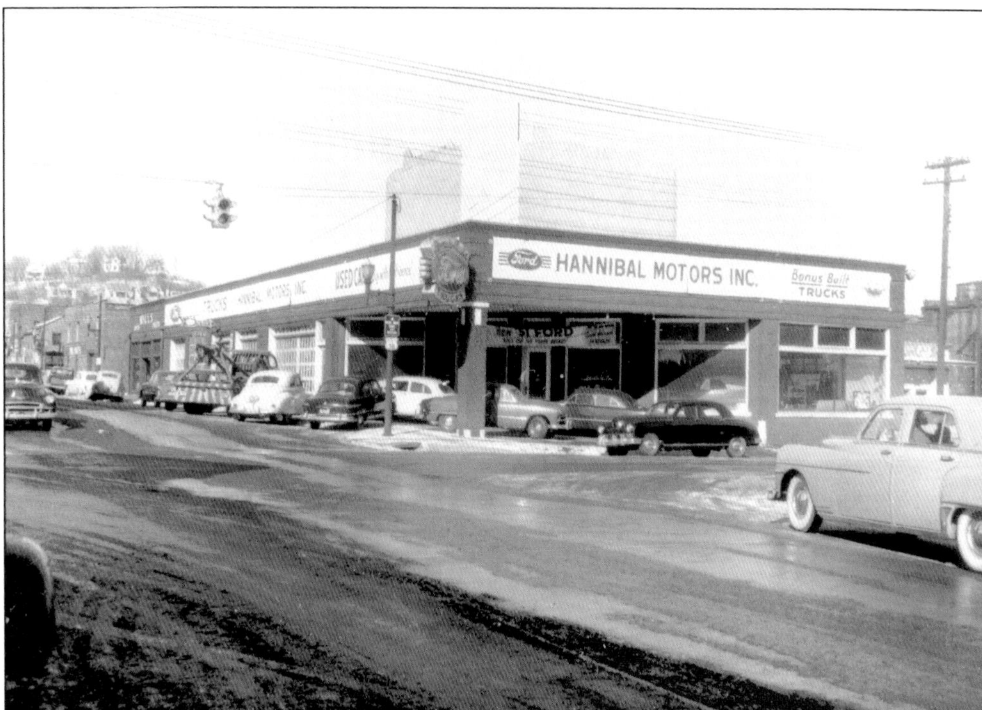

The building that is now home to the *Hannibal Courier-Post* was once Hannibal Motors, a Ford automobile dealership. Before the end of the year Hannibal Motors would move out to McMasters (see page 38, top). (February 1951)

This old building at 312 Center looks to be a candidate for demolition. It had just been purchased by Willard Reavis of Paris as warehouse for his wool business. As can be seen by the lettering at the top of the structure, it had at one time been used as a warehouse for Avery Burch Furniture. We know the building better today as the old Standard Printing Warehouse. Note the residential structure to the left, which no longer stands. (March 1951)

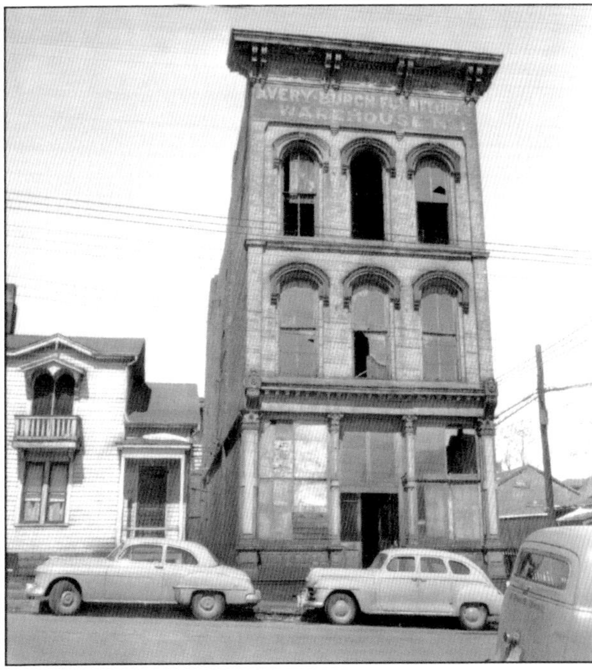

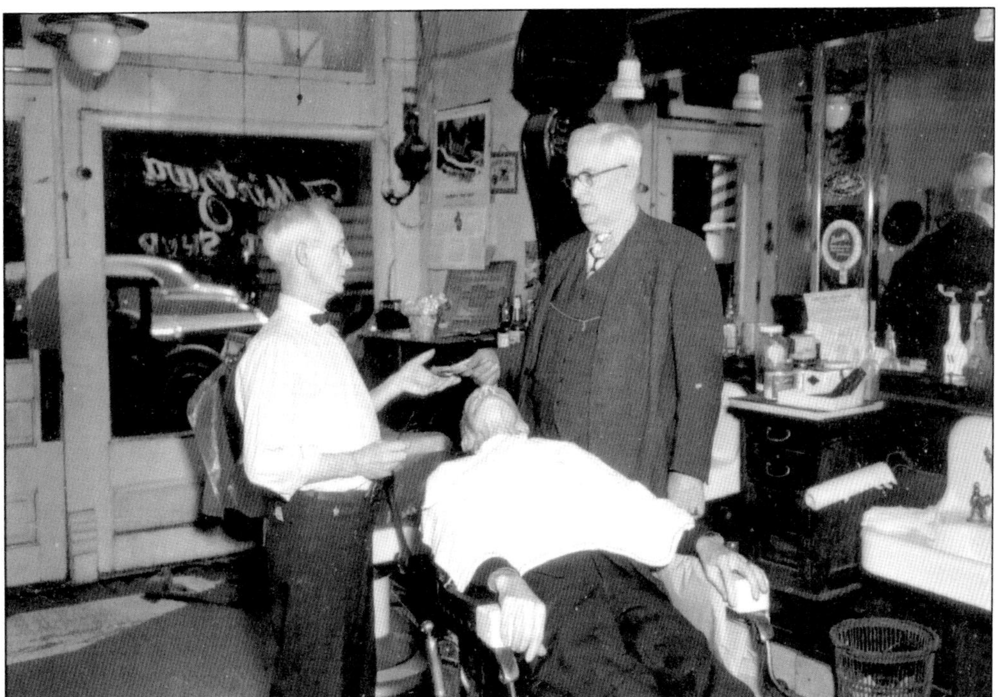

This scene could have been lifted from a Norman Rockwell painting. It is the inside of Fred Mirtzwa's barbershop, which stood at 114 Bird Street. Mirtzwa is remembered for giving free haircuts to the children at the Home of the Friendless. The building that housed his barbershop was razed in 1968 (for an outside view of this building, see page 64, top). The photo dates from March 1951.

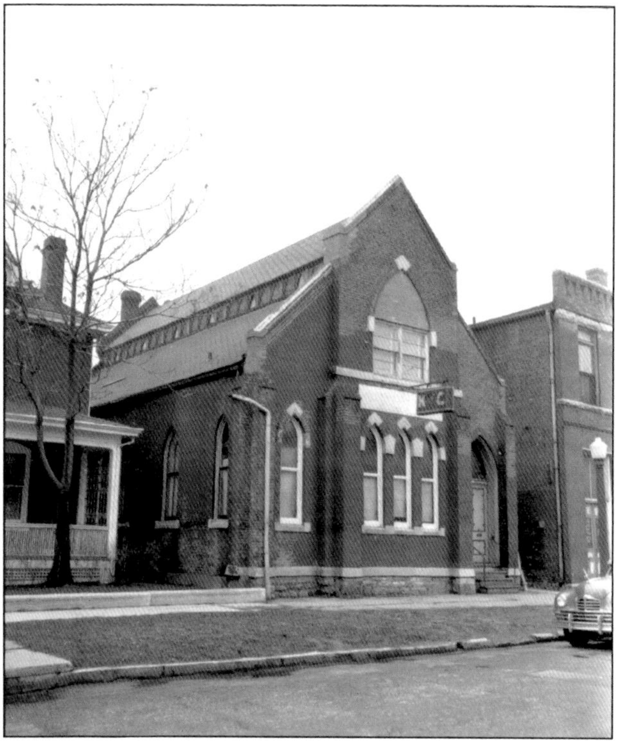

The old Knights of Columbus hall stood at 105 South Fifth Street. Originally built for the Women's Christian Temperance Union, this building served the K of C for many years. It fell to the wrecking ball in the late 1960s, and today Farmers & Merchants Bank stands on the site. (March 1951)

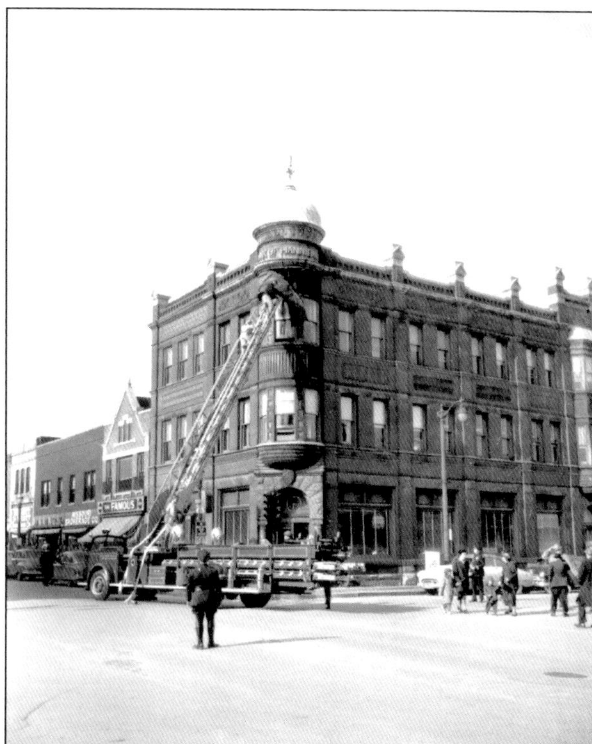

Firemen remove a section of sheet tin from the tower of the Hannibal National Bank at Main and Broadway after it had been blown loose in a storm. The piece was never reinstalled and the damage called attention to the aging condition of the structure. The following year a bank official, Morton Weaver, announced that the bank's exterior would be completely redone with a modern façade. (March 1951)

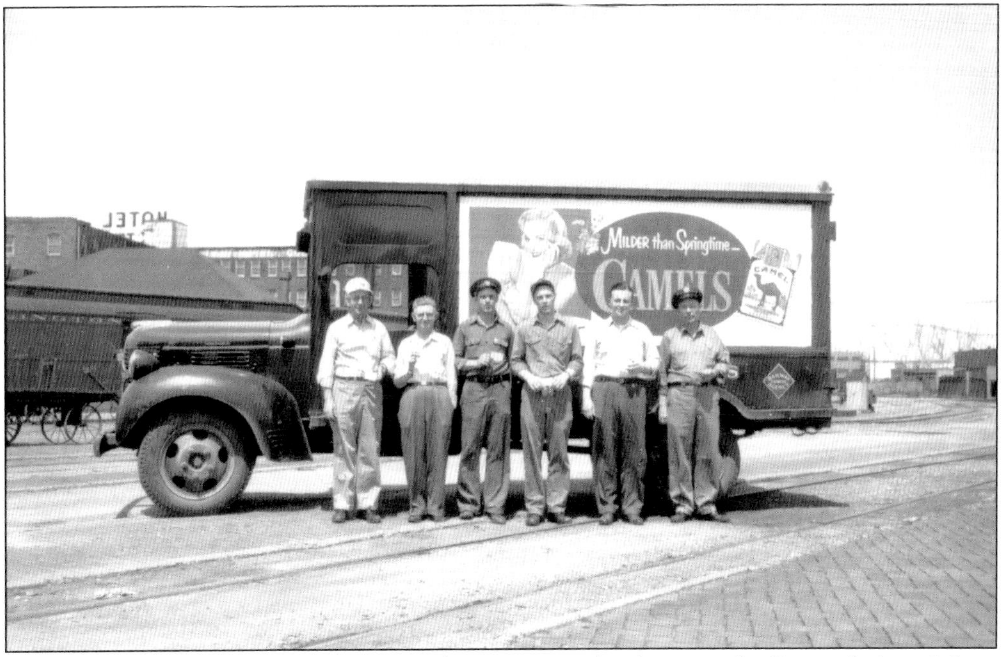

In May 1951, Railway Express Agency drivers received safety awards. Pictured, from left to right, are W.P. Strube, G.A. Likes, J.R. Redman, George W. Gundling, E.C. Buxman, and J.B. Tapley. The photo was taken behind the old Union Depot.

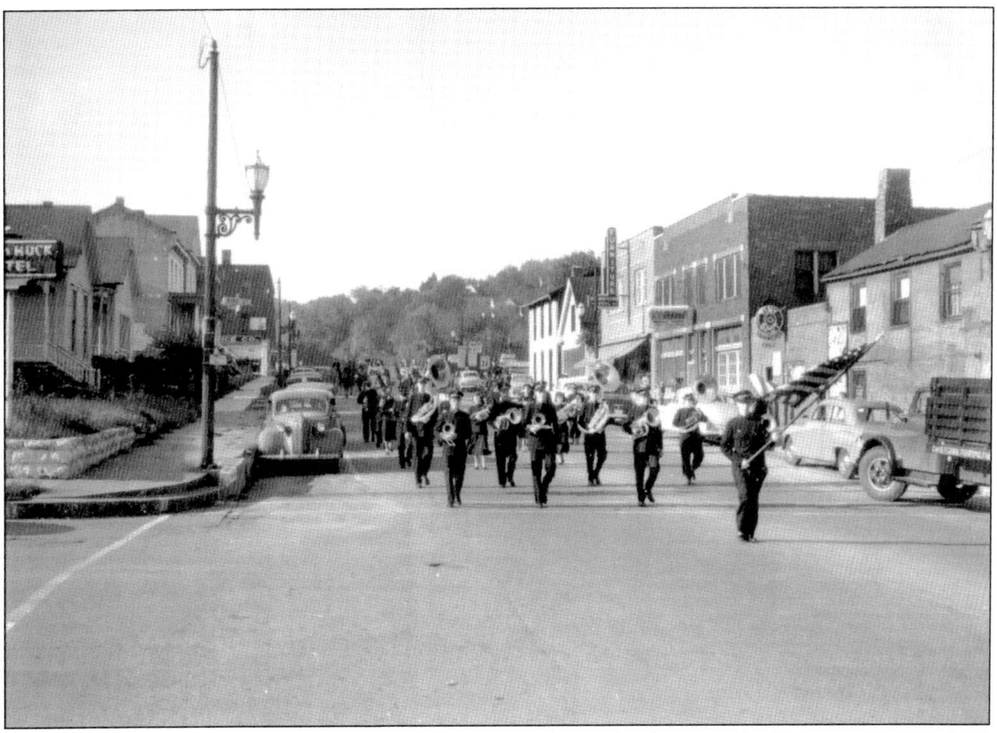
Everyone loves a parade. The backdrop of this parade is Third Street, looking north from Bird Street. (September 1951)

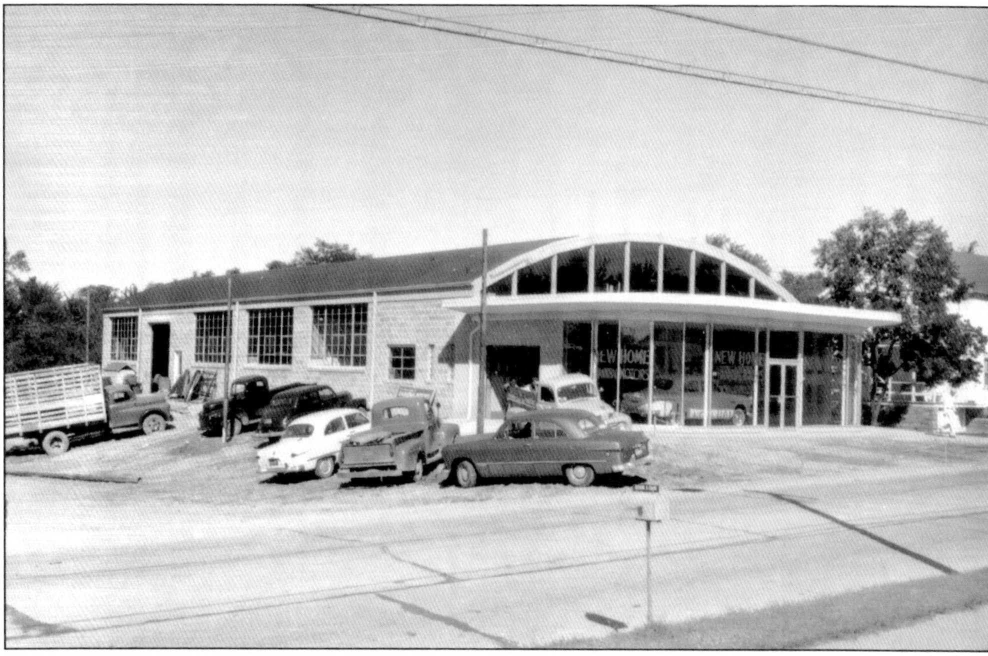

In the summer of 1951, Hannibal Motors moved into this new building at 4215 McMasters. This building would later be the location of Links' Superama, and as of 2004 houses Martin's True Value Hardware.

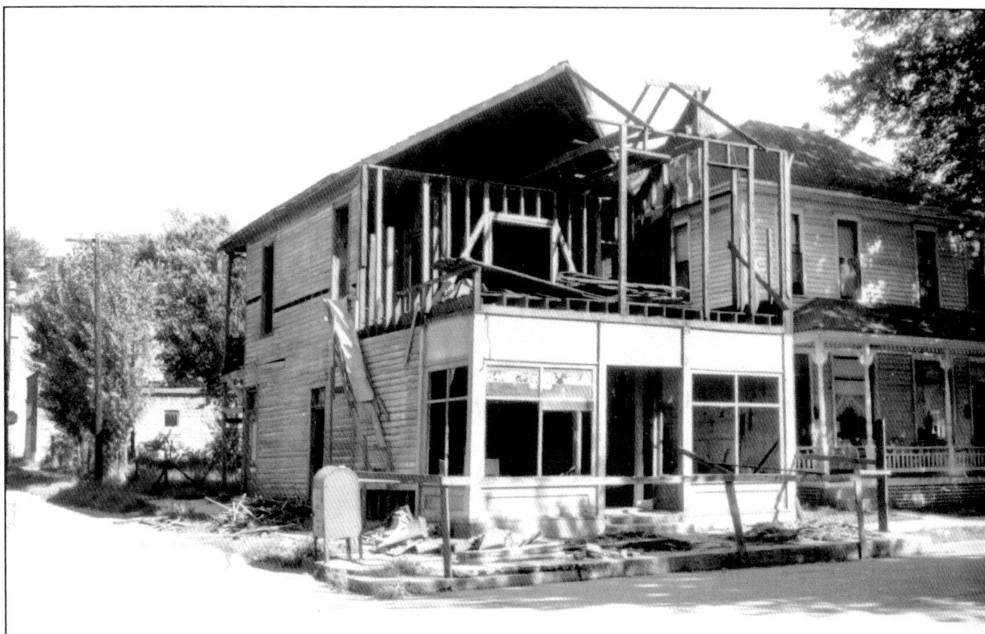

This two-story frame store building at 600 Union Street was built in 1867 by J.L. Buchanan, with lumber purchased from the Hannibal Planing Mill. Mr. and Mrs. Eddie Hall, who were having the building torn down, were going to use some of the materials to build a new home on the site. (September 1951)

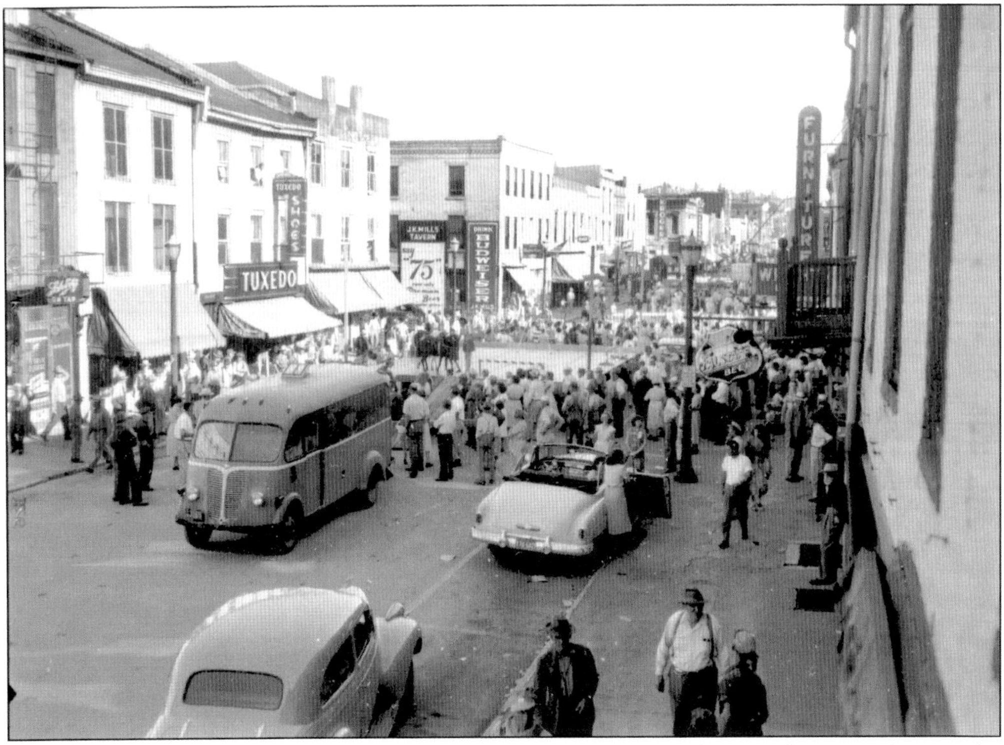

This photo, taken from the balcony of the Planter's Hotel, shows the crowds on North Main for the Fall Festival. Notice the stage set up in the middle of the street. Many of the buildings in this photo are now parking lots. (September 1951)

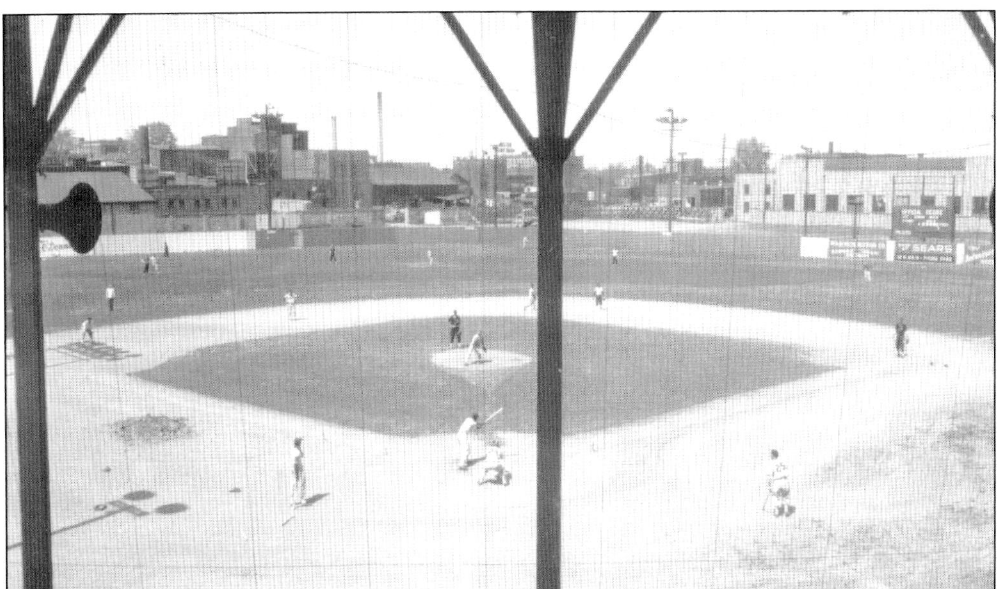

Spring is a time for robins and tulips . . . and baseball! This was the season opener for the Hannibal Stags, played at Clemens Field. The Stags, part of the Mississippi-Ohio Valley League, would finish in an impressive second place when the season ended in September. (March 1952)

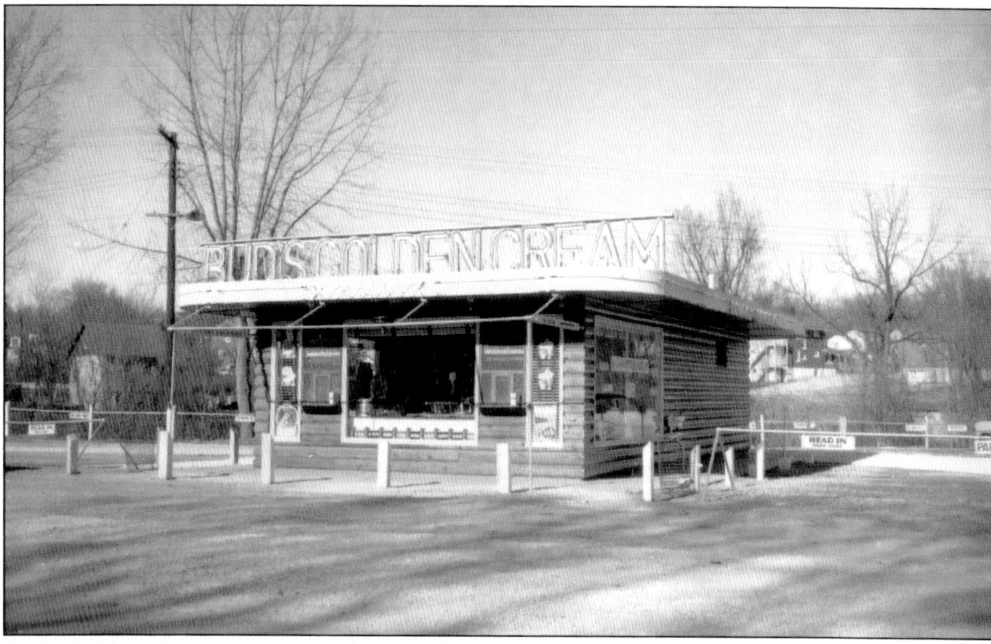

Bud's Golden Cream was a popular stop for the kids. Bud's was located at the intersection of U.S. 61 and U.S. 36 (now U.S. 61 and Highway MM). There are still those who remember the yellow and red pinback buttons that said "I made a pig of myself at Bud's," and how you received one. This photo dates from March 1952, when Bud's first opened.

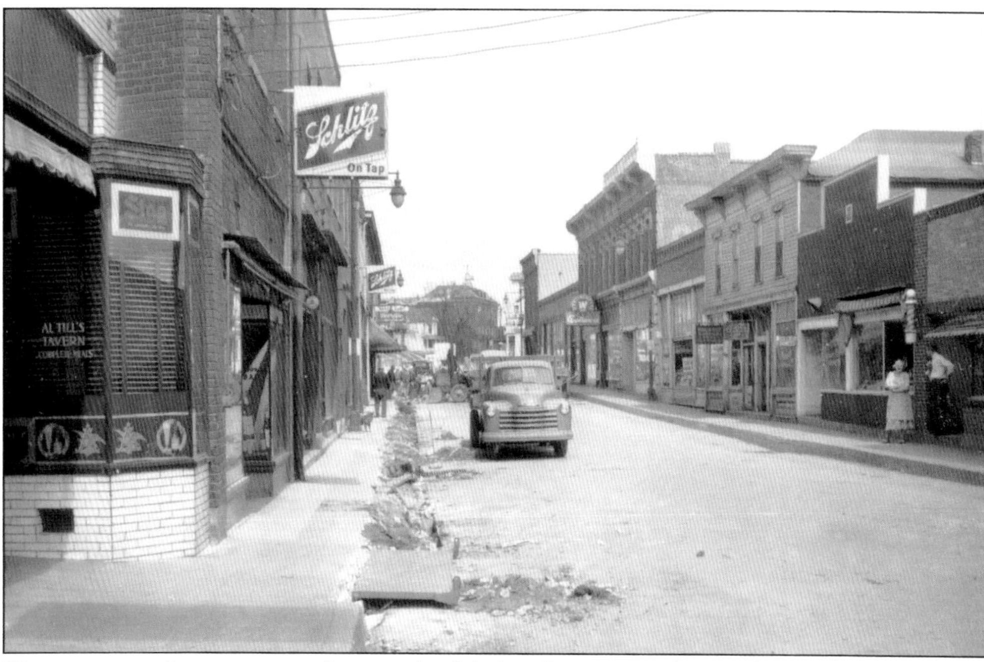

The city street department works to widen Market Street near the Wedge. The narrow street, laid out long before the automobile, had been very treacherous to navigate, especially with cars parked along the curb. Market Street near the Wedge was once a thriving business area, with hardware, grocery, and dime stores, as well as a bank. (April 1952)

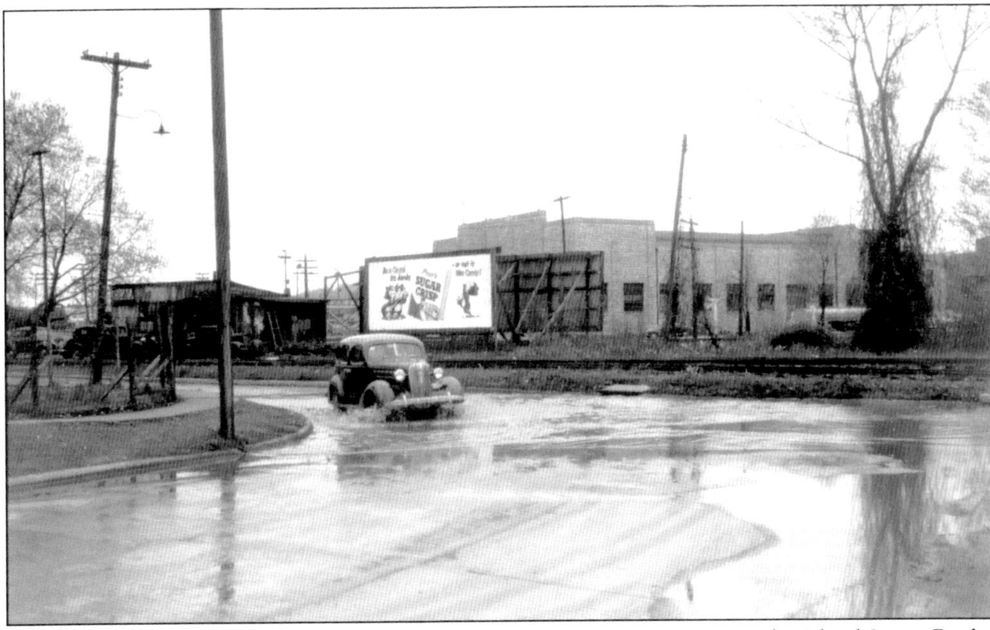

A car rounds the corner on Monroe Street on the south side after crossing the Third Street Bridge over Bear Creek during high water. The Third Street Bridge was often closed due to flooding, and this situation would eventually lead to the construction of the Third Street Viaduct, which replaced the bridge. The Admiral Coontz Armory is visible in the background. (March 1952)

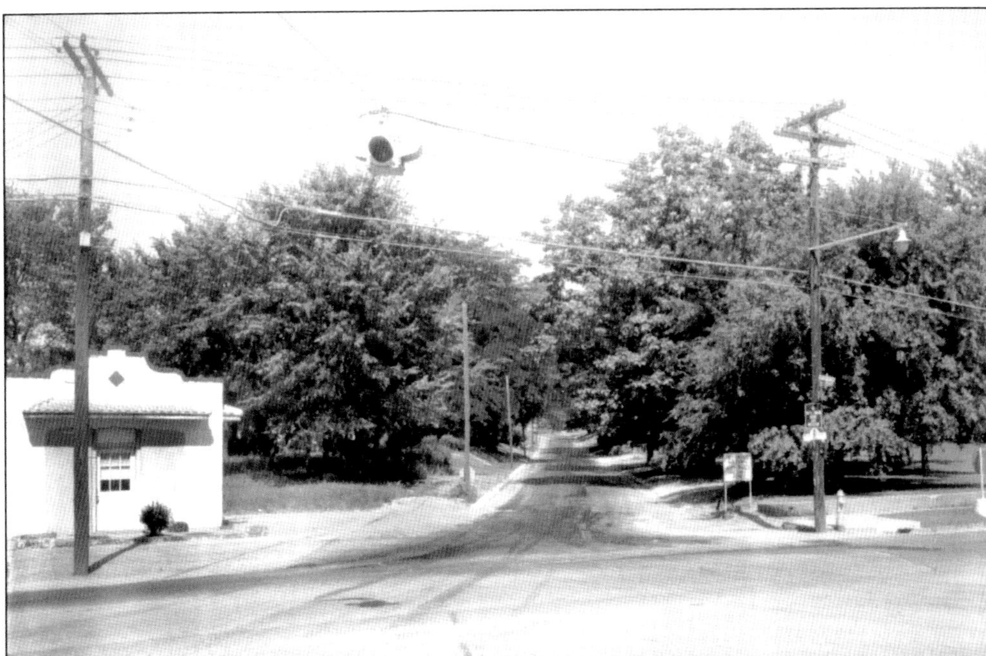

Here is the intersection of Pleasant and U.S. 61 when this was the outskirts of town. The white building partially visible at left was the old Dutch Mill, a popular restaurant dating back to the 1930s. It would be replaced by the Immanuel Baptist Church. The traffic light had just recently been installed, as this intersection had been the scene of numerous accidents. (May 1952)

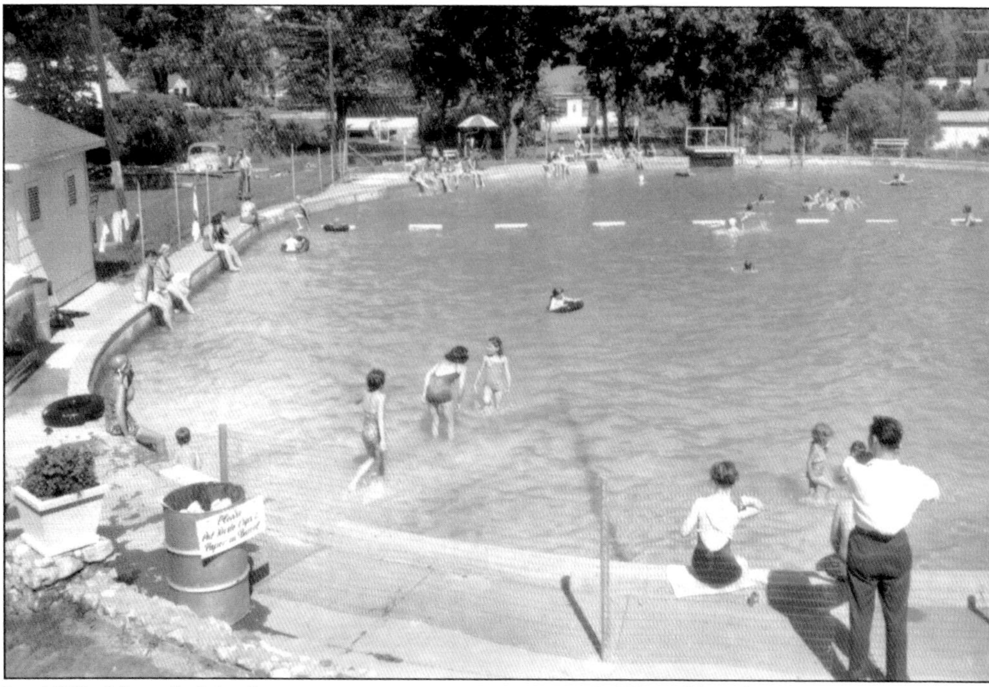

In 1952, Hannibal had no community swimming pool. The old Indian Mound Swimming Pool had fallen into disrepair and was acquired by the Moose Lodge. The lodge renovated the pool and opened it for their members. On the June day when this photo was taken in 1952, temperatures had climbed into the 90s, and the pool saw very heavy use. When construction on the U.S. 36 overpass began, the pool was removed.

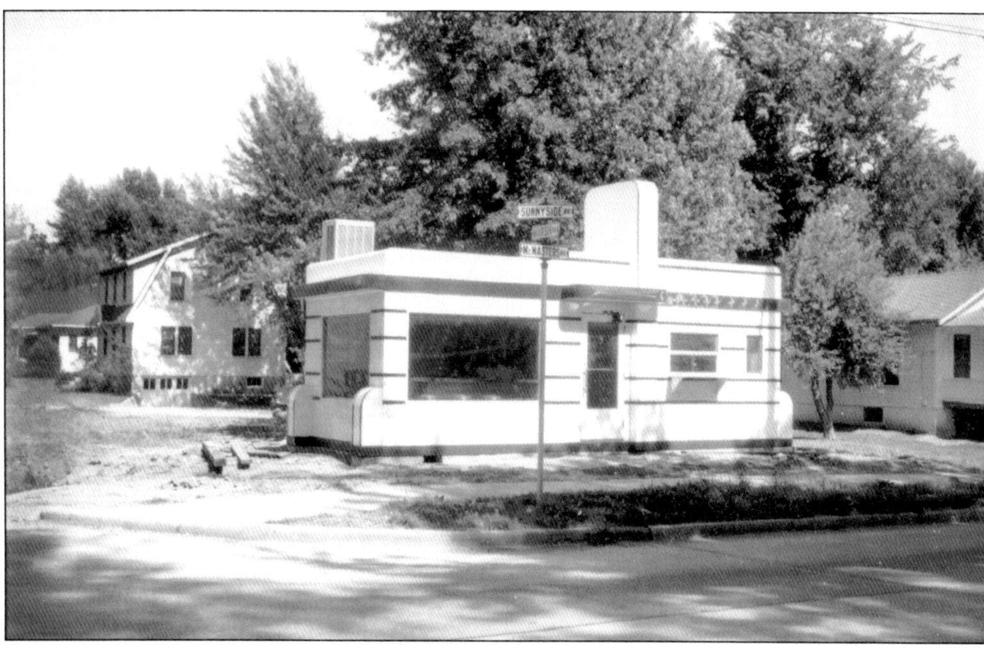

In June 1952, a new burger bar opened at 3906 McMasters Avenue. The building was a pre-fabricated metal unit that was trucked in and set down on a concrete foundation.

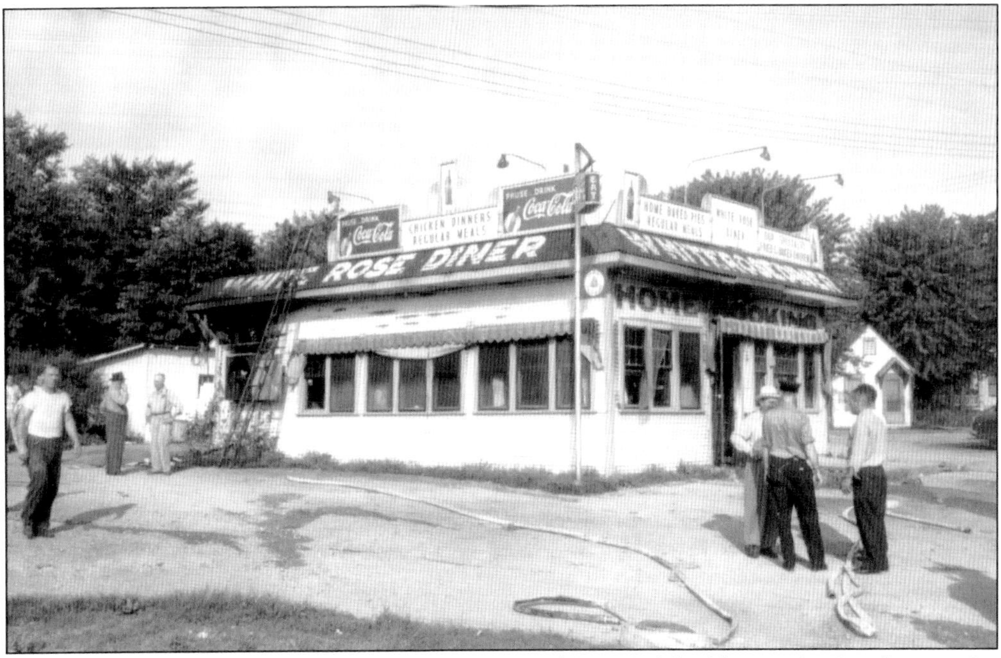

The White Rose Diner at the Junction (U.S. 61 and U.S. 36) had been a landmark since the 1930s. In July 1952, the little diner suffered damage from a fire, which started from grease in the kitchen area. This photo was taken after the fire had been extinguished.

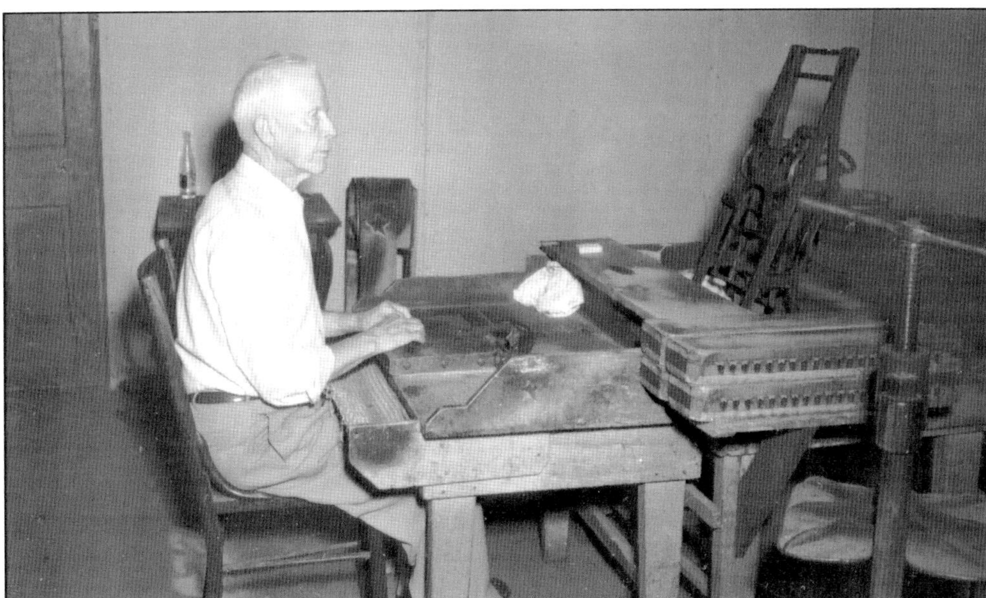

This photo documented the end of an era. Fred Harrow, aged 79, was the last cigar maker in Hannibal and was retiring. As owner and operator of the Red Star Cigar Factory on Market Street, he opened his business in 1908. At that time there were over 200 people working in cigar manufacturing in Hannibal. When the Red Star Cigar Factory was at peak production, Harrow had eleven workers and produced 70,000 cigars per month. Harrow's most expensive cigars sold at two for a quarter. (July 1952)

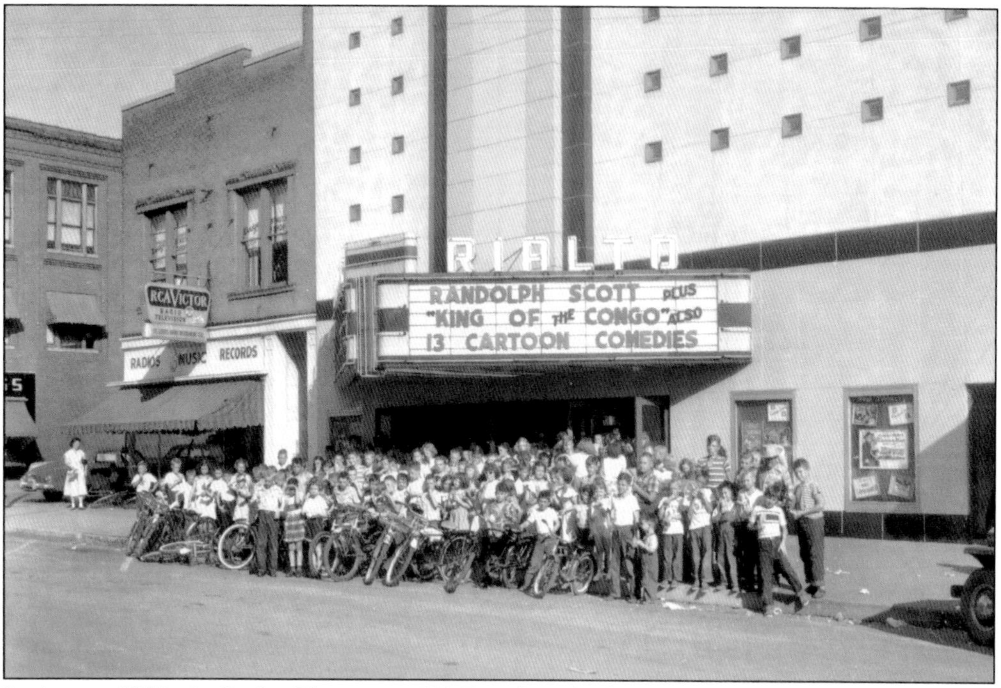

In August 1952, the Rialto Theater at 603 Broadway had a special back-to-school event, and some of the crowd of children posed for this photo. From the billing on the theater marquee, it looks like they had quite a show.

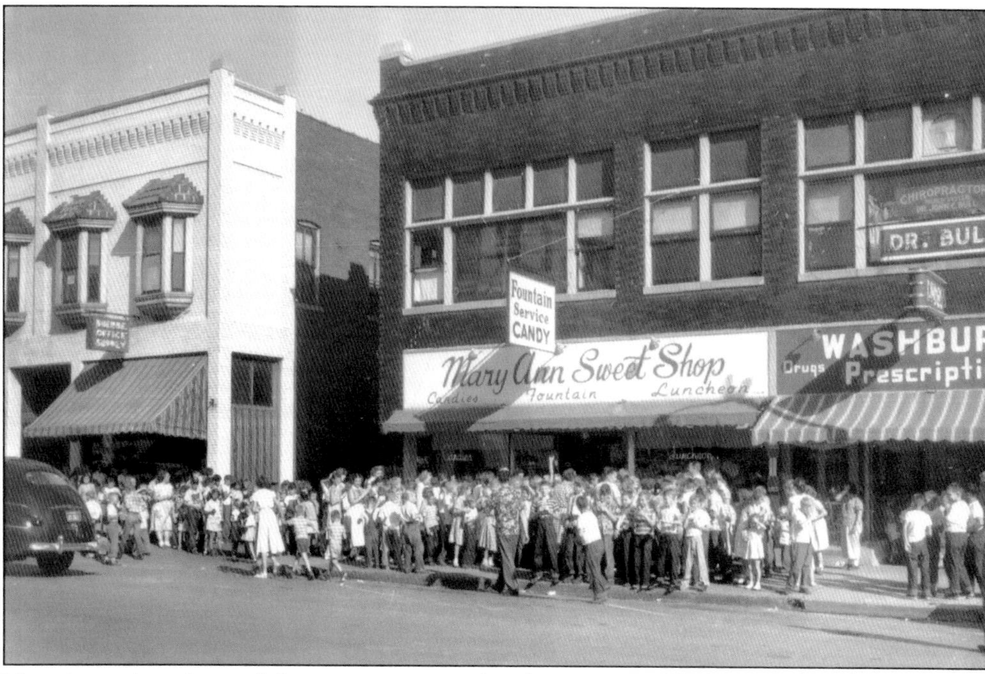

Here is another photo of the same event, with a large group of kids just a few doors down in front of the Mary Ann Sweet Shop. They were given a free popsicle, and if you look carefully you will see several children with their treat. (August 1952)

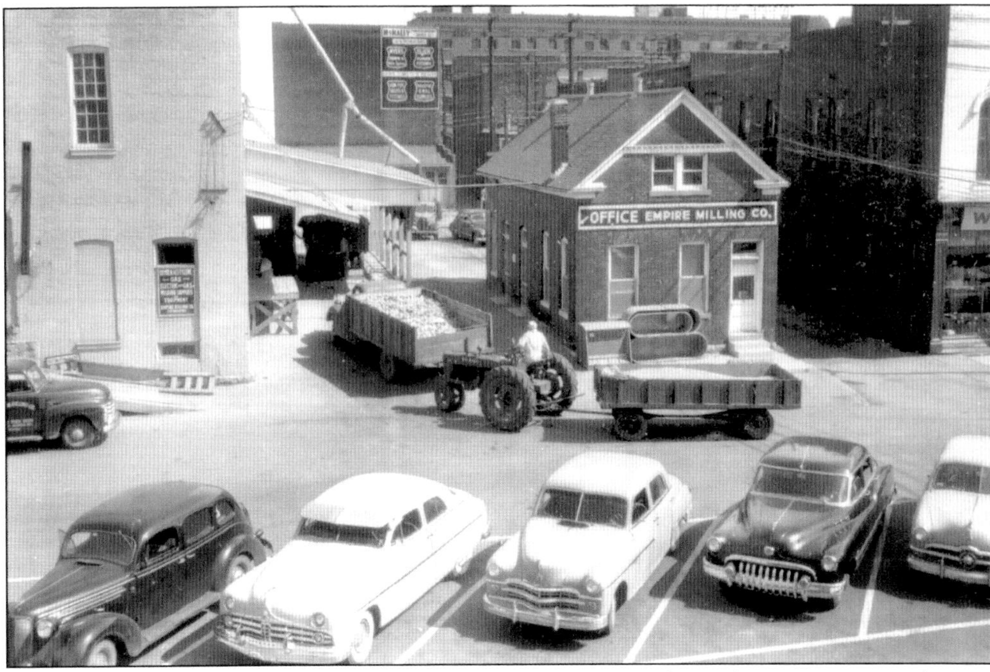

The Empire Mills, which stood on East Broadway, was a very busy place every year at harvest time. This August 1952 photo shows grain trucks and a tractor and farm wagon waiting to unload their grain. Empire Mills, built in the 1870s, closed in the late 1960s and the buildings were demolished in 1971. Notice the angle parking in the center of East Broadway.

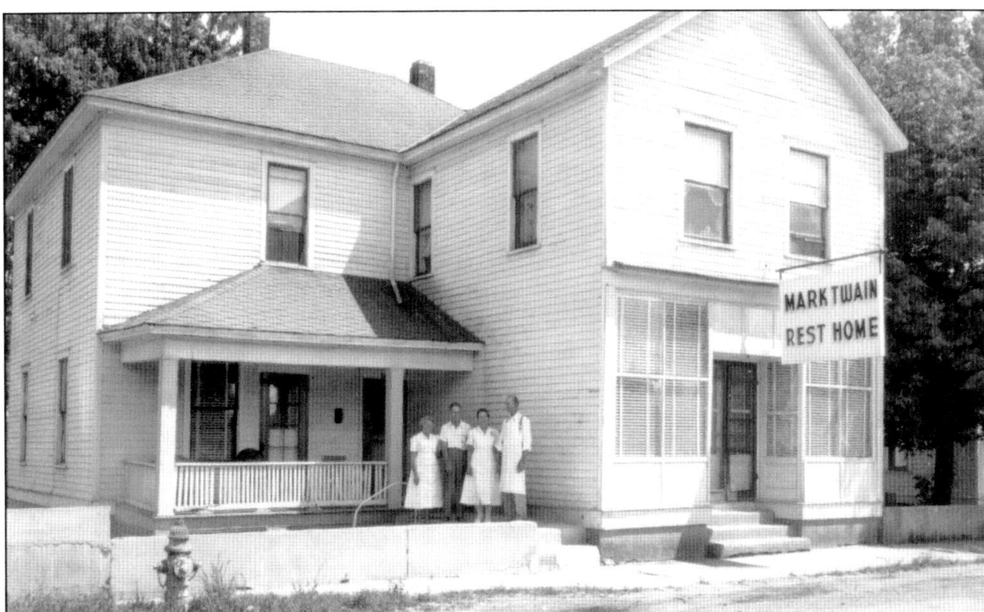

The Mark Twain Rest Home was located at 1220 Lindell Avenue. Operated by Mr. and Mrs. E.M. Smallwood, the home accommodated twenty patients. Here posed in front of the home are, from left to right: Mrs. Meatia Bryant, cook; Robt. Cochran, custodian; Mrs. Smallwood, and Mr. Smallwood. (August 1952)

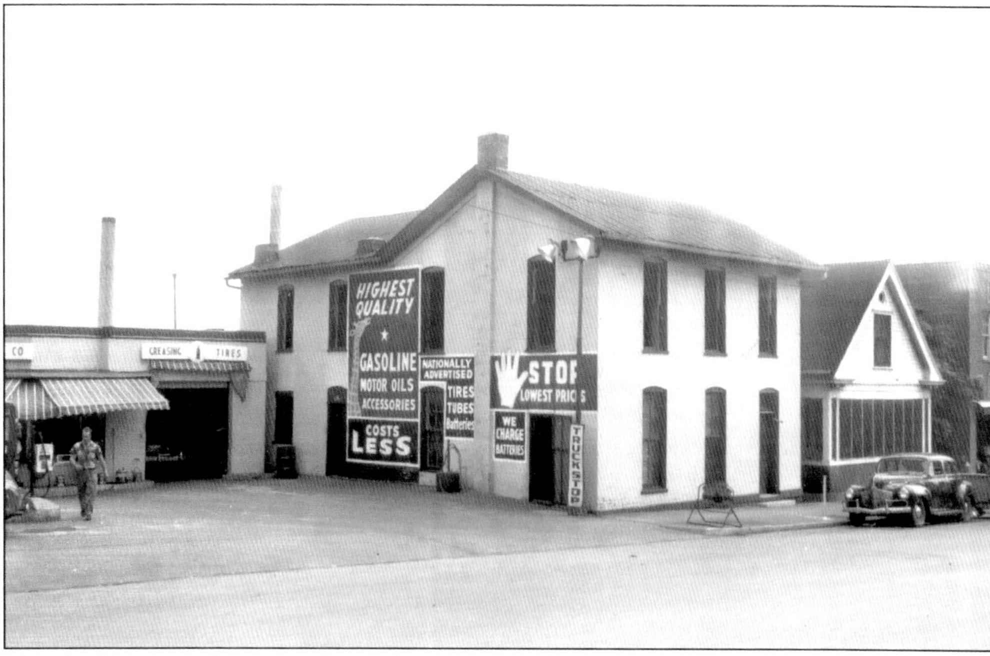

This building, on the east side of the 300 block of North Third, is pictured just prior to demolition. The site was being cleared for the expansion of the Consolidated Oil filling station, which is partly visible at far left. (October 1952)

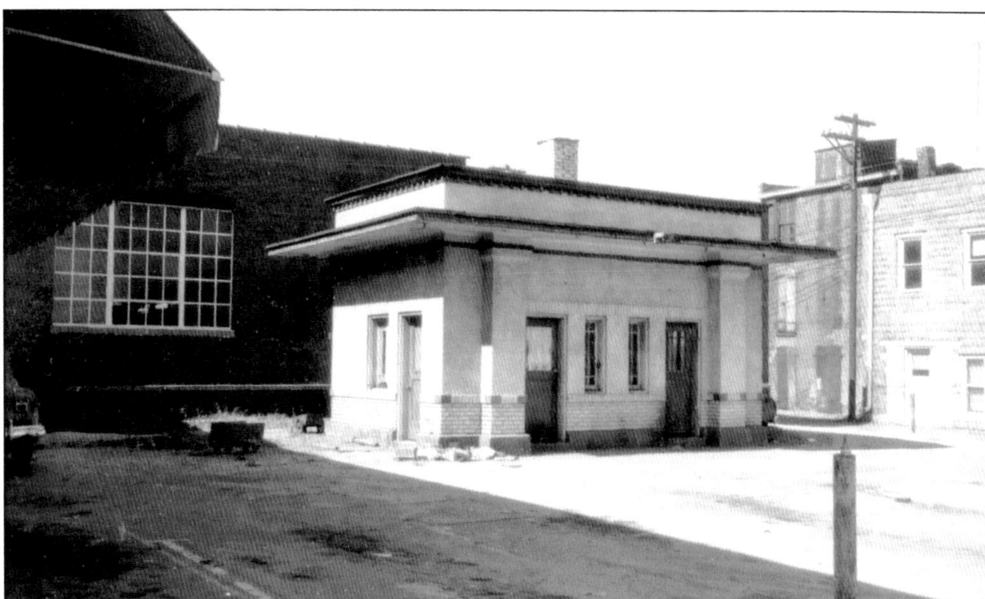

On the subject of filling stations, this is a photo of one of Hannibal's early stations on the eve of demolition. This one stood in the 200 block of Center Street, in the middle of what is today the parking lot for the *Hannibal Courier-Post*. According to a note in the paper on September 20, 1952, this building, once a Standard Oil filling station, may have been the third one that Standard Oil had built, dating back to 1916. Such a distinction, however, did not save it from the wrecking ball.

Pictured left to right are Girl Scouts Jackie Hudson, Ann Conner, and Sharon Ellis. The girls pose in front of the Community Chest Red Feather at Main and Broadway. The annual Community Chest drive was a major event in Hannibal and the red feather sign was a very familiar sight in downtown Hannibal. The Community Chest was a forerunner of the United Way. (October 1952)

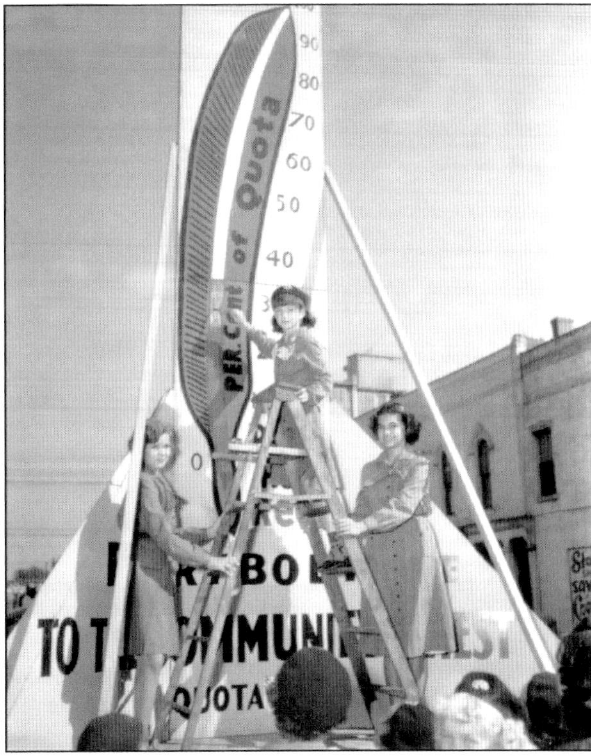

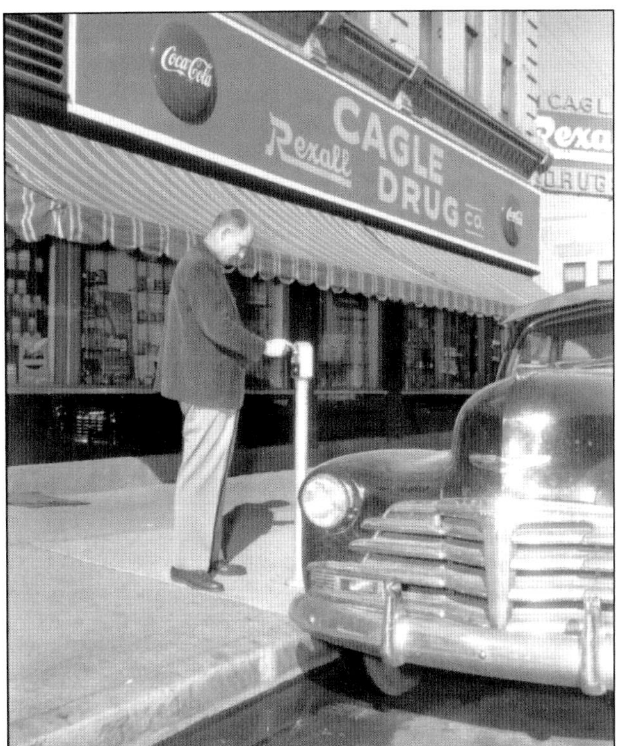

In September 1952, Hannibal installed parking meters along the commercial streets. Revenue was to be used for the purchase of property for municipal parking lots. Archie Craig, manager of the Surplus store on East Broadway, demonstrates how easy it is to use the new parking meters. In the first month of use nearly $8,000 in pennies and nickels were collected from the new meters. Photo taken in 100 block of South Main, with Cagle Drug Store in the background.

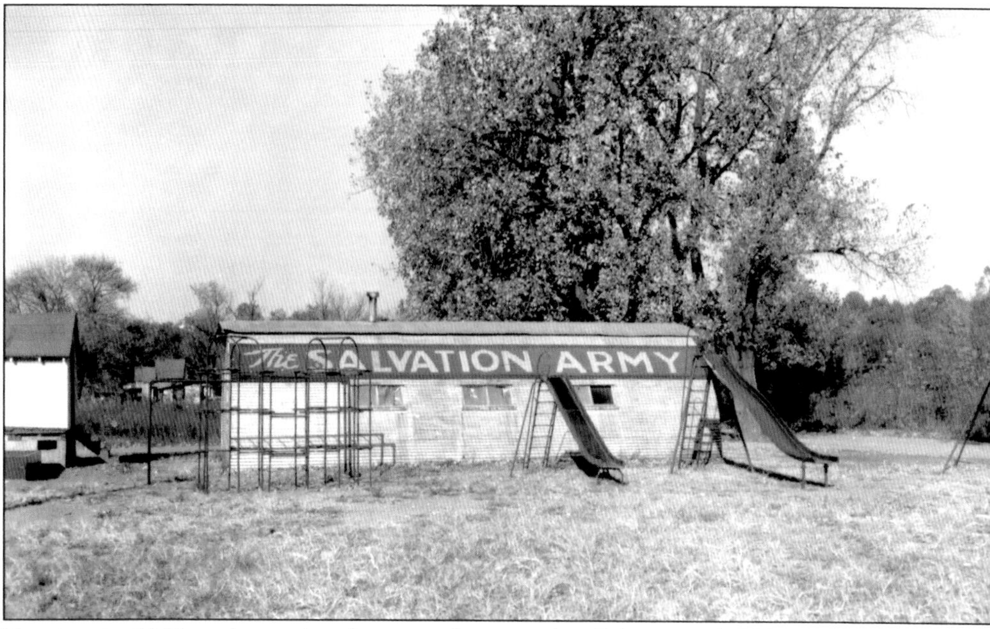

Starting in 1947 and running for several years, the Salvation Army ran an "outpost"on Patchen Street, which consisted of an activities center in a Quonset hut and some playground equipment. This photo shows the Patchen Street outpost as it appeared in October 1952, its fifth anniversary of operation.

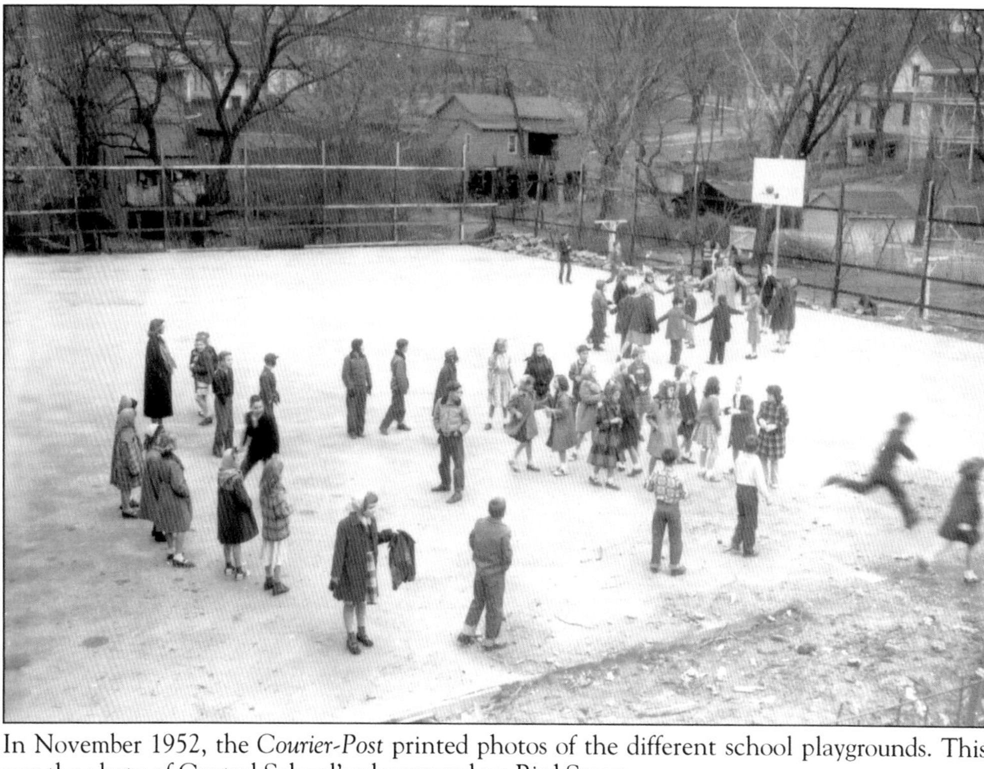

In November 1952, the *Courier-Post* printed photos of the different school playgrounds. This was the photo of Central School's playground on Bird Street.

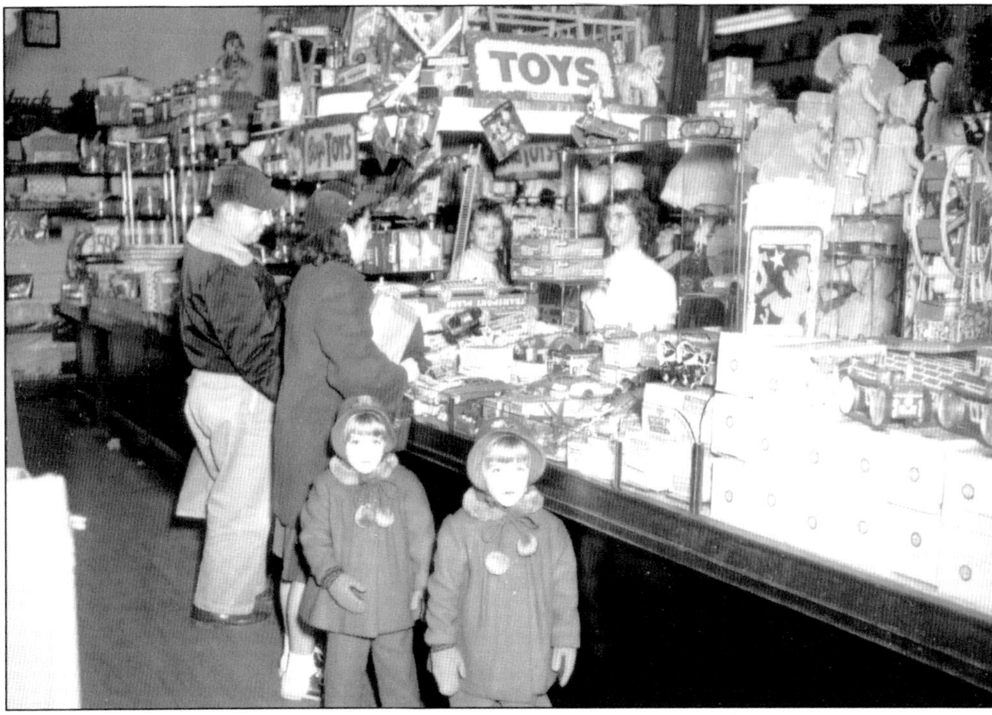

This is the toy department of Kresge's Department Store during Christmas season. Pictured here are Mr. and Mrs. Nova Givan and their three-and-one-half-year-old twin daughters Mary and Martha. The two girls know exactly what they want Santa to bring them—cowboy hats and guns! (December 1952)

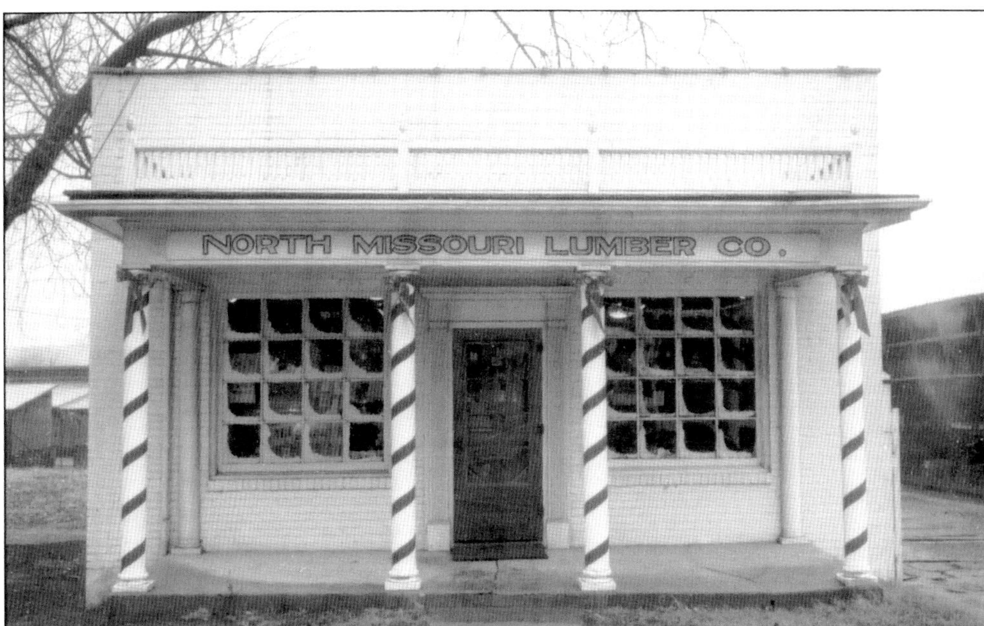

Here is the North Missouri Lumber Company office building decorated for Christmas. Located at 2401 Market, it is now the Hannibal Homestore. (December 1952)

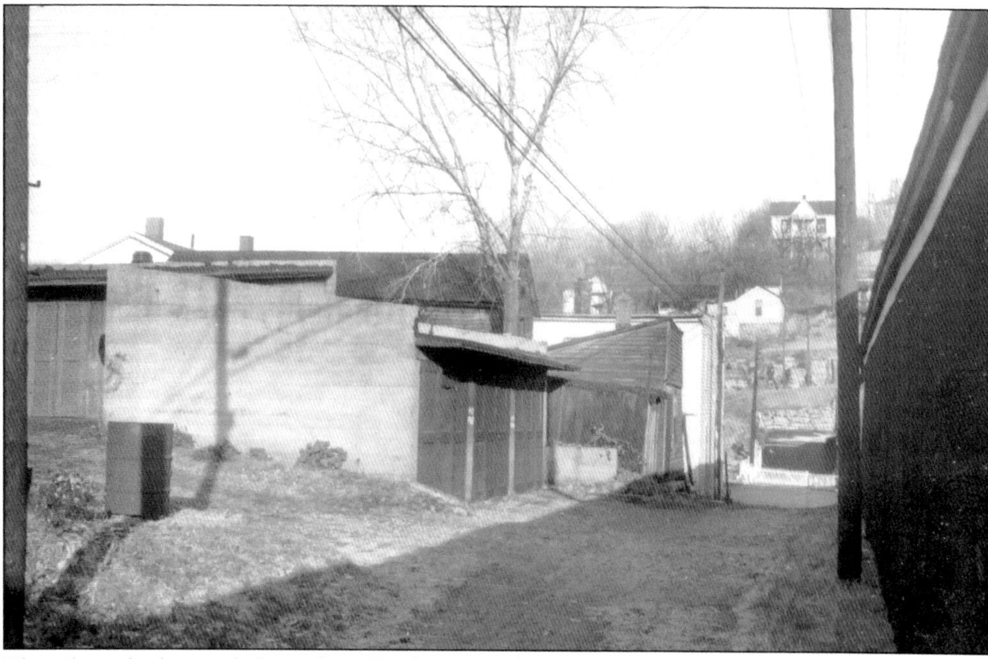

This photo looks north from the alley between the 200 block of North and Hill Streets. The city was cleaning up the alley, known as "Dead Man's Alley," removing dilapidated sheds and outdoor toilets. At right is the rear of Cruikshank Lumber Company. (November 1952)

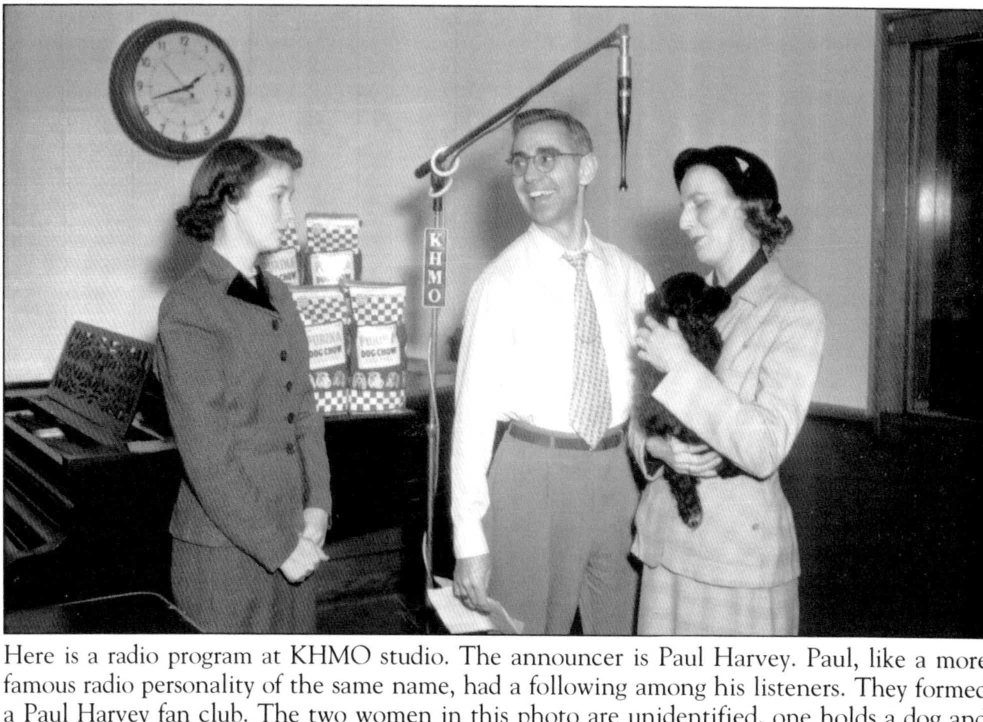

Here is a radio program at KHMO studio. The announcer is Paul Harvey. Paul, like a more famous radio personality of the same name, had a following among his listeners. They formed a Paul Harvey fan club. The two women in this photo are unidentified, one holds a dog and there are bags of Purina Dog Chow on the piano in the background. Purina was one of KHMO's sponsors at the time. (January 1953)

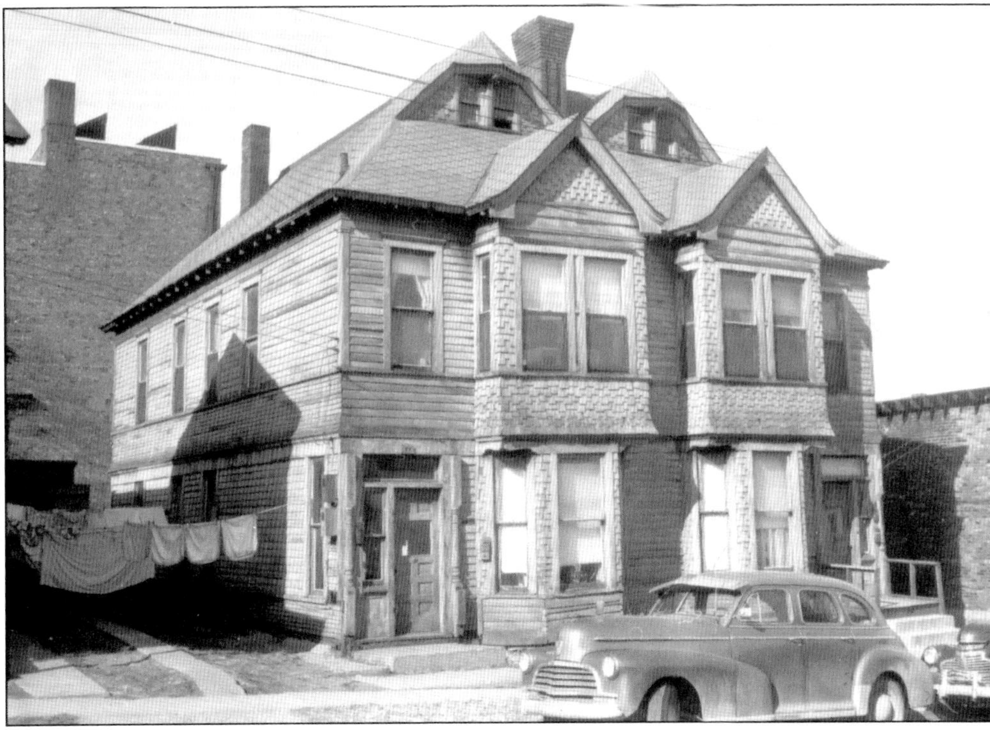

Here is a duplex located at 412–414 Church Street. It would be razed in 1994 for parking for the public library. At the time of the photo it had been purchased for use as a nursing home. (February 1953)

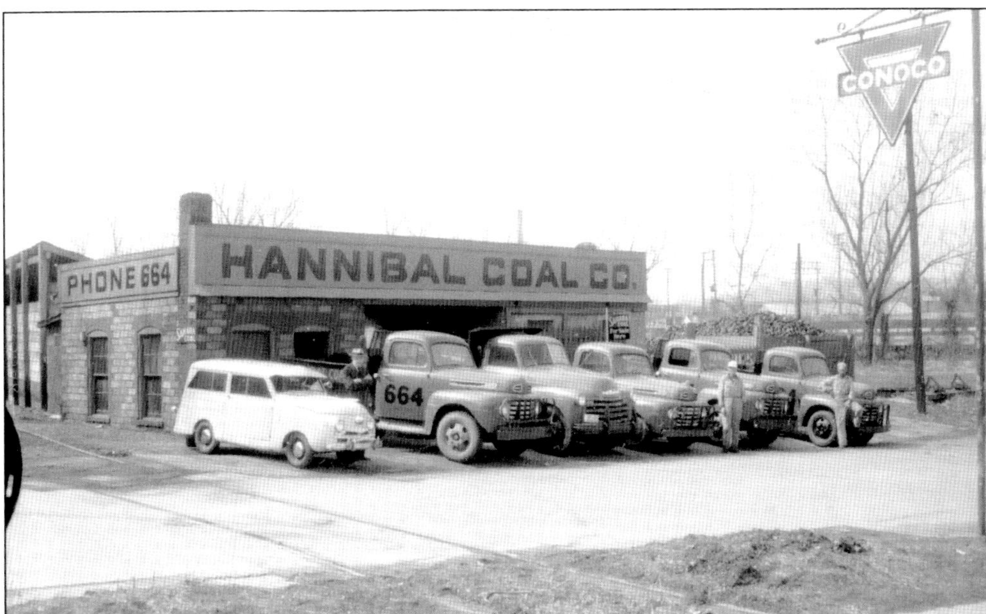

Once many homes and businesses were heated with coal, and the coal truck was a common sight. Here is the Hannibal Coal Company with their fleet of delivery trucks at 501 Birch Street. Note the Crosley station wagon. (March 1953)

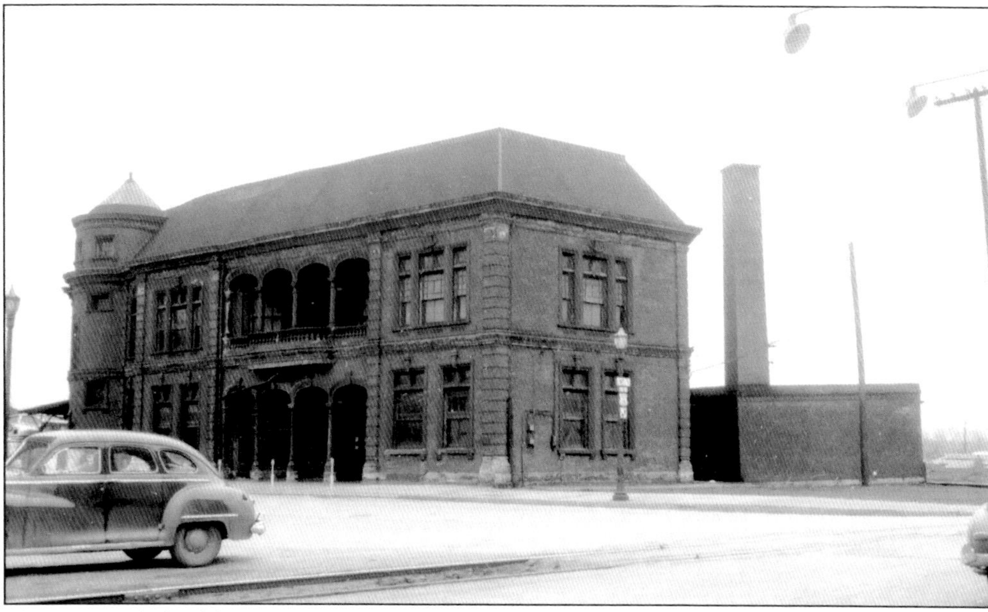

This is Hannibal's old Union Depot right before demolition work began. Work would be completed by June of 1953, hastened by a fire, which destroyed part of the ruins. The old tower, one of the last sections to be removed, was the source of an amusing rumor that the city had appropriated $2,200 to purchase and renovate the old tower as a refuge for pigeons. Apparently the story had a wide circulation, as it took an article in the *Courier-Post* to discount it. (March 1953)

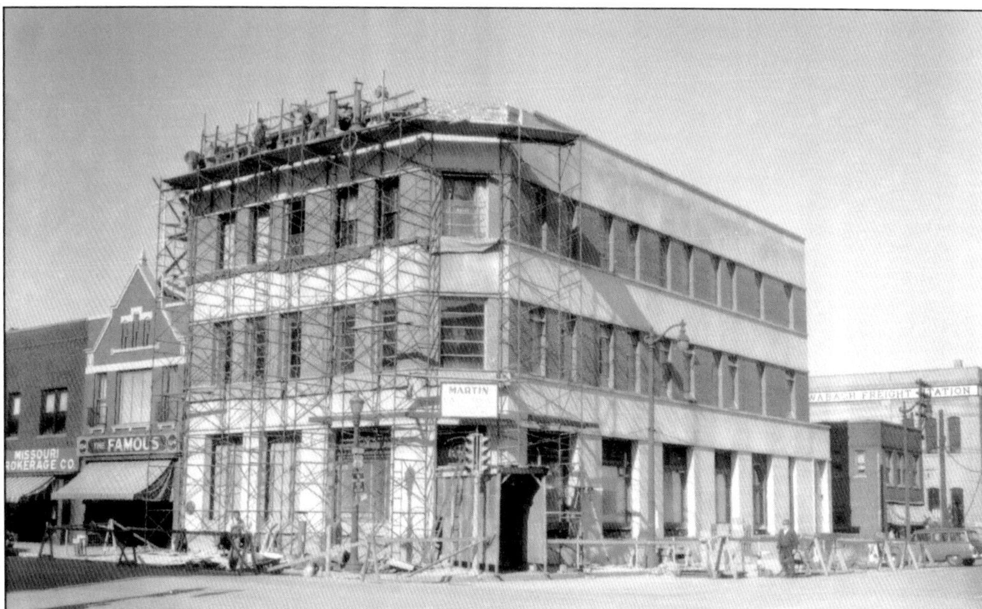

Refacing of the Hannibal National Bank building at Main and Broadway is in its final stages in this photo (compare with photo on page 36, bottom). Workmen from Martin Construction Company atop scaffolding are removing the last of the ornate roofline trim on the Main Street side of structure. The old tower was gone and the new exterior was almost complete. Note the new windows are yet to be installed on the side of the third floor facing Main Street. (March 1953)

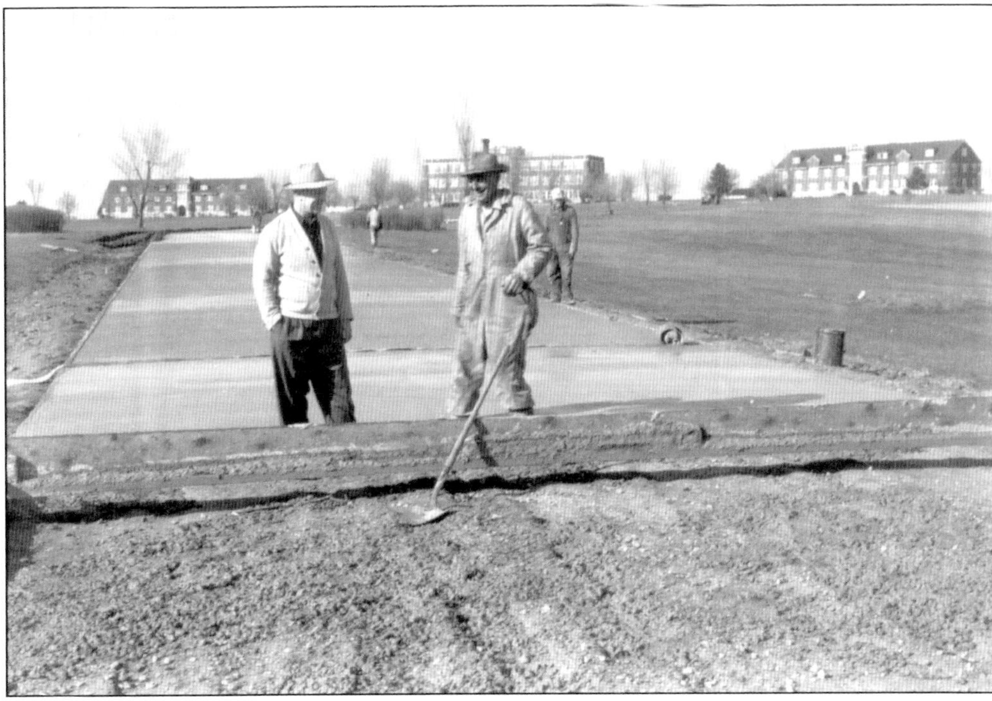

Hannibal-LaGrange College, a pathway to higher learning, is getting a new pathway to its front door, made of concrete. At left is L.W. Riney, contractor, and at right is Joe McDonald, superintendent of construction. About 1,000 feet of reinforced concrete was put down, with the remaining portion of the driveway to be completed as funds were raised. (March 1953)

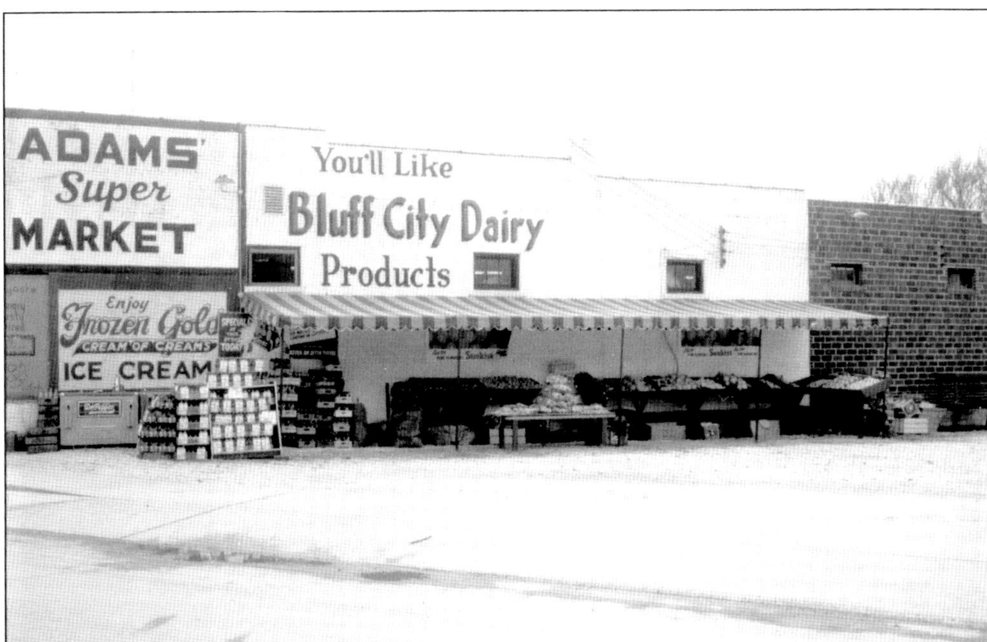

Here is a side view of Adams Supermarket at 2923 St. Mary's Avenue as it looked in April 1953. Note the produce and soda (in glass bottles, of course) displayed for sale under the canopy.

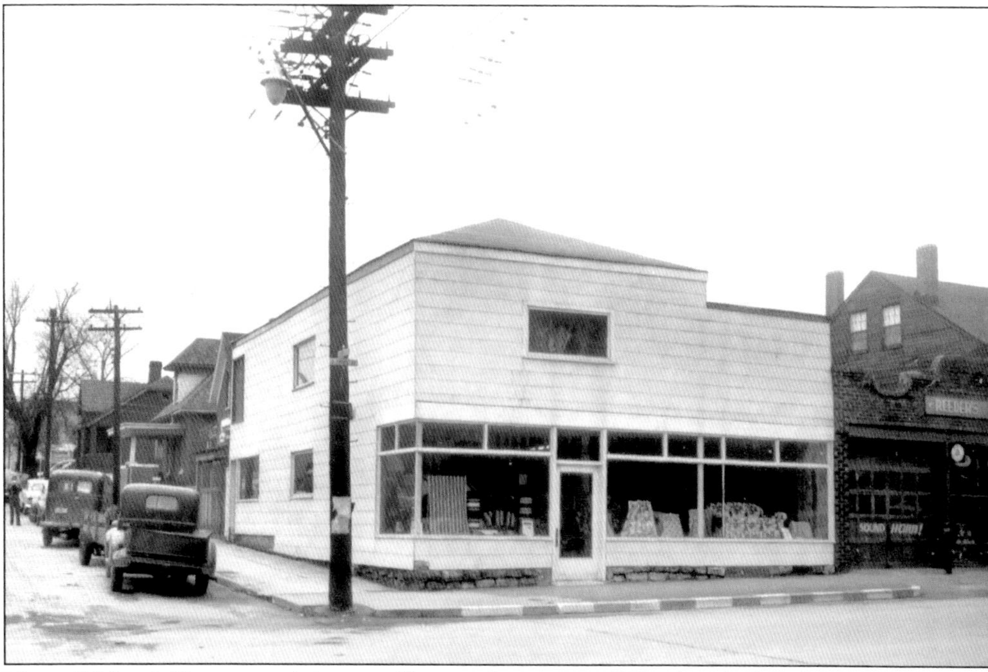

This is Wilson's Drapery and Awning Shop at the corner of Third and Church. Reeder's Garage is visible at the far right. (April 1953)

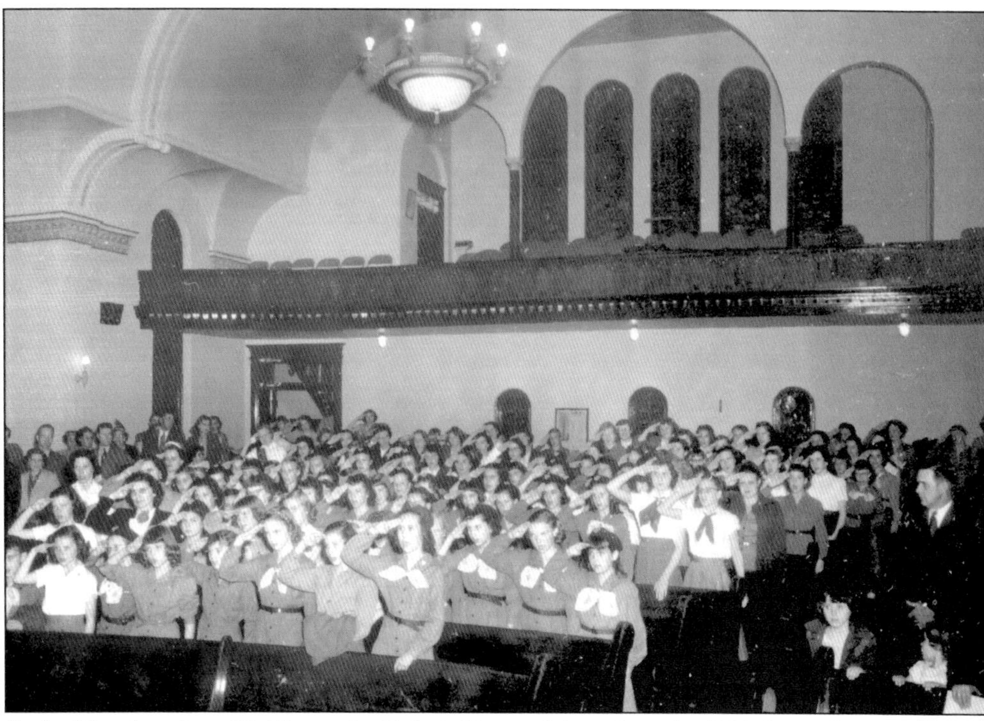

Becky Thatcher Area Girl Scouts hold their Court of Awards at the Fifth Street Baptist Church on May 14, 1953. The scouts are standing as they recite the Girl Scout Promise. Rev. Leon Pigg of First Christian Church was the speaker for the ceremony.

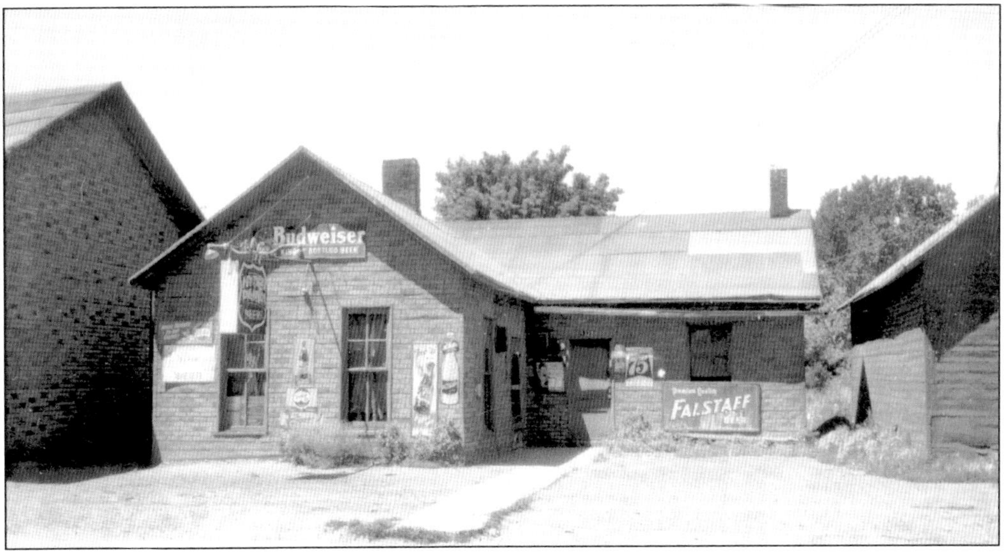

This old house, at 1322 Gordon Street, covered in beer and soda signs was a tavern. It was operated by Clifford Burton when Otis took this photo of it in May 1953. Perhaps today the old advertising signs would be worth more than the old house!

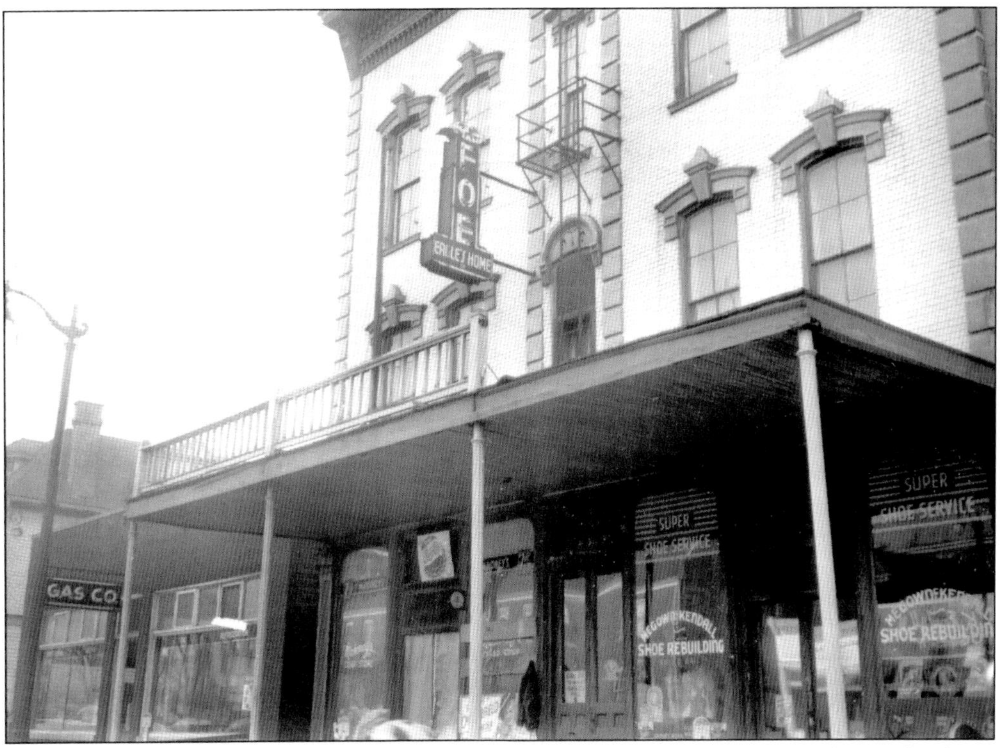

This photo shows the Eagles' Hall at 517 Broadway, as the building is being modernized. Like at the Maryland Hotel several years earlier (see page 26, top), the large front porch was removed. This old building was formerly known as the Labinnah Hall in the early 1900s. It was torn down in 1994. Note the first floor, that at the time was occupied by the Mahoney Cigar Store and Megown & Kendell Shoe Repair. (May 1953)

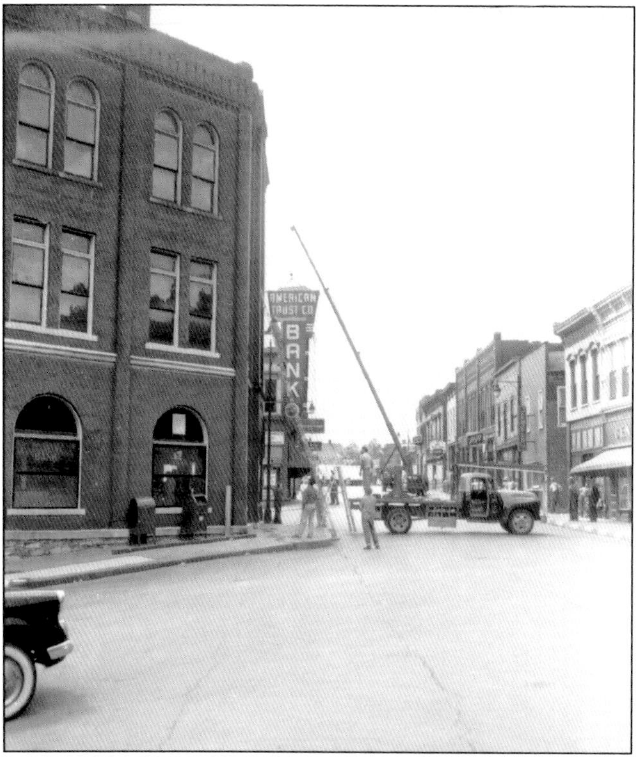

Workers install a new sign for the American Trust Company bank at the intersection of Market and Church Streets. The building formerly housed the old German-American Bank. Visible also are buildings along the north side of Market Street, including part of the Ben Franklin. This bank building was torn down in 1989. (July 1953)

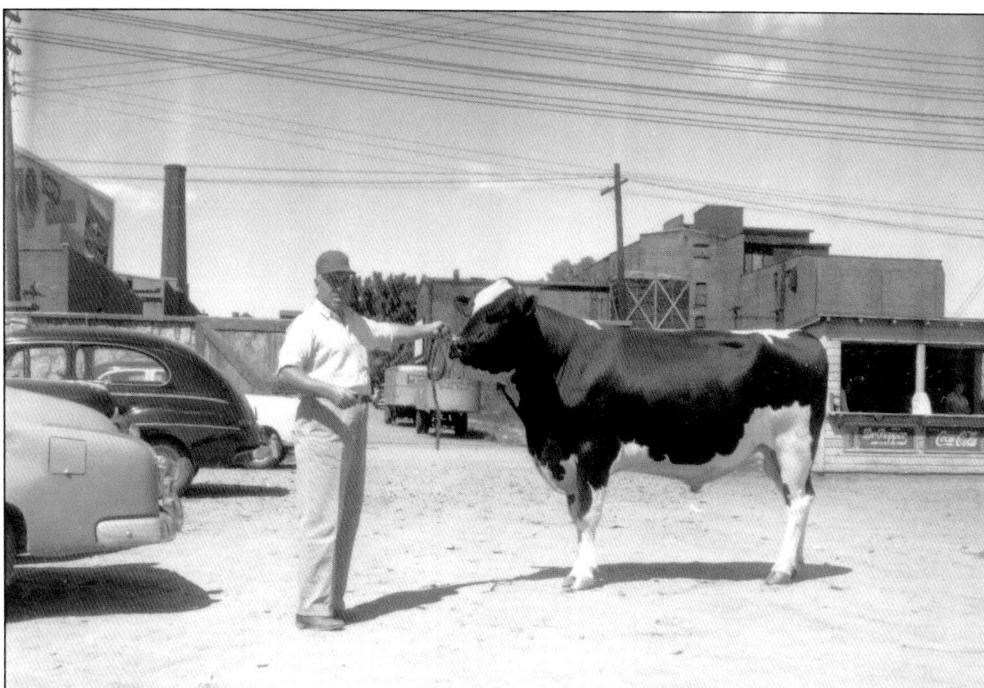

An unidentified man displays a bull at Clemens Field during livestock judging at the Hannibal Fall Festival. The old Hannibal Ice & Cold Storage building is visible in the background. (September 1953)

Two

Tailfins and TV Antennas

1954–1959

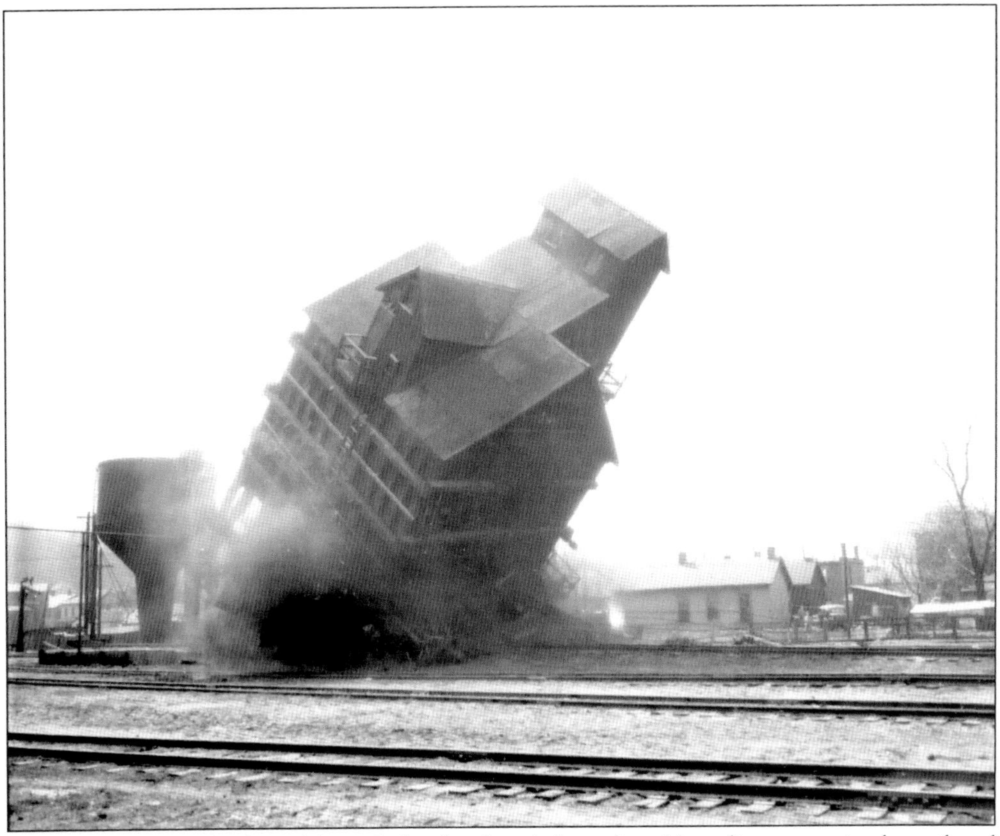

TIMBER! With a loud rumble and clouds of coal dust, the old coaling tower in the railroad yards is pulled down with switch engines. With the retirement of the last steam locomotive, the equipment that serviced them, such as this old tower, were scrapped. (March 1954)

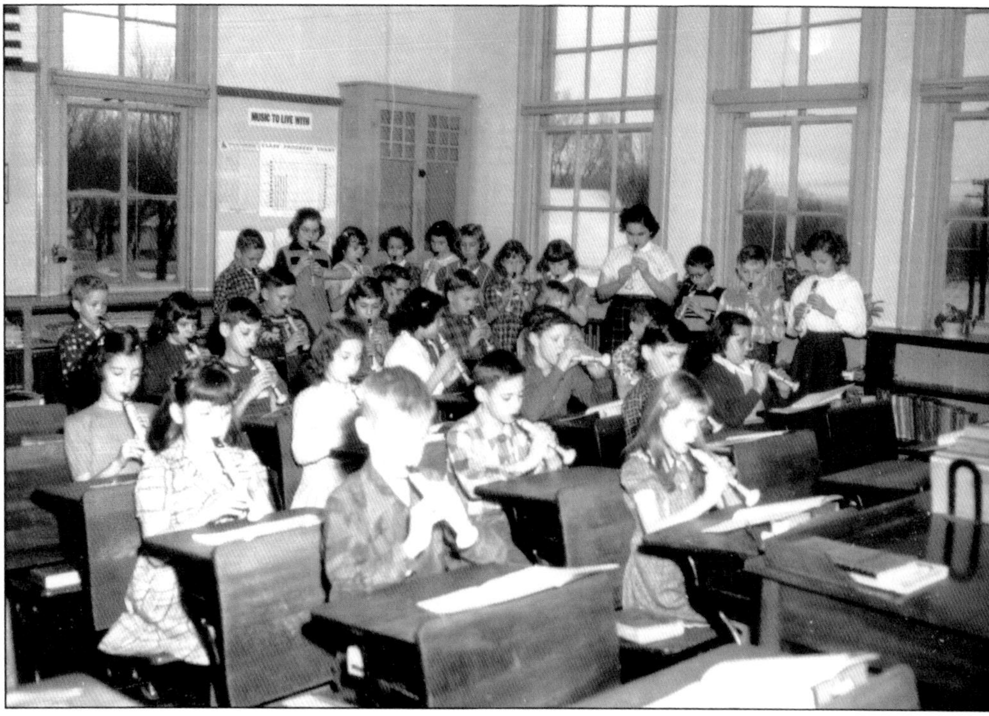

This photo shows the third grade flutophone band of Tilden School. Tilden School, located at 4001 Market in Oakwood, closed in the late 1950s and, for a time afterward, was used by a local nursery and landscaping business (see page 114, bottom). (January 1954)

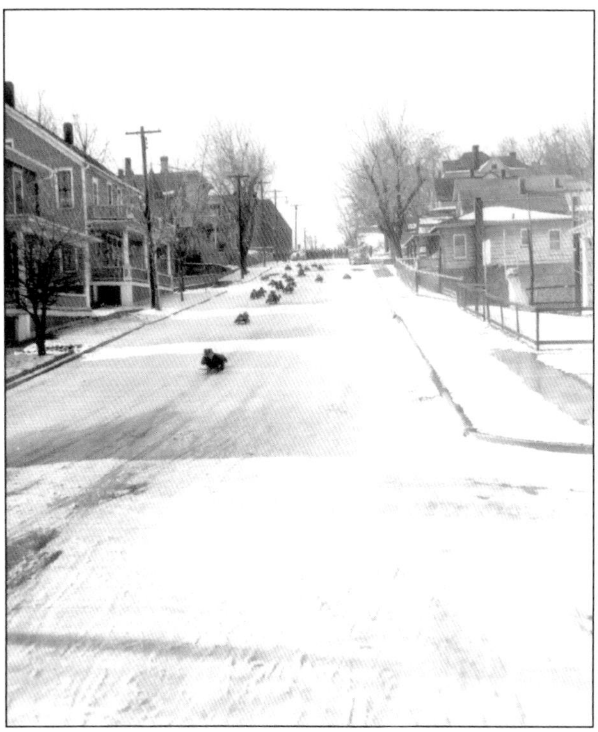

When the snow falls, Hannibal's hills offer a multitude of sledding opportunities for kids. This photo shows children sledding down Bird Street in January 1954. Central School is visible at the top of the hill to the left.

Russell Krigbaum, of the City Maintenance Department, and Police Capt. John Walmsley install decals on parking meters, urging motorists to feed dimes into the meters as a contribution to the March of Dimes. The meters had normally accepted only pennies and nickels to register time, with dimes passing straight into the coin box. All dimes collected from the meters would be turned over to the March of Dimes campaign. This photo was taken in the 300 block of Broadway, with the old Brittingham Hall building in the background. (January 1954)

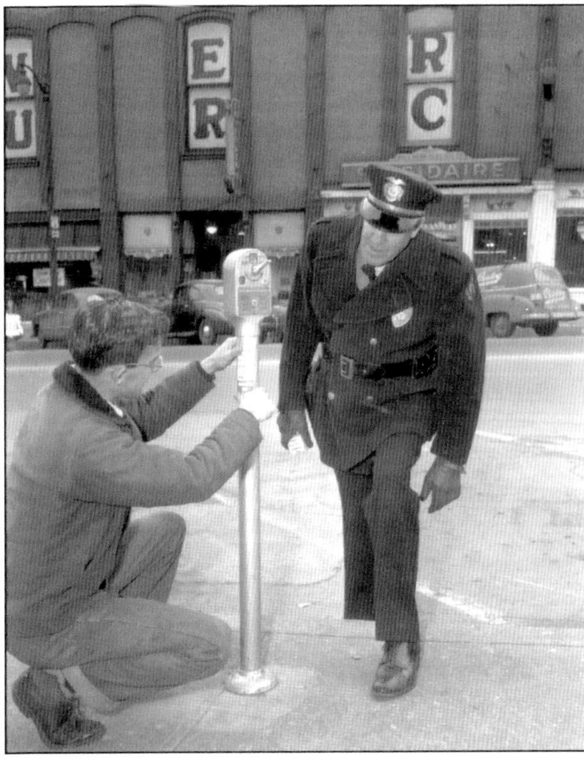

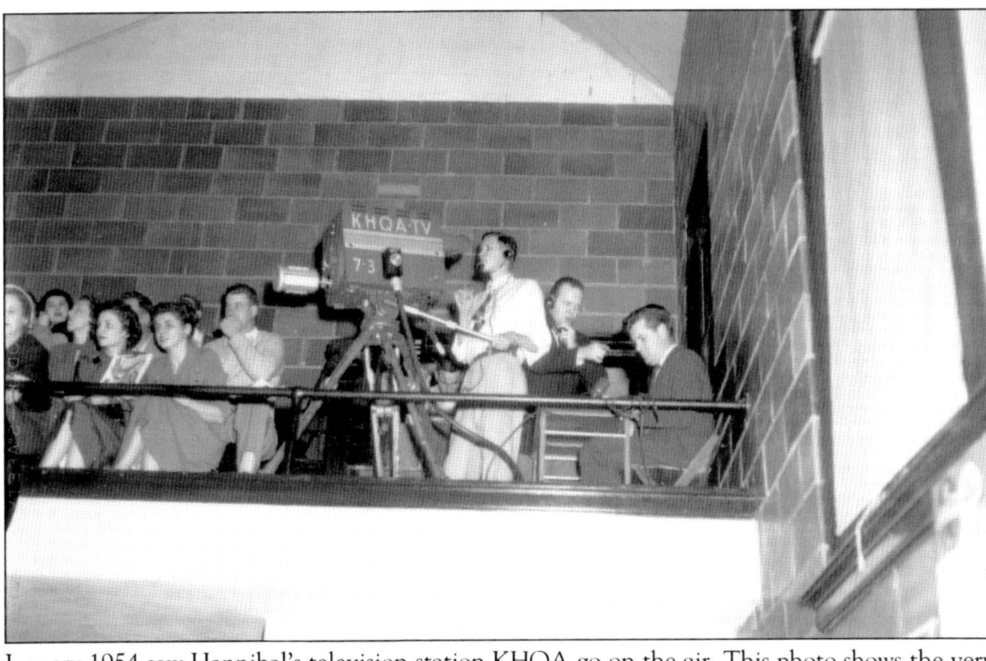

January 1954 saw Hannibal's television station KHQA go on the air. This photo shows the very first remote telecast. The event was a basketball game between Hannibal-LaGrange and Moberly Community College. Pictured here, from left to right, are: Gene Brhaensiek, cameraman; Tom Robey, resident manager KHQA-TV; and Bill Crews, sports director. The game, seen by thousands of viewers, was won by Hannibal-LaGrange, 82-68. (January 15, 1954)

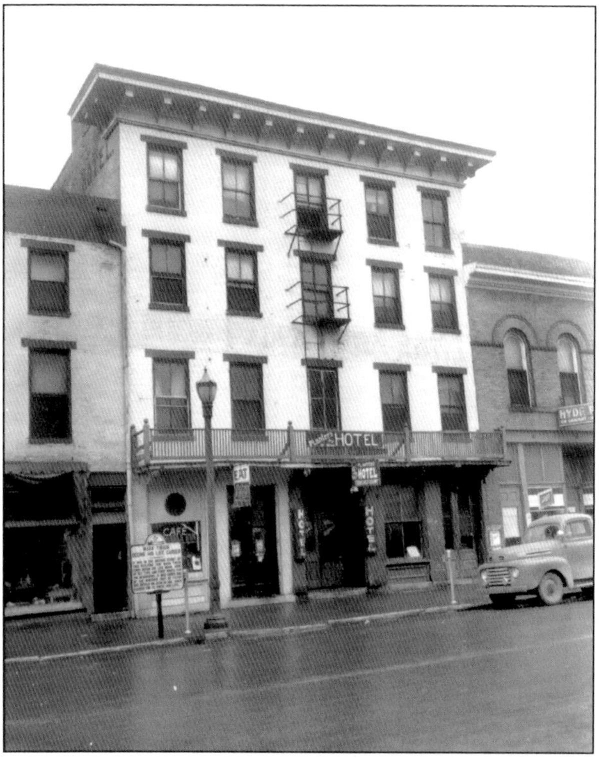

Hannibal's old Planters' Hotel at 317 North Main was a part of the town's early history (as were the buildings in the next three photos), but that could not save it from demolition in 1954—the lot was used as additional parking for a furniture store on the block. (March 1954)

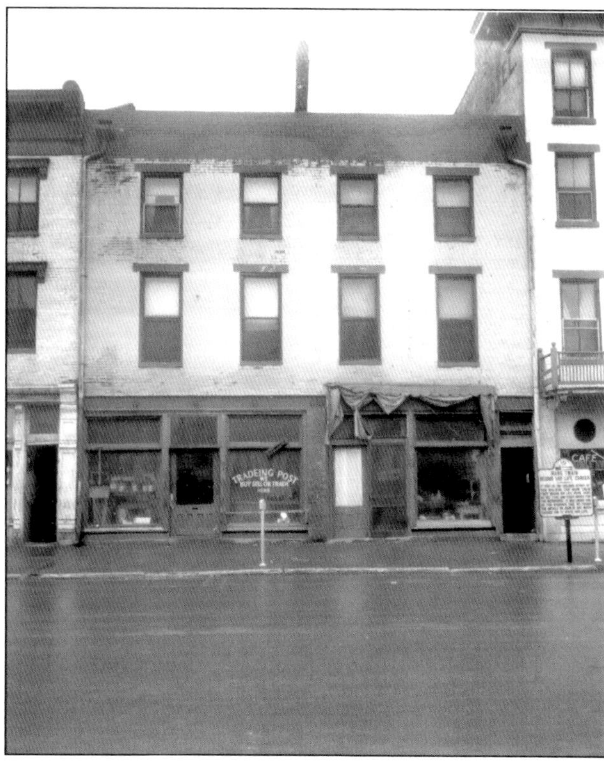

As can be seen by a historic marker in front of this building at 313–315 North Main, this building had special significance. It was on the second floor of this structure that Sam Clemens began his life's work. As a newspaper printer's apprentice setting type, he found an article on Joan of Arc which caused him to write a story on her life. When this building was torn down, along with the old Planters Hotel, the historic sign disappeared as well. (March 1954)

Perry and Annie's Tavern at 311 North Main was the third of the condemned buildings. Visible are the marks where a second-floor balcony was once mounted (see page 31, top, for an earlier view of this building with its balcony). (March 1954)

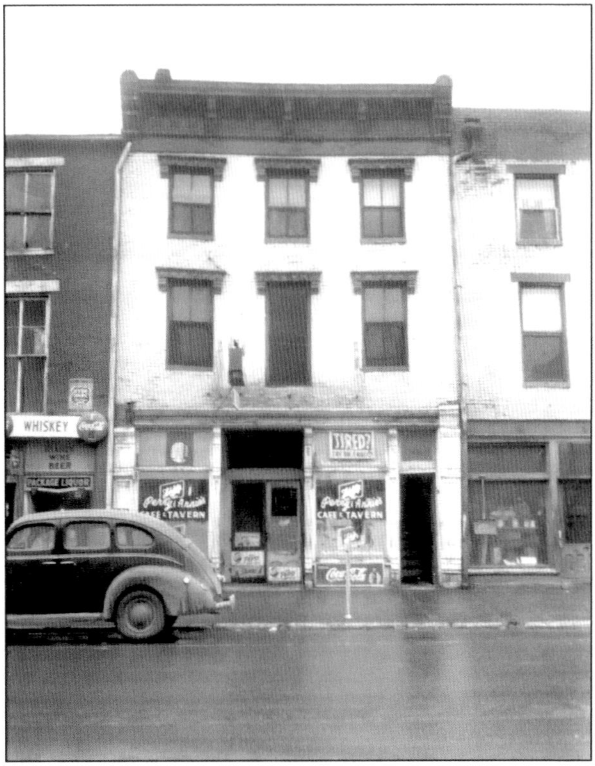

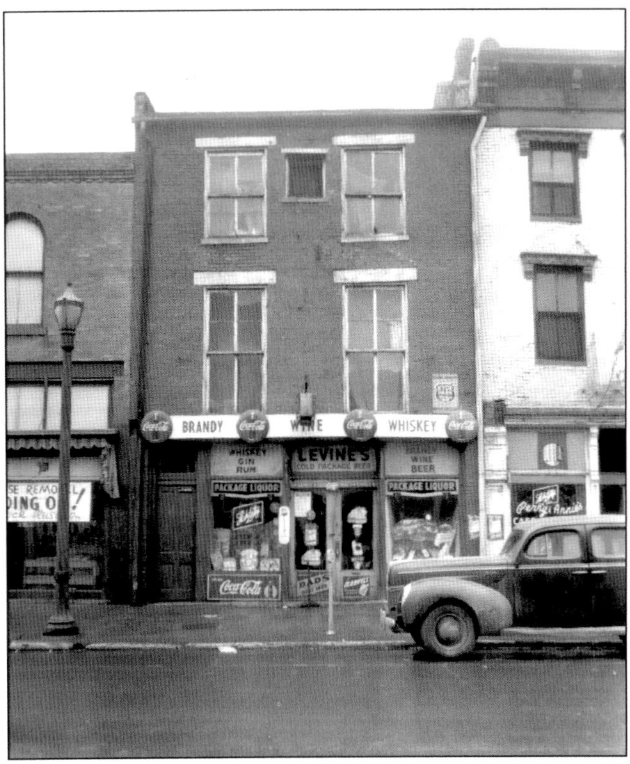

The fourth of the condemned structures was Levine's Package Liquors at 309 North Main. (March 1954)

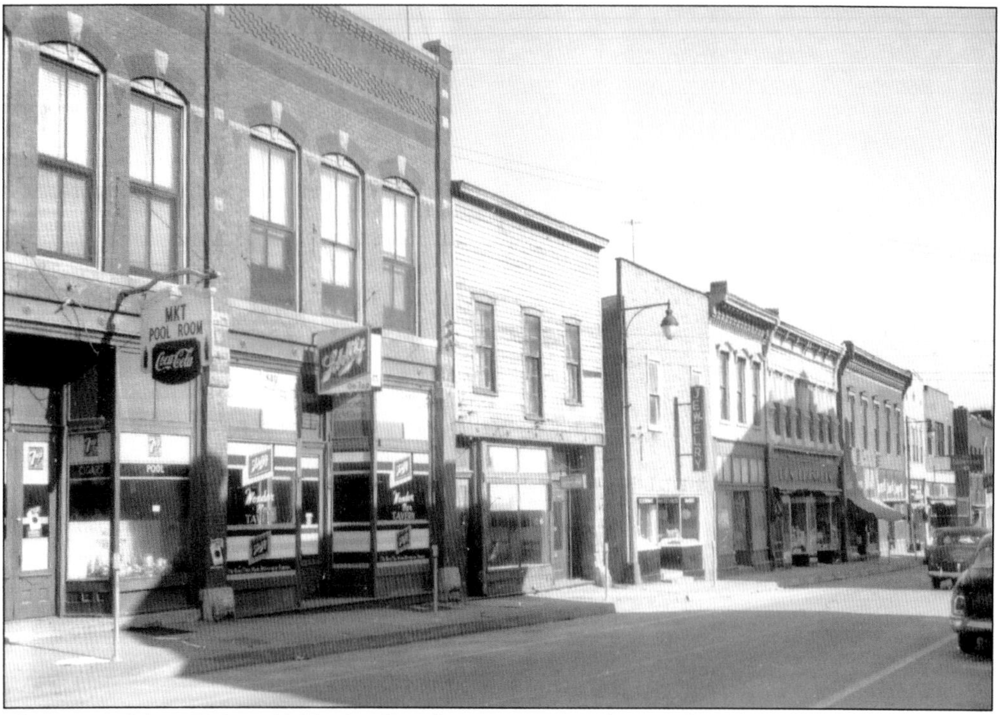

This view of the 1300–1400 block of Market Street near the Wedge shows an unbroken sweep of commercial buildings. The three structures in the center of the photo (starting with the two-story frame next to the large brick building on the left) were about to be removed for a parking lot. Today none of these buildings remain. (March 1954)

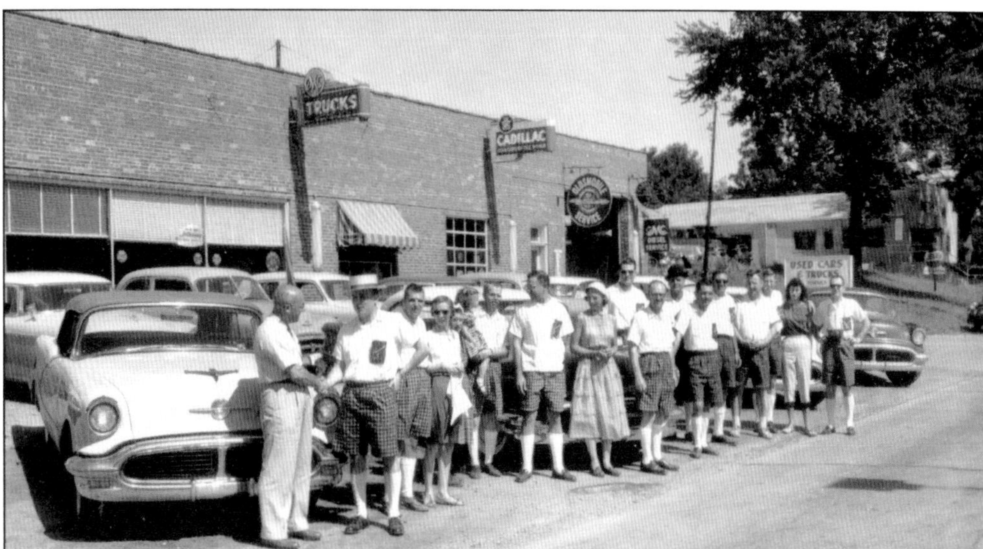

Mayor Jack Schroder greets the Flint, Michigan delegation of the Junior Chamber of Commerce in front of Warnick Motors on June 27, 1956. Warnick Motors was located at 3801 McMasters where the westbound entrance ramp of the U.S. 36 overpass is today. Part of the old Rol–Arena skating rink is visible in the background.

This photo shows the "Silent Salesman" newspaper rack that the *Courier-Post* was installing around town. The customer simply dropped a nickel into the slot and took a newspaper. Obviously the *Courier-Post* was counting on people to have strong consciences! This rack was set up just outside the newspaper's own building at Third and Center. Part of Ellis Tire Co. is visible in the background. (May 1954)

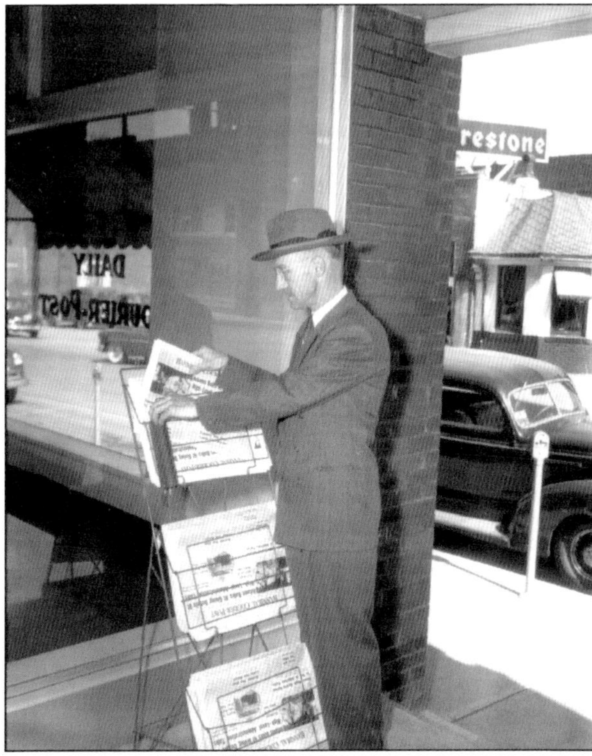

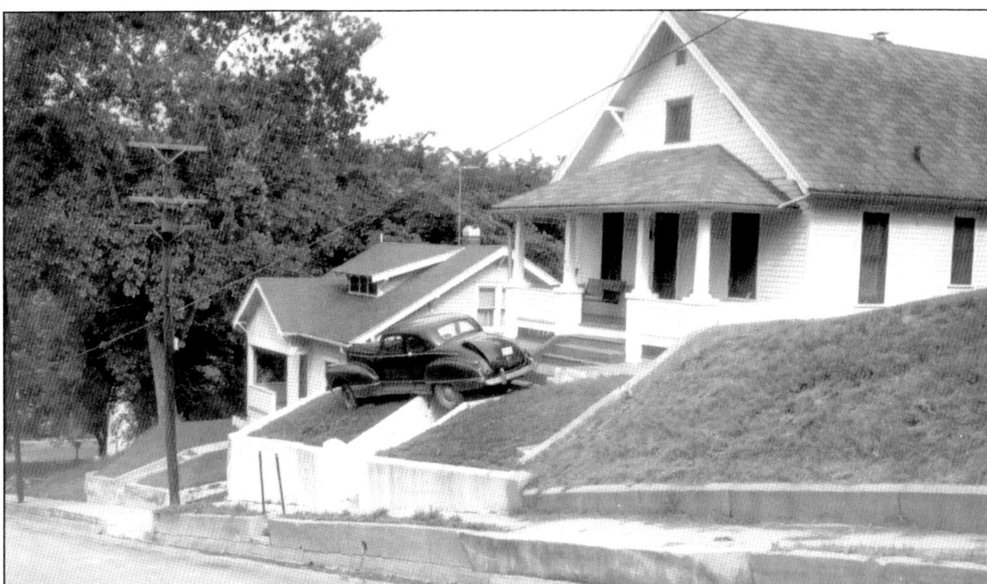

This car perched precariously across the front entrance of Jack Sederwall's home at 418 Oak Street had been parked uphill from the Sederwall home and rolled out of gear across two yards before coming to rest where it did. There were no injuries except to the car and property. It took puzzled workers more than a day to figure out how to remove the car. (June 1954)

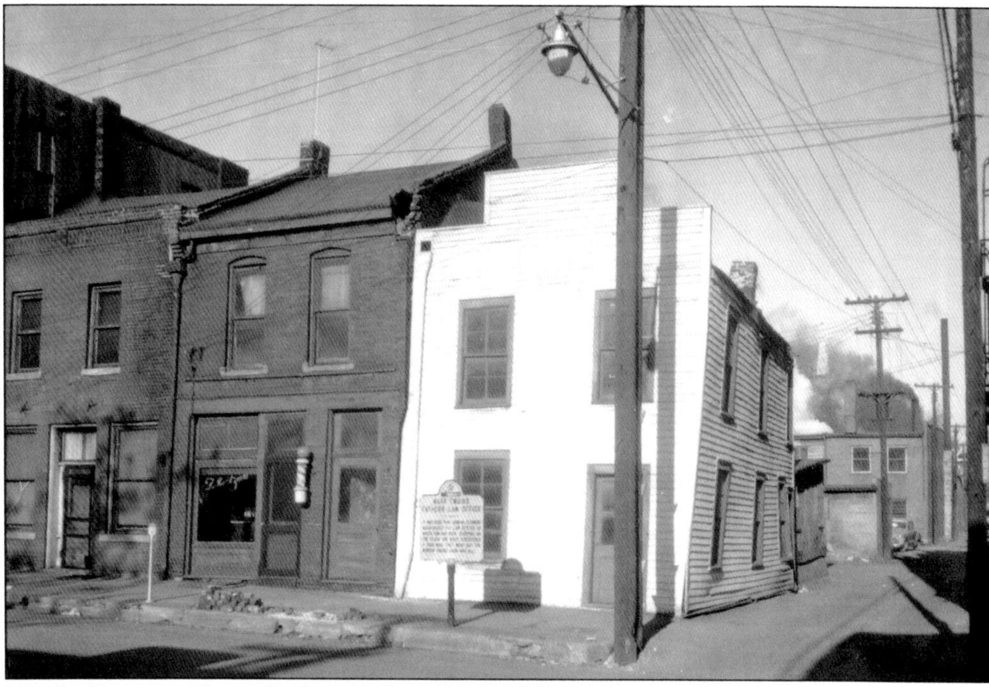

The building that housed where Judge Clemens' (Mark Twain's father) Justice of the Peace office is today is a popular tourist attraction just across from the Mark Twain boyhood home on Hill Street. This 1954 photo shows the old building at its original location on the 100 block of Bird Street. At the time of this photo there had been some renovation done to the structure, but it was in serious danger of collapse, partly due to a crumbling wall of the adjoining building, Fred Mirtzwa's barbershop.

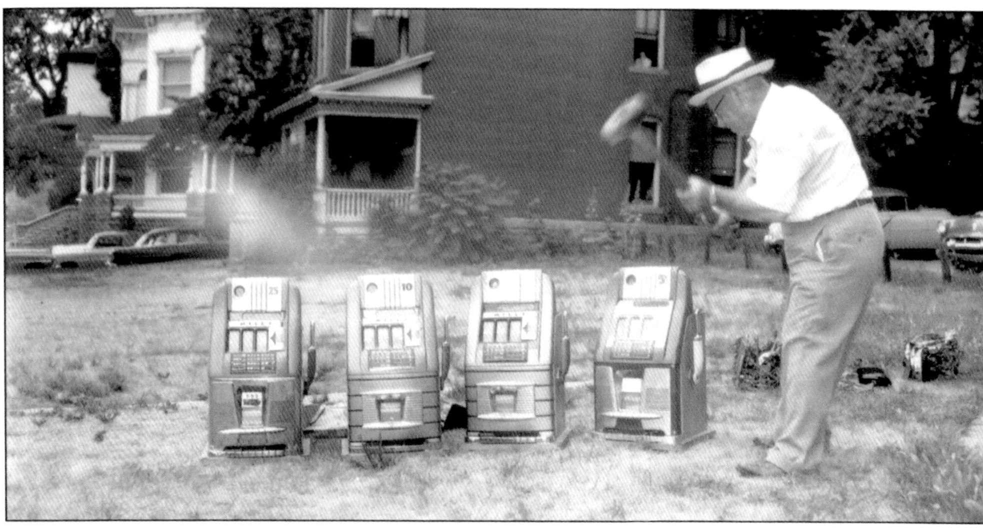

An official breaks up confiscated slot machines on the lawn of the courthouse in Hannibal, during the summer of 1954. Now and then "games of chance" would be found and destroyed, but those shown here had belonged to a local organization that called police to report a theft of some money. The responding officer noticed the slot machines and had them hauled off. Today these machines would be worth a small fortune. Notice Schwartz Funeral Home visible in the background.

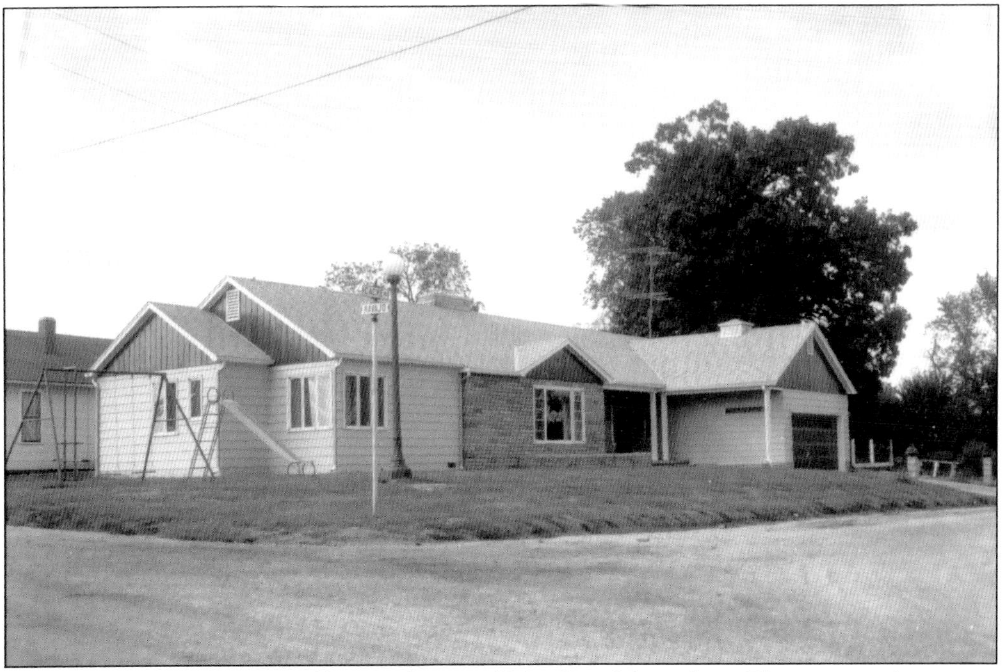

Here is the newly constructed home of Mr. and Mrs. Pete Merendino. The six-room house was located at 3801 Cache in the Indian Mound Subdivision. Many new homes were being built in Indian Mound at that time. (October 1954)

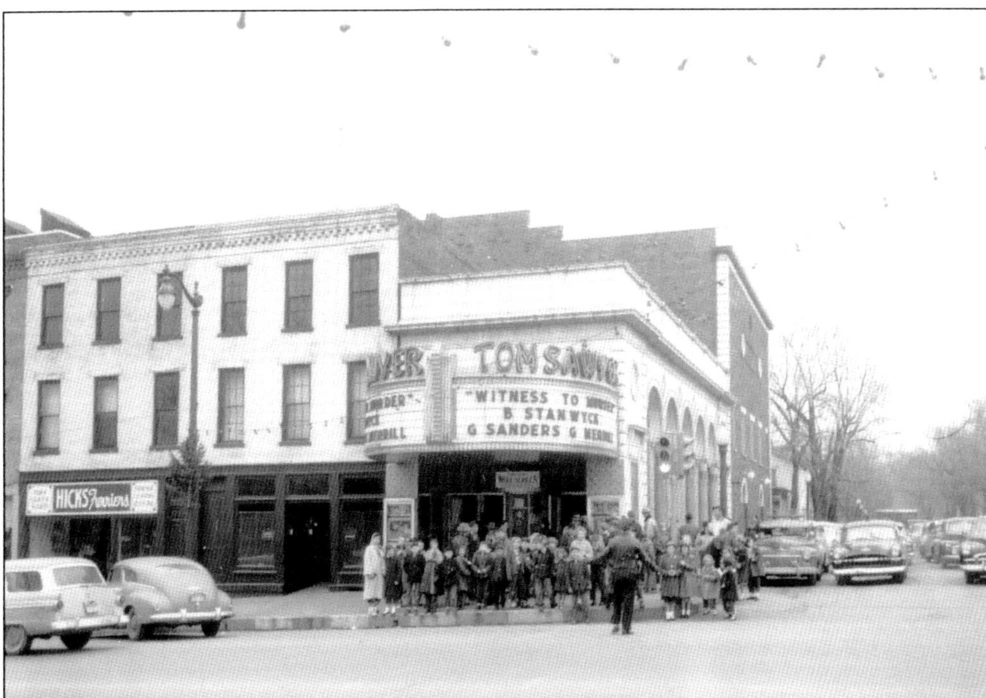

A crowd of children gathers outside the Tom Sawyer Theater for a special attraction there in December 1954. Looks like the police officer has his hands full!

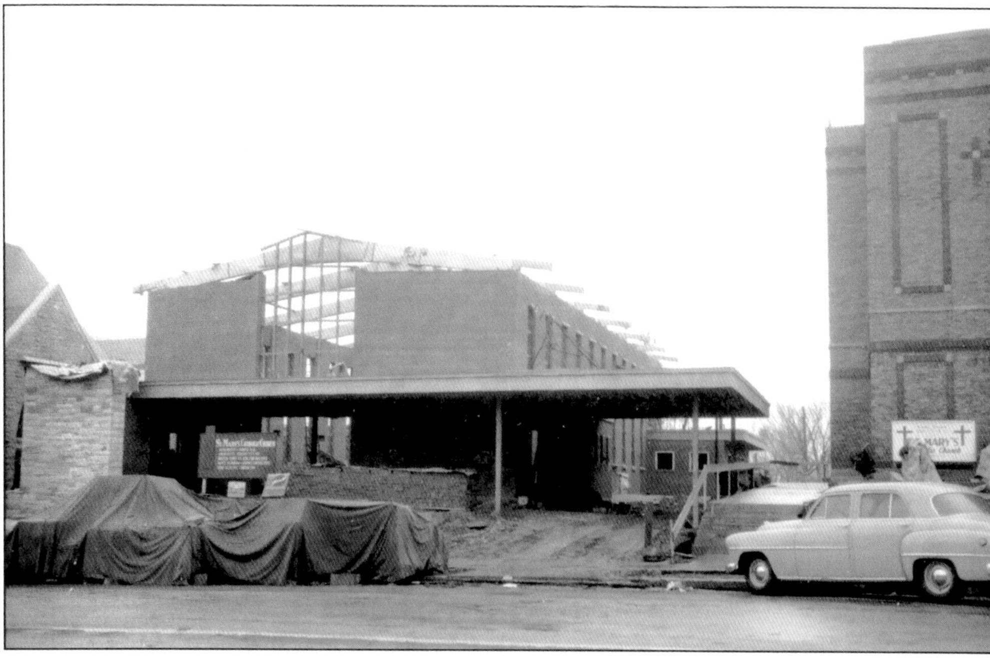

Construction progresses on St. Mary's Catholic Church as roof trusses are set in place. It took some of the older parishioners some time to get used to the new modern styling as compared to the ornate décor of the old Immaculate Conception Church. St. Mary's is the present day Holy Family Catholic Church and combines both the old St. Mary's and Blessed Sacrament parishes. (January 1955)

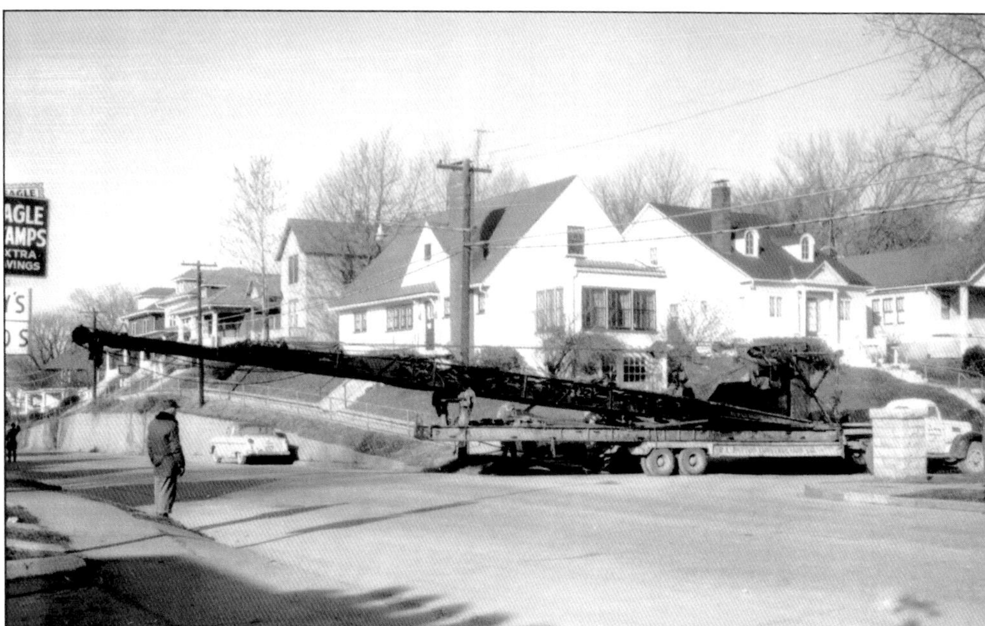

This is the intersection of Magnolia and St. Mary's Avenue as a 30-ton steam pile driver is removed from the construction site of the 75-bed addition to St. Elizabeth Hospital. In the foreground the shadow of Harold's Standard filling station can be seen. (January 1955)

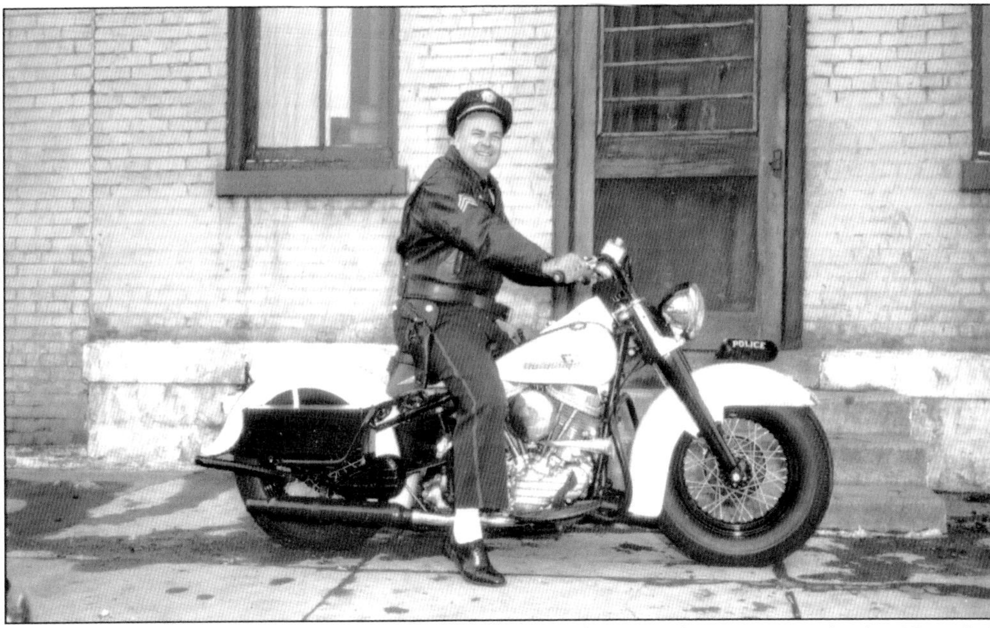

Traffic officer Carl Brink poses with a brand new Harley Davidson motorcycle the Hannibal Police Department just acquired. Two older cycles were traded in on this one, which was purchased from a St. Louis dealer. This photo was taken in front of the old police station at Fourth and Church. (January 1955)

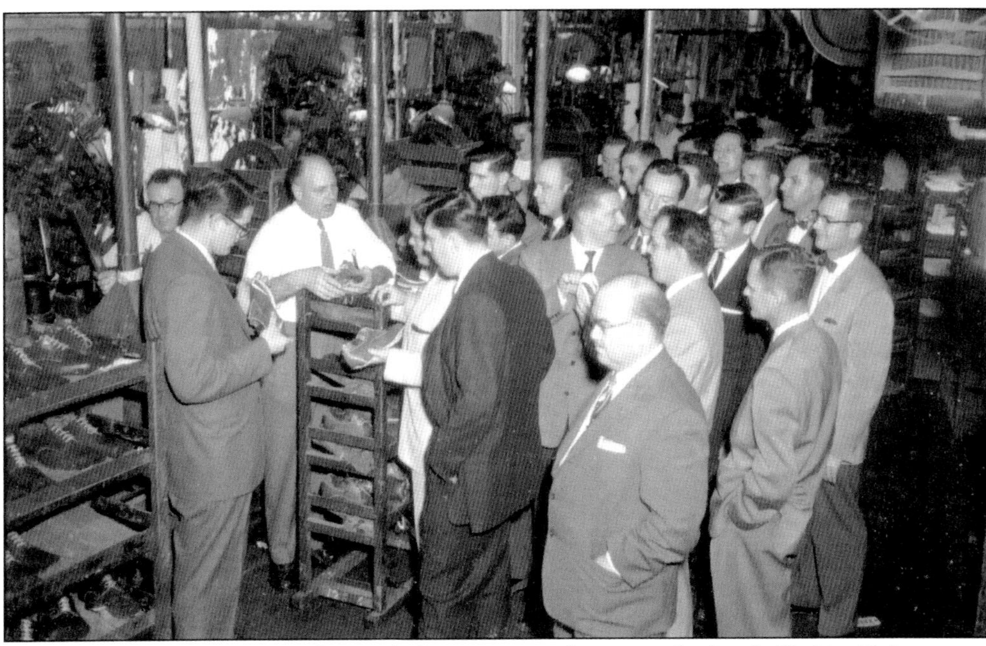

Shoe manufacturing was one of Hannibal's mainstay industries in the first half of the 20th century. In 1910, over 1,500 people were employed in the trade. By the 1950s, shoe manufacturing began to taper off—the work could be done cheaper overseas and by the end of the 1960s the shoe industry in Hannibal was gone. This photo shows International Shoe Company sales trainees touring the Bluff City plant in February 1955.

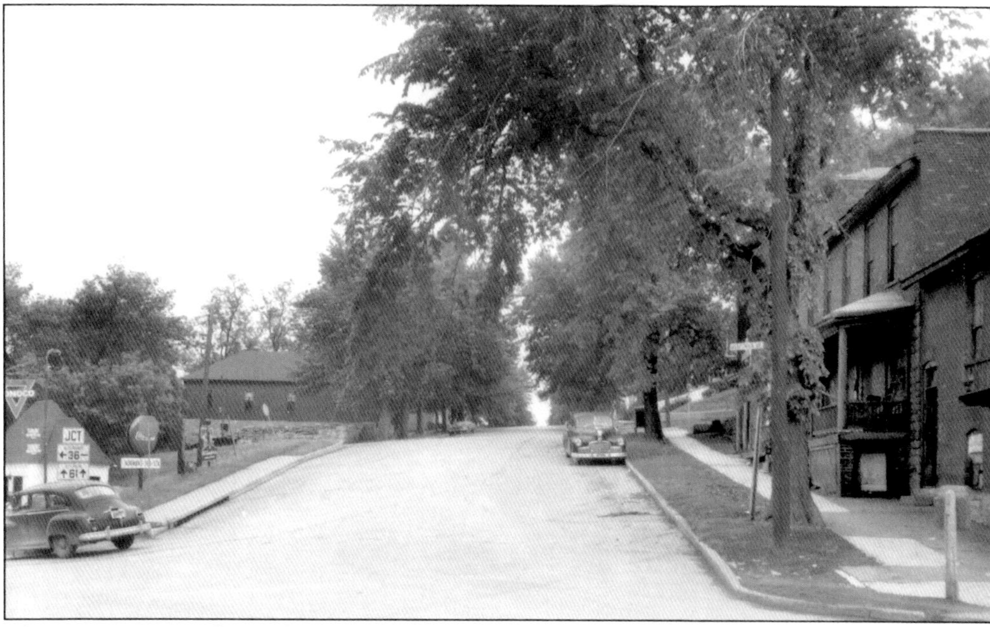

This intersection of Fourth Street and Mark Twain Avenue no longer exists. Prior to the widening of the avenue and routing U.S. 36 along its length, both Rock Street and Fourth Street spilled out onto Mark Twain Avenue at right angles, forming a small triangle. Norman's Conoco, partly visible at left, sat in that triangle. A small portion of the old Garth Tobacco Factory, where Molly Brown once worked, is visible at the far right. All of this would disappear in the summer of 1956 when the highway work began. (May 1955)

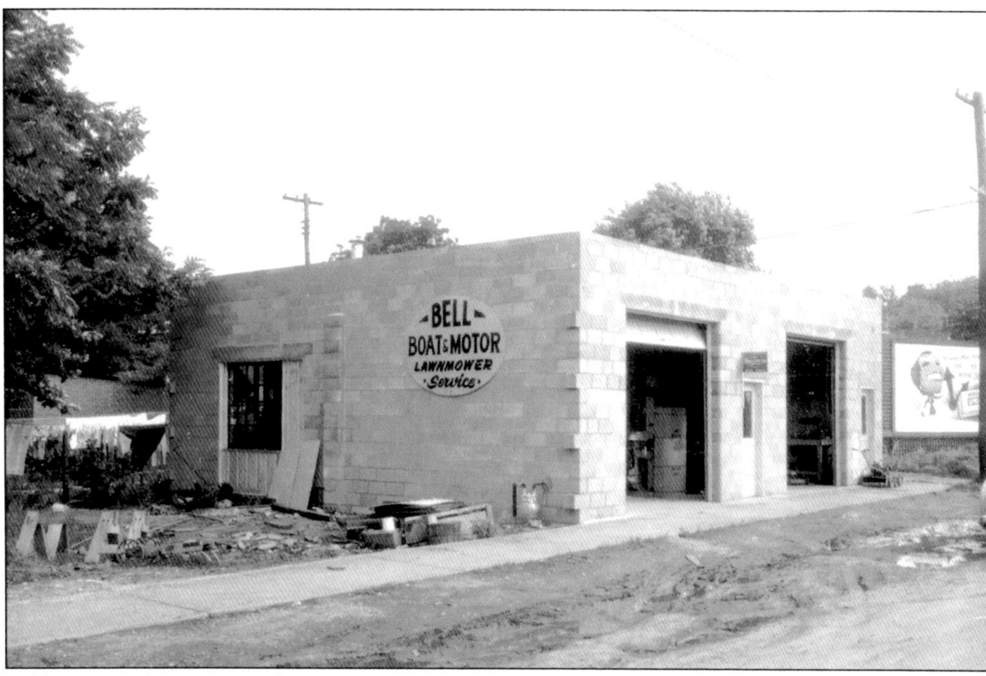

Bell Boat and Motor was located at 701 South Main on the south side. This photo shows the new building of the small engine and lawnmower repair service. (May 1955)

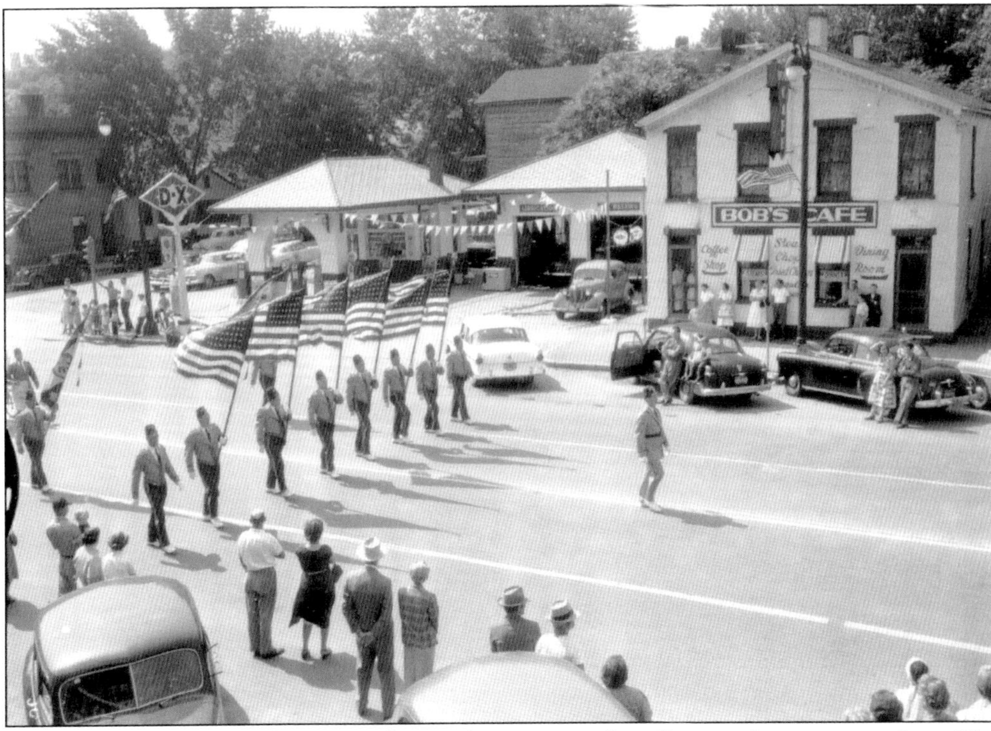

This photo of a Memorial Day parade is truly a picture of small-town America at its best. The Diamond D-X station and Bob's Lunch form the perfect backdrop for the row of waving flags. This was the 600 block of Broadway during May 1955.

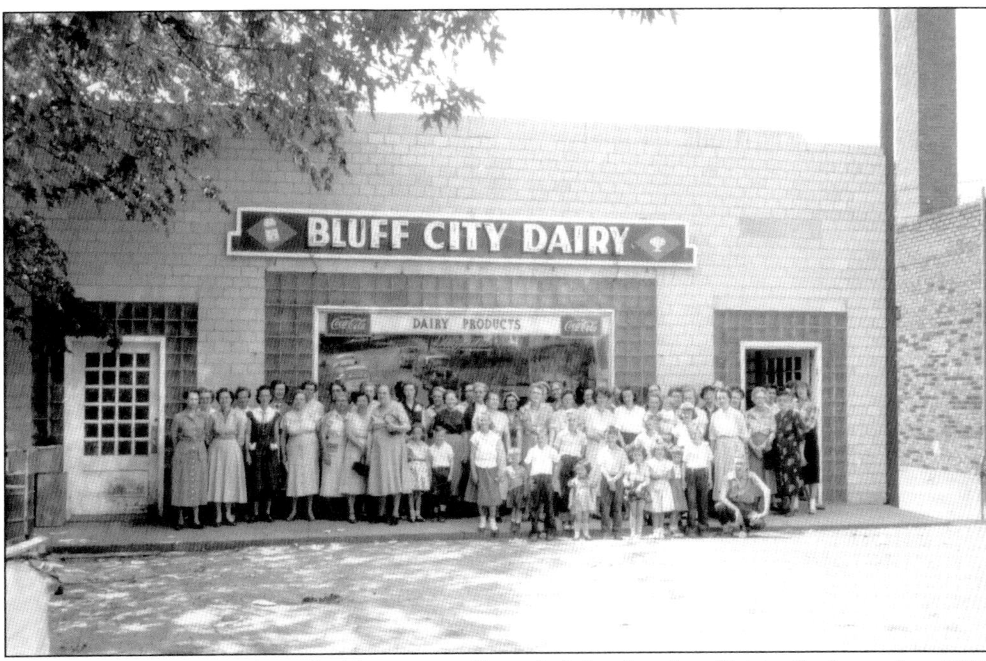

Bluff City Dairy was a household name in Hannibal for decades. Originally located at 2300 Market, Bluff City moved to 2903 St. Mary's Avenue, where this photo was taken in May 1955.

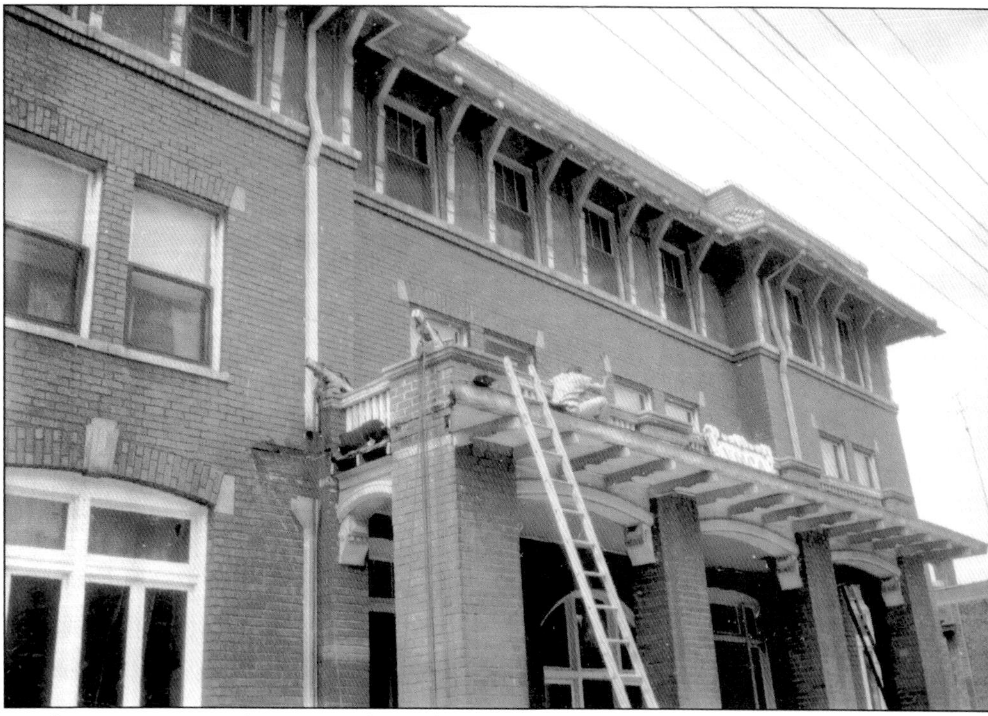

Workers remove trim from around the front porch of the old YMCA Building at Fifth and Center in May 1955. The trim near the roofline of the building would also be removed.

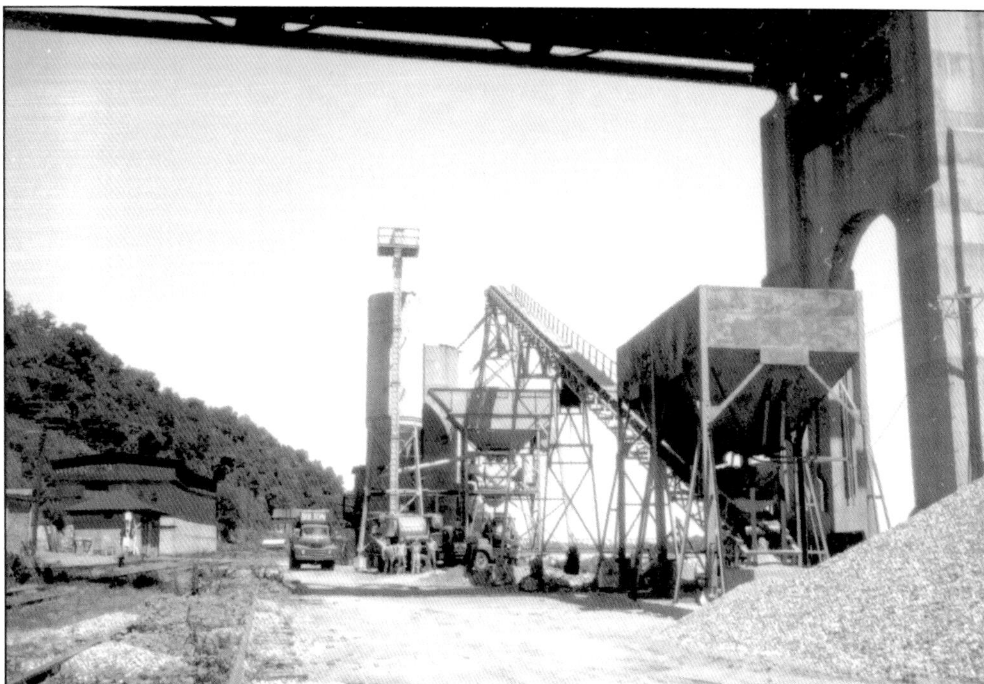

Bolton Sand and Gravel Co. was located at 506 Bridge Street. The old Storrs Ice House is visible in the background. (June 1955)

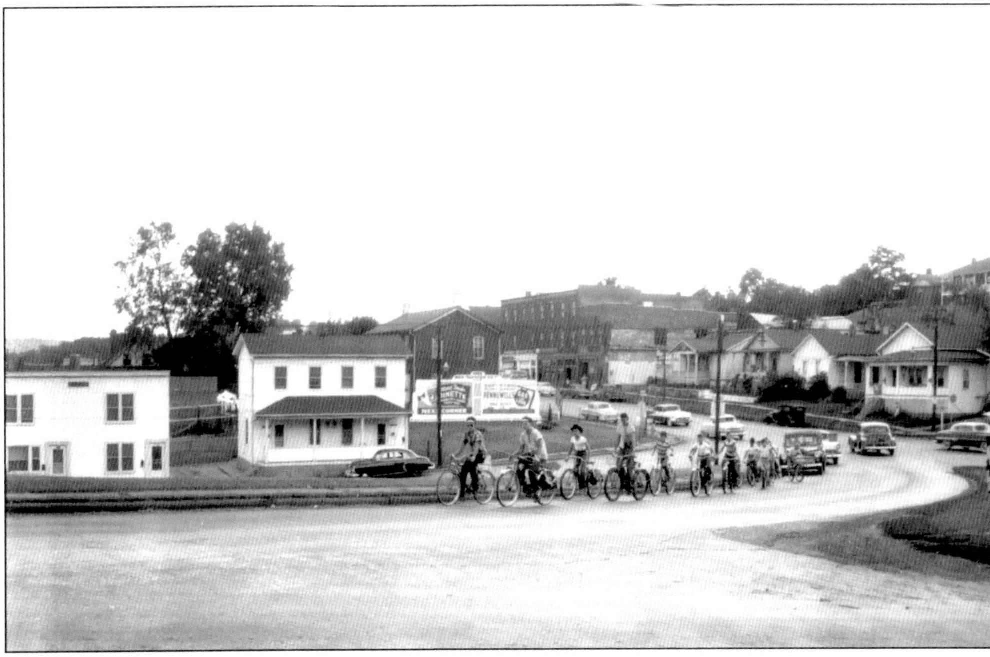

On July 28, 1955, the swimming class at the YMCA took a "bicycle hike" from Hannibal to Hull, Illinois. The children ranged in age from nine to fifteen. The photo was taken as the group rode onto the Missouri approach of the Mark Twain Bridge, with buildings along North Third in the background.

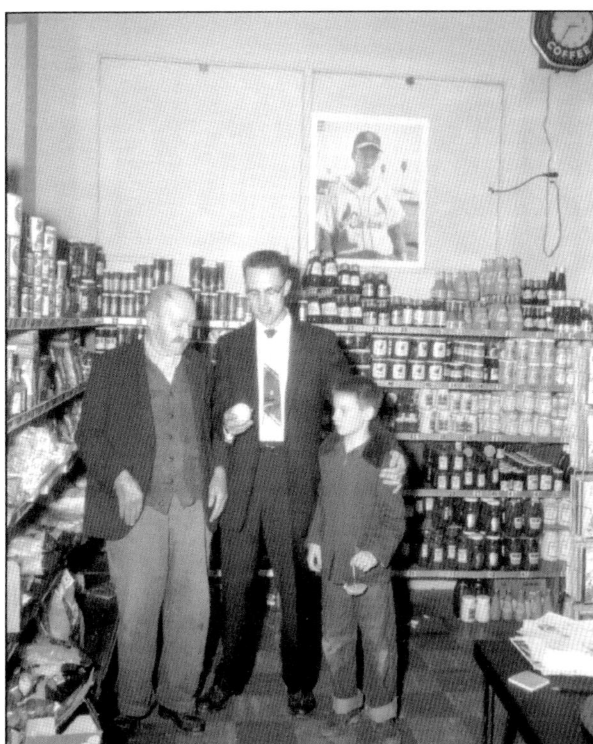

Cardinals baseball player Bill Virdon appeared at Gooch's Market, at 696 Grand, on October 29, 1955 to sign autographs. Twelve autographed baseballs were given away that day. Pictured with Virdon are Thomas Wright, age 91 and Larry Ritter, age 8. Virdon, who played center field for the Cards, was named Rookie of the Year. He would be traded the next year, and went on to manage several clubs.

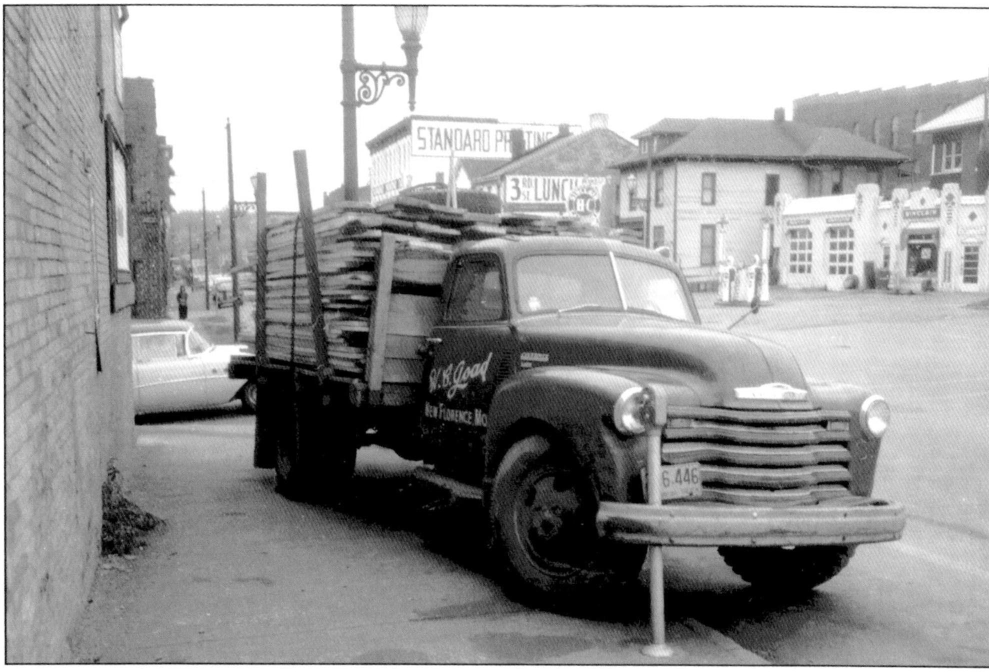

Otis was always ready with his camera to capture an amusing moment. This rather embarrassing incident happened when the driver of this truckload of wood hooked a parking meter with his front bumper while trying to parallel park. The photo was taken in the 300 block of Third Street in November 1955.

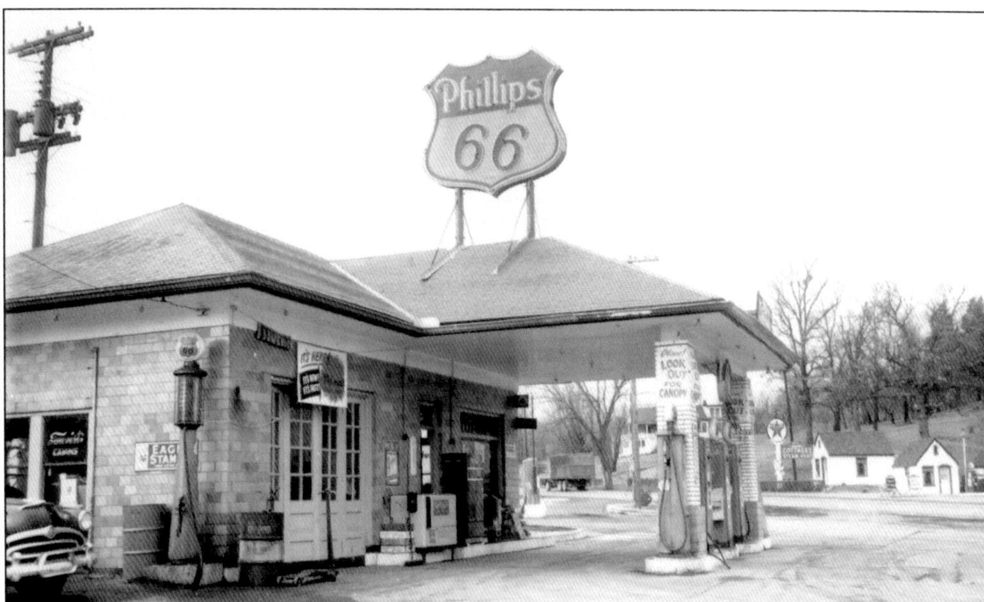

We go back to the Junction for this view of Piper's Phillips 66 filling station and motor courts at 2901 James Road. Piper's would be replaced by a more modern looking station in 1964. Notice the old gravity gas pump at the corner of the station. In the background some of the cabins of Miller's Cottages are visible.

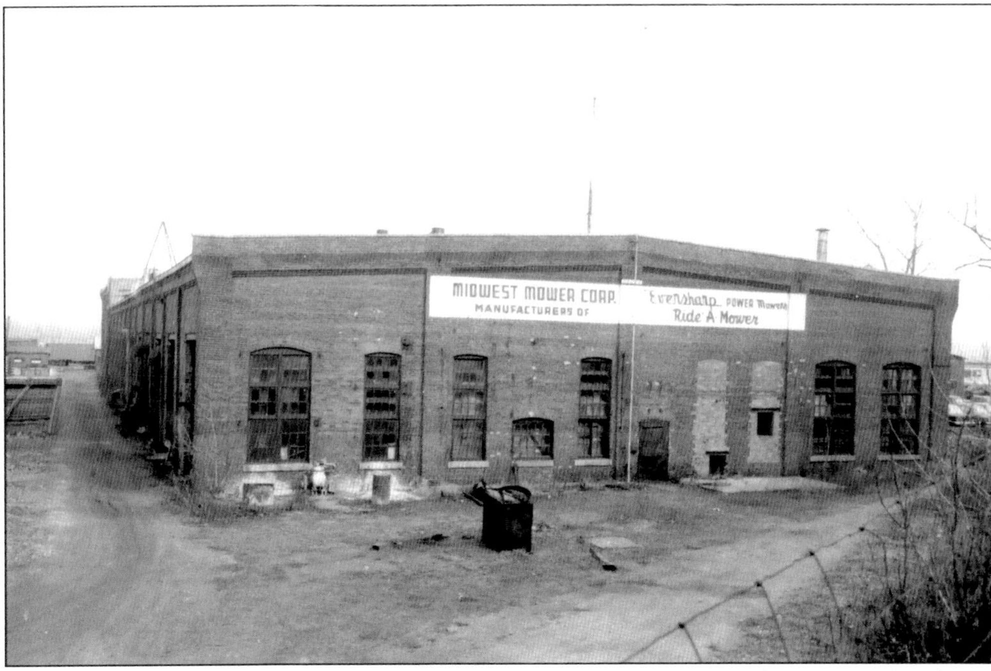

Midwest Mower Company manufactured riding and push mowers in the 1950s. They began operation in the old Durasteel building on Lindell, but then moved to this location at 916 Bluff (part of the old Burlington shops). (January 1956)

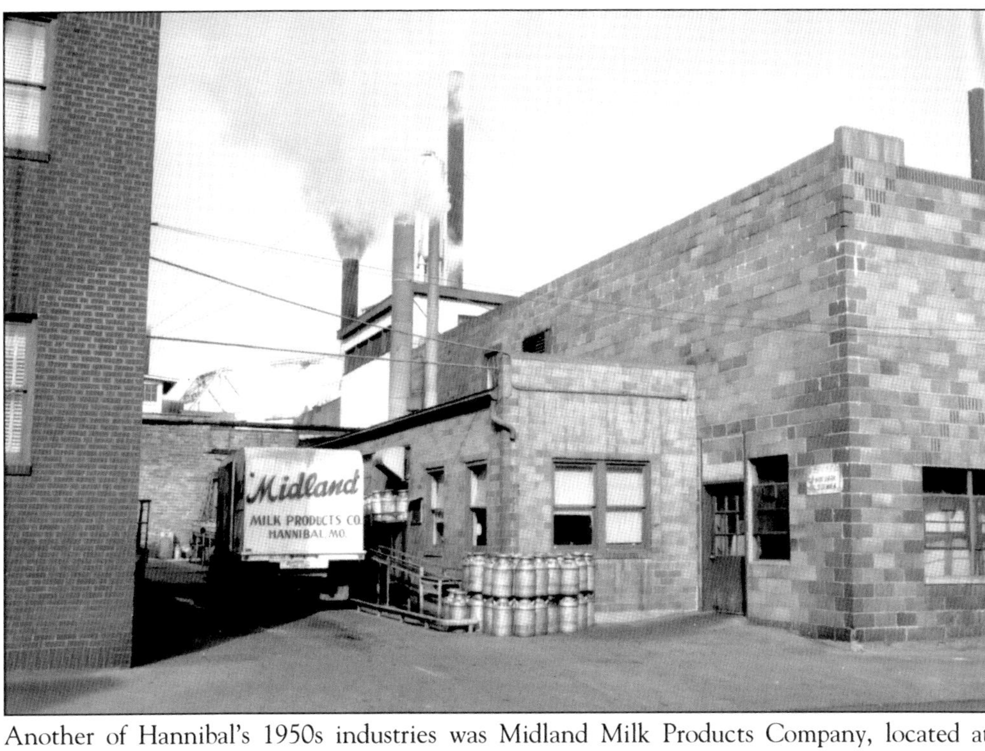

Another of Hannibal's 1950s industries was Midland Milk Products Company, located at 118 Hill Street. Midland manufactured a powdered milk product. (January 1956)

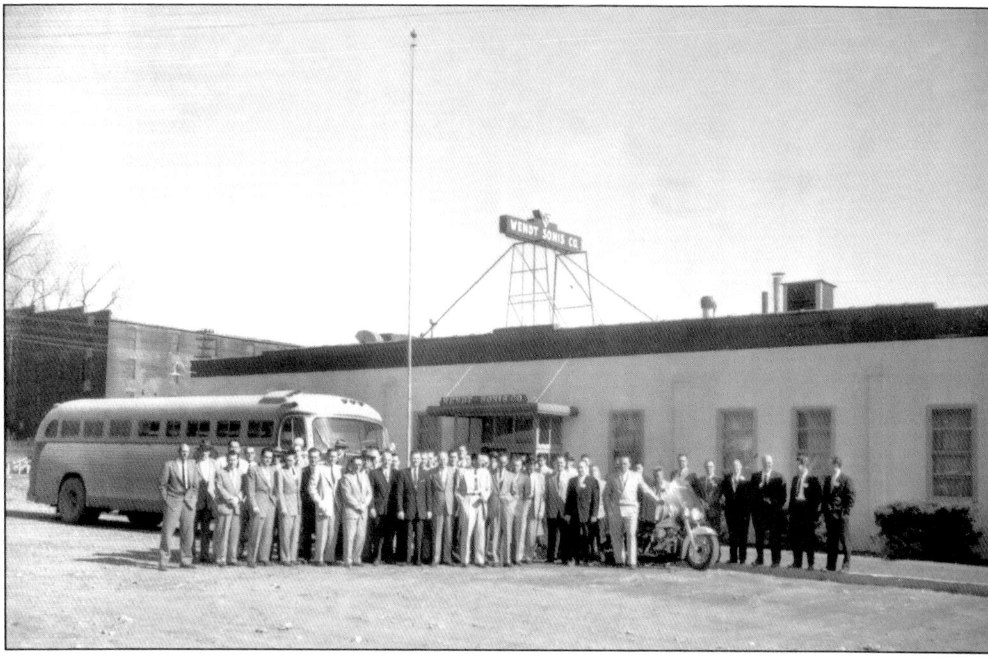

This is the Wendt-Sonis Company, located at 929 Collier. Wendt-Sonis made quality carbide cutting tools. This photo was taken of a production clinic sponsored by Wendt-Sonis. The men posing in this photo were attendees from various St. Louis manufacturing firms. (March 1956)

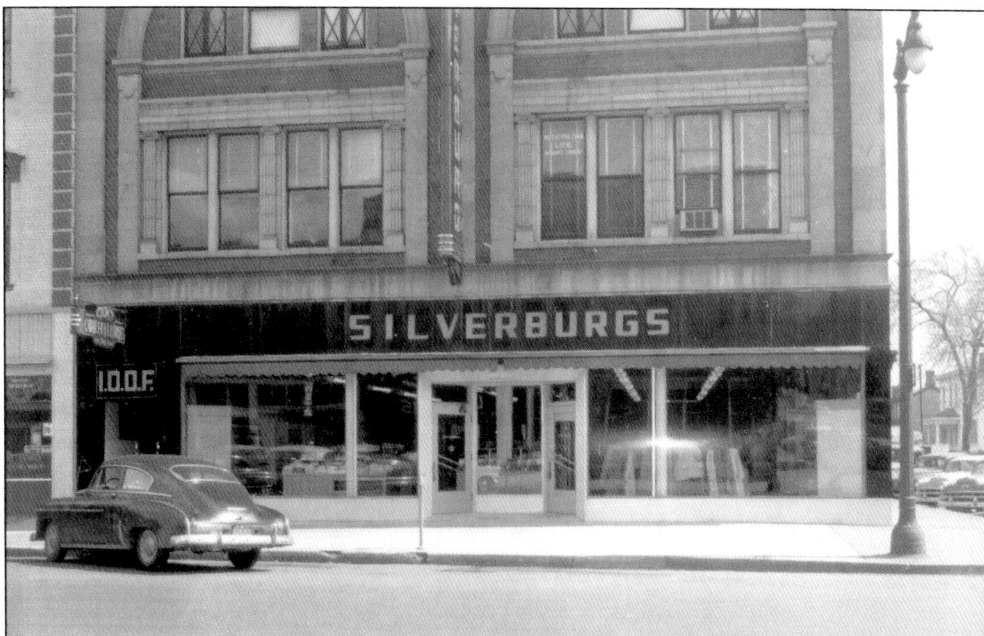

Silverburg's Department Store was located on the main floor of the IOOF Hall at 521 Broadway. The IOOF Hall was built in 1915 on the site of the old Broadway Methodist Church, and this building would in turn be destroyed by fire in 1975. Silverburg's had just undergone a major remodeling and modernization when this photo was taken in March 1956.

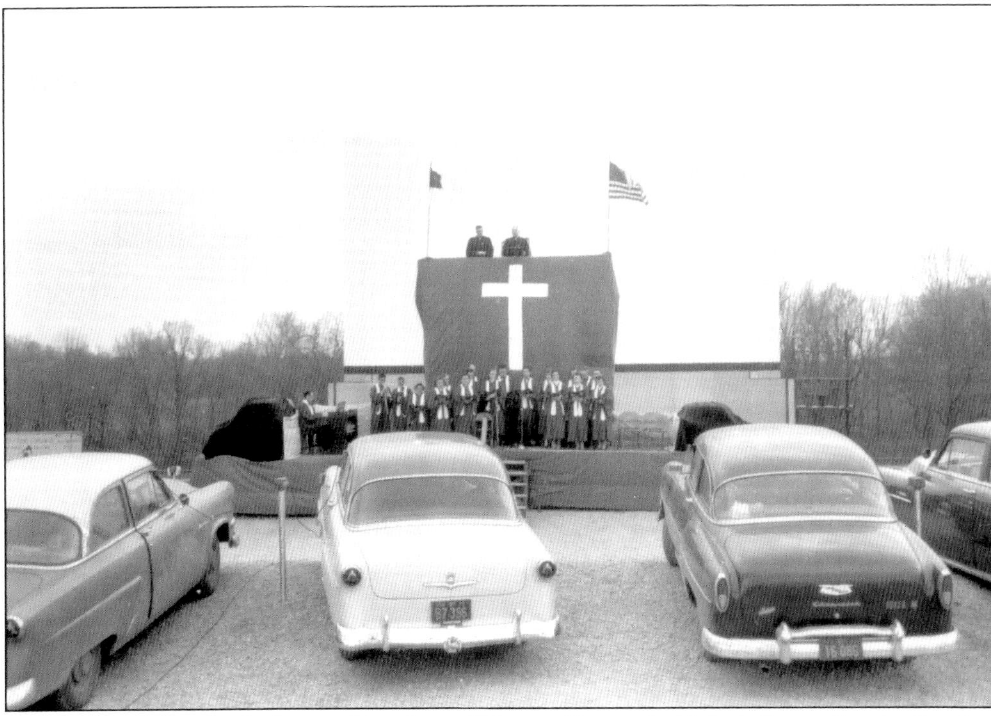

During the 1950s, the Lutheran Churches of Marion County held their Easter Sunrise Services at the Sky-Hi Drive-In. The 1956 service pictured here was led by Rev. A.J. Becker, pastor of the Zion Lutheran Church of Palmyra. Rev. Clinton Koch of the West Ely church was liturgist, and Harold Radewahn led the choir. Attendees sat in their cars and listened to the service through the car-side speakers.

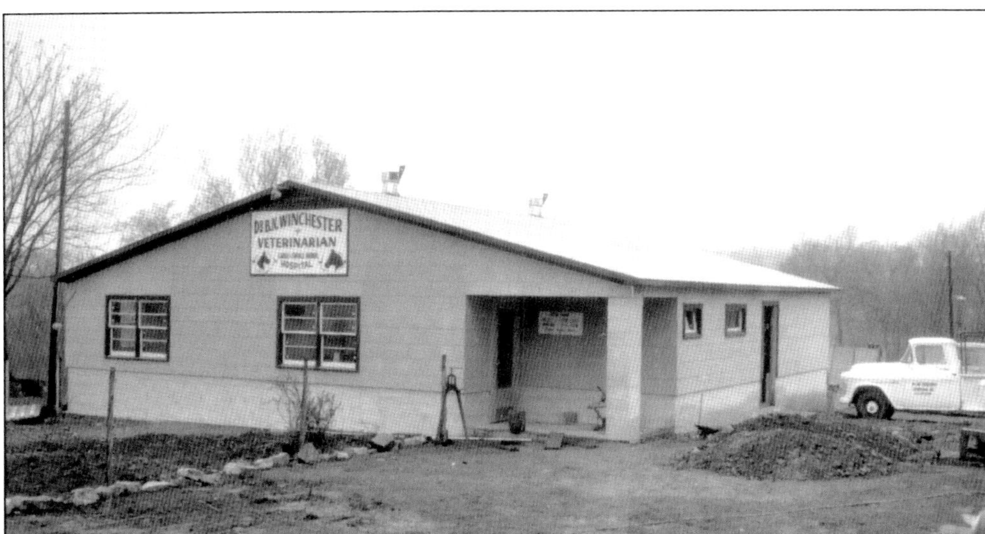

In April 1956, Dr. B.N. Winchester opened a new veterinary clinic at 4805 McMasters at the site of the present-day Hannibal National Bank North facility. This building became a Hannibal landmark when a life-size horse was placed atop the roof. Dr. Winchester was also noted for his collection of western artifacts and for years operated the South River Fort museum on his property.

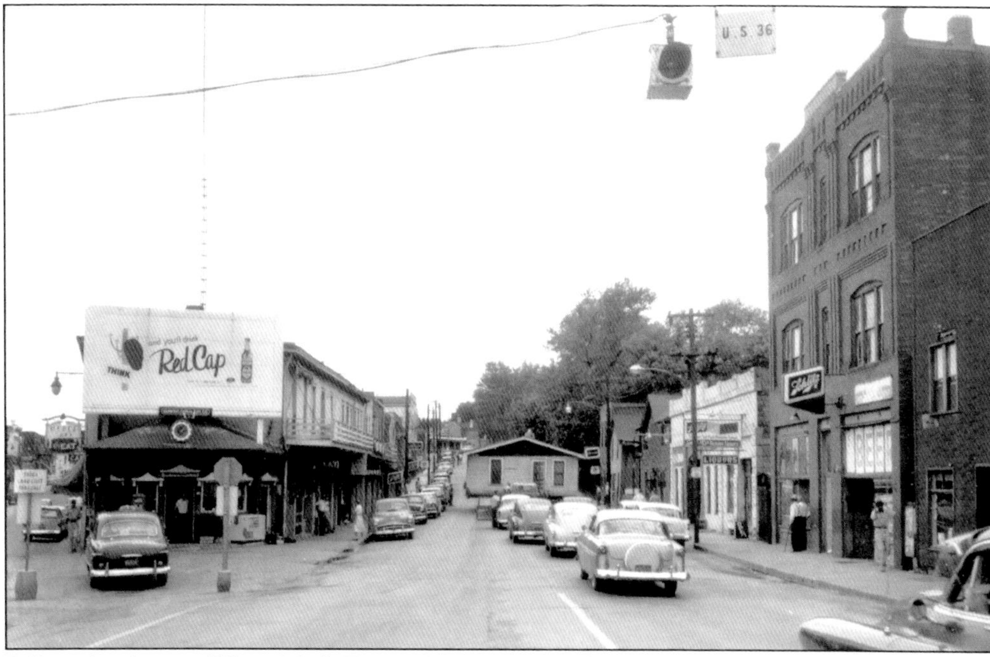

Follow that house! When Mark Twain Avenue was widened, structures in the way of progress were auctioned and demolished or moved. This photo of one of the homes chosen to be moved is also a nice view of the Broadway side of the Wedge. (May 1956)

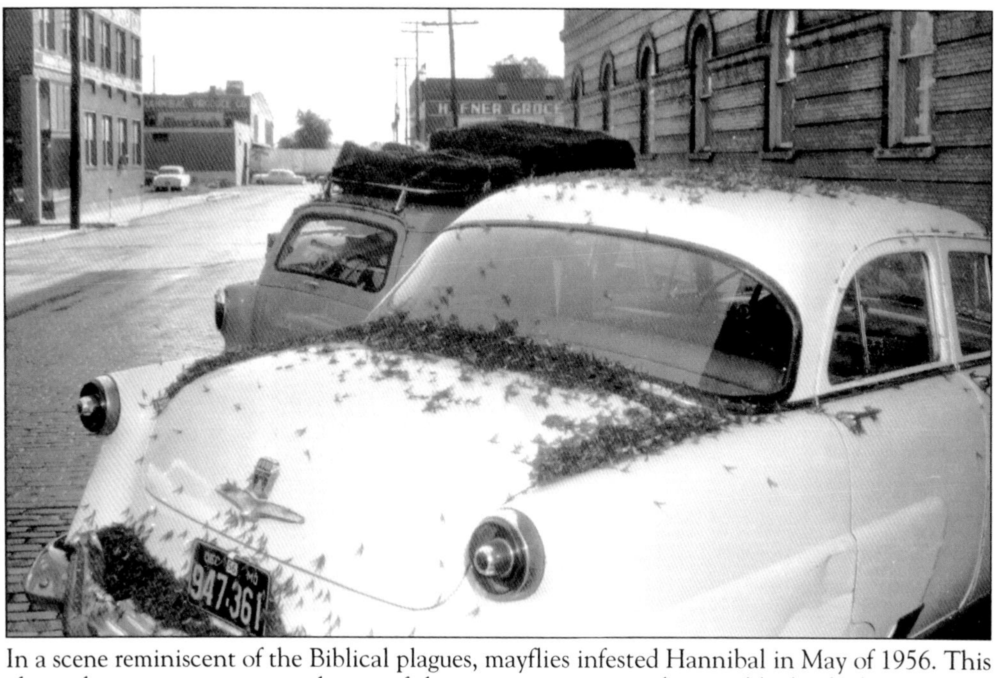

In a scene reminiscent of the Biblical plagues, mayflies infested Hannibal in May of 1956. This photo shows quite an accumulation of the insects on cars in the 100 block of Church Street by the Mark Twain Hotel. Streets became so slick with dead insects they became hazardous. In some places they were piled so high that the street department had to use snow removal equipment to clear the roadways.

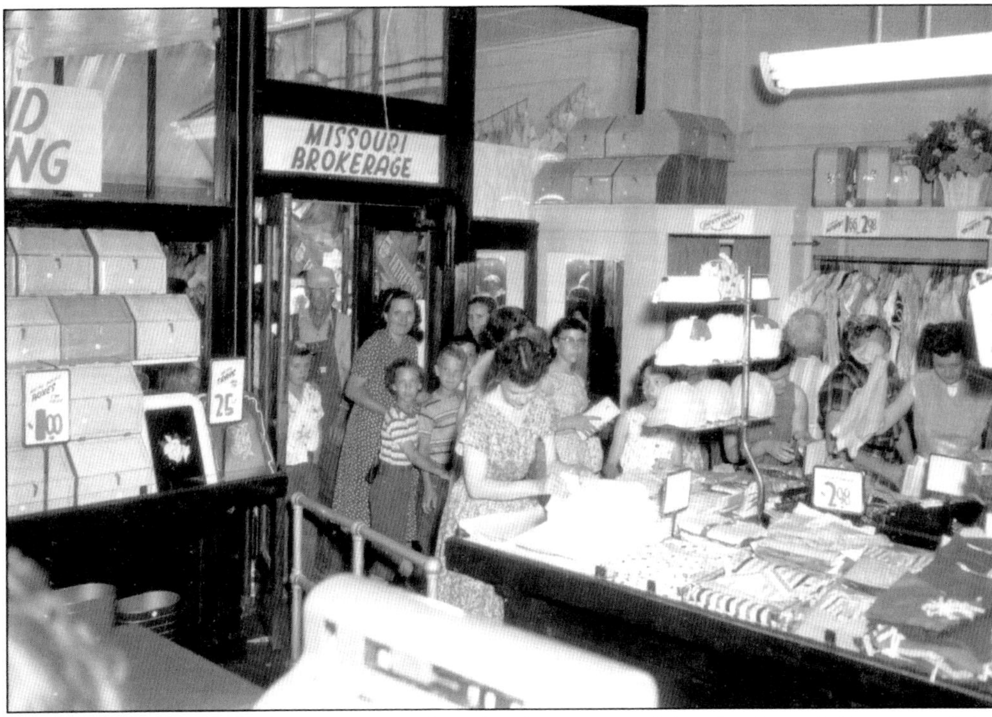

This photo records the first minutes after the doors opened for the Grand Opening of the Missouri Brokerage store at 106 North Main. Do you wonder how many of those one dollar breadboxes sold that first day? (June 1956)

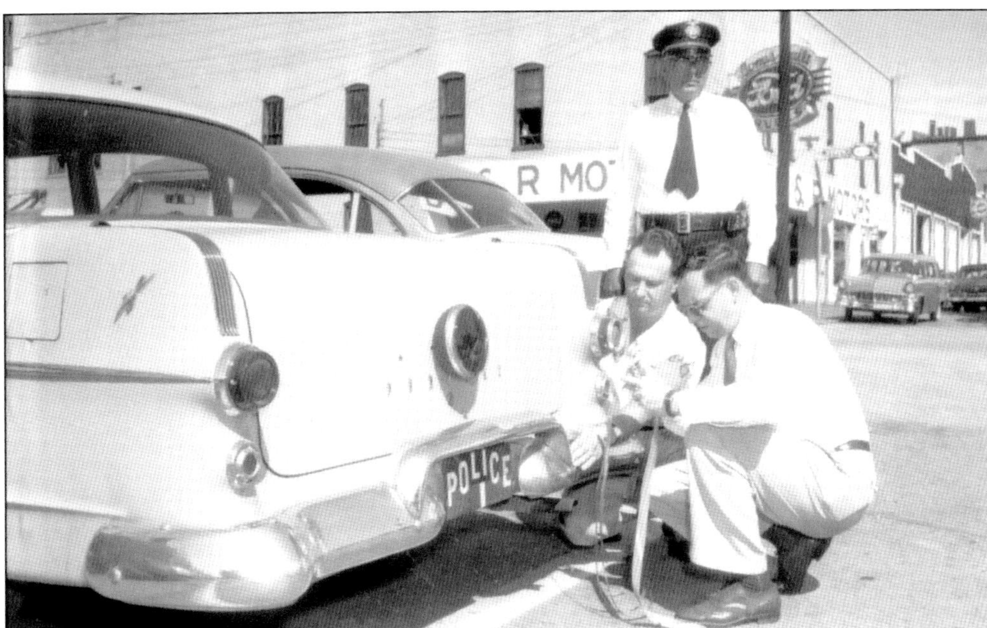

Hannibal Jaycees Roy Auten and Bob Welch affix a safety reflective tape kit to the Hannibal Police Chief's patrol car. The Jaycees were selling these kits as part of their safety campaign, and Chief of Police John Lawson (standing) purchased the first kit. (July 1956)

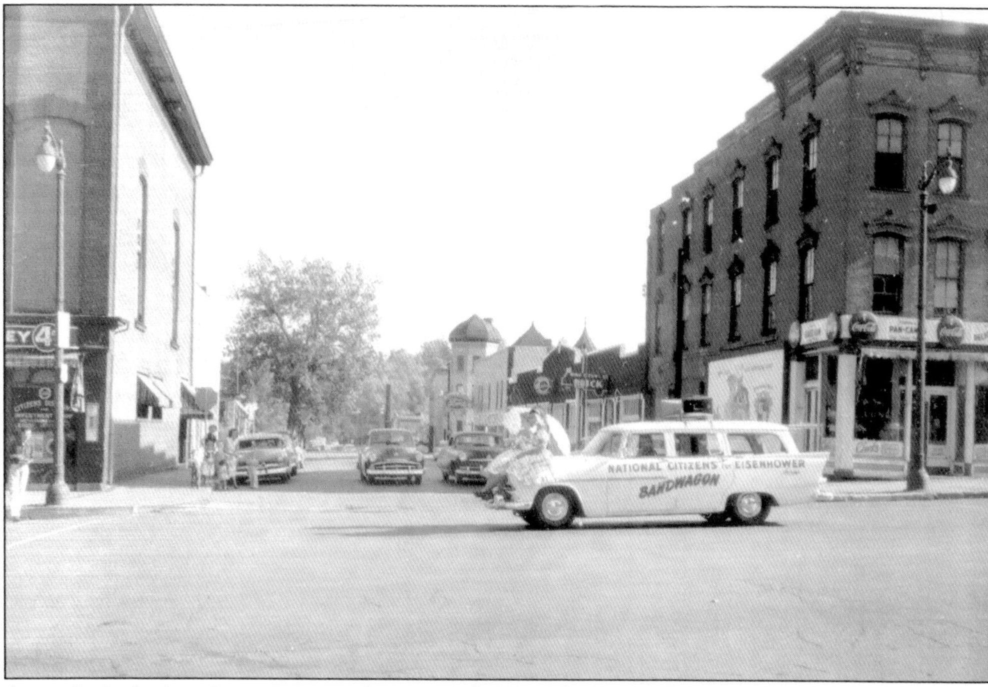

A car bedecked with campaign advertising for Eisenhower cruises down Broadway at Fourth during the summer of 1956.

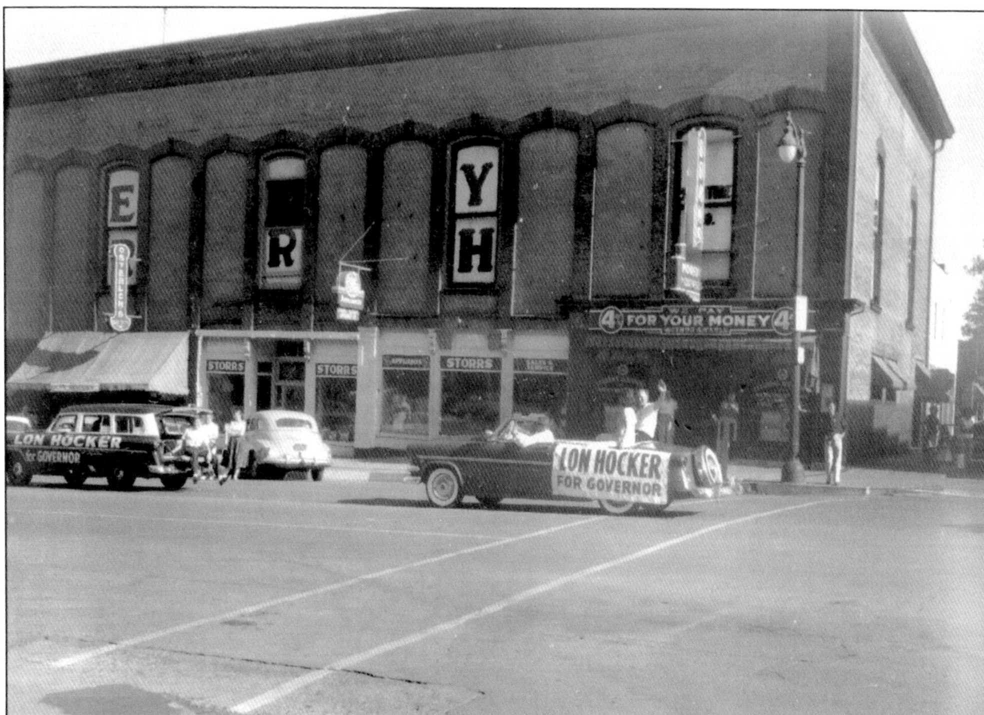

Here two vehicles proclaim their support for Lon Hocker for governor. This was part of a local rally to nominate Hocker as the Republican candidate for Missouri governor. (July 1956)

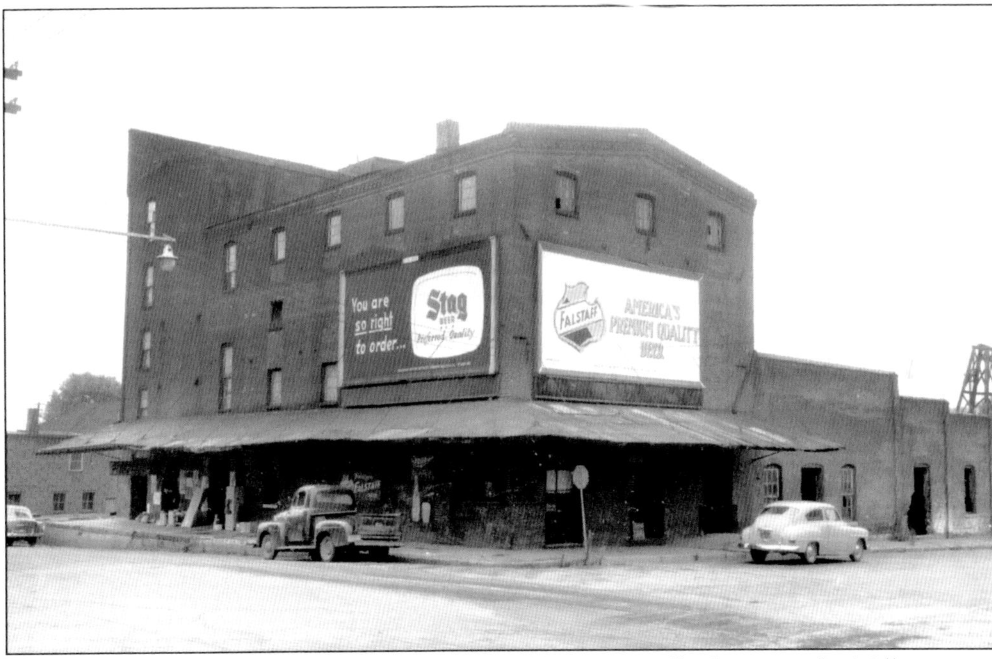

This was the Hannibal Ice and Cold Storage building, originally the Magnolia Mills, prior to demolition. Built about 1867, it stood at the southeast corner of Fourth and Lyon. This huge structure was one of several between Third, Lyon, Fourth, and Collier that were slated for demolition in order to make room for the new National Foods store. (August 1956)

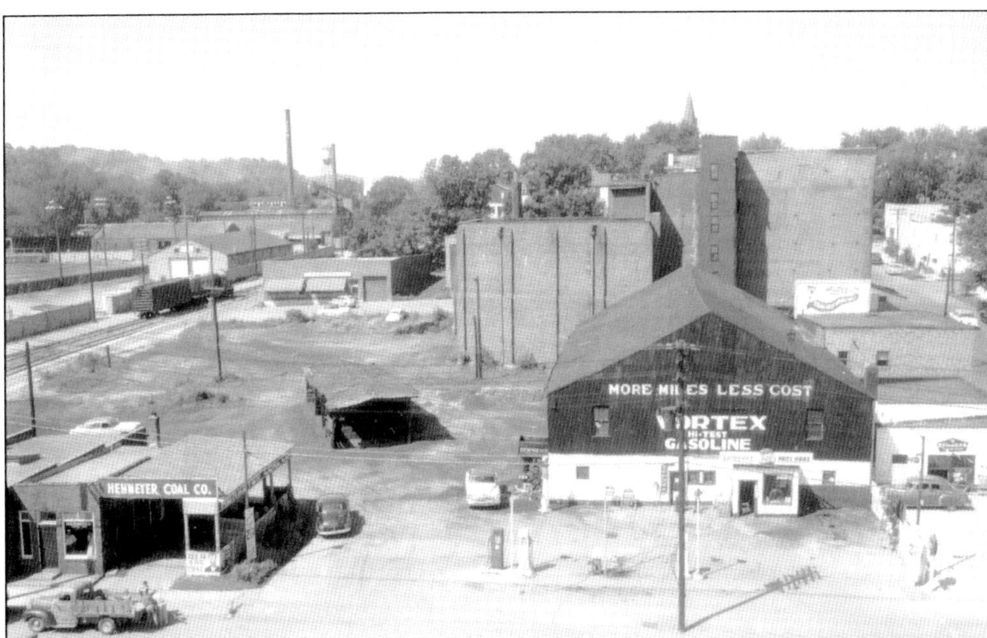

In this photo Hehmeyer Coal Company and Vortex filling station are both visible along South Third. Both of these would be demolished to make way for the new National Foods. In the background is the back of the Hannibal Ice and Cold Storage building. (August 1956)

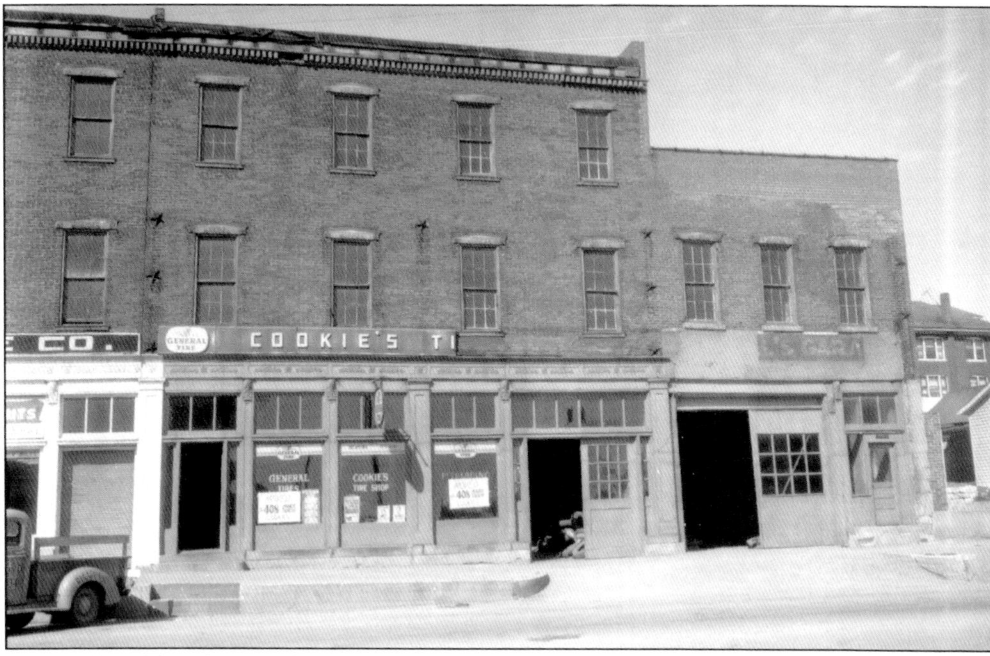

This is the old Helm Building on North Third being vacated prior to demolition in August 1956. It once housed a paper box factory. The most recent tenant, Cookie's Tire Shop, had moved to Mark Twain Avenue. Today the Hotel Clemens sits on this site.

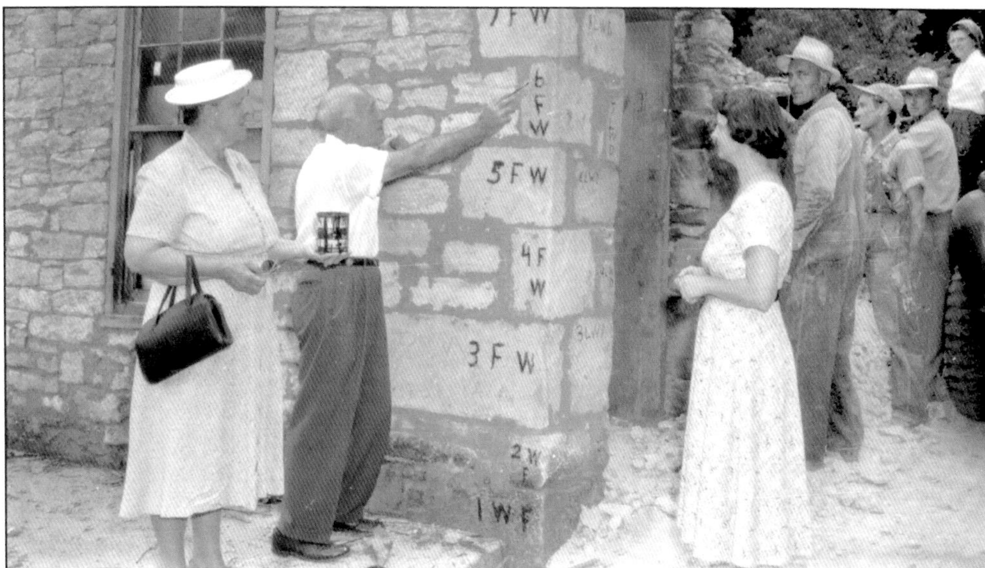

Dismantling work is in progress on the old Welshman's House on Mark Twain Avenue at Denkler's Alley. This historic structure dating back to Hannibal's very early days was endangered when Mark Twain Avenue was to be widened. The newly-formed Marion County Historical Society sought to preserve it, and it would ultimately be moved to the intersection of North Third and Mark Twain Avenue. In this photo, Kate Ray Kuhn holds a can of paint, Charles Walker holds the paintbrush, and Mrs. Frank Berry looks on. The others were workers assisting the historical society in their work. (August 1956)

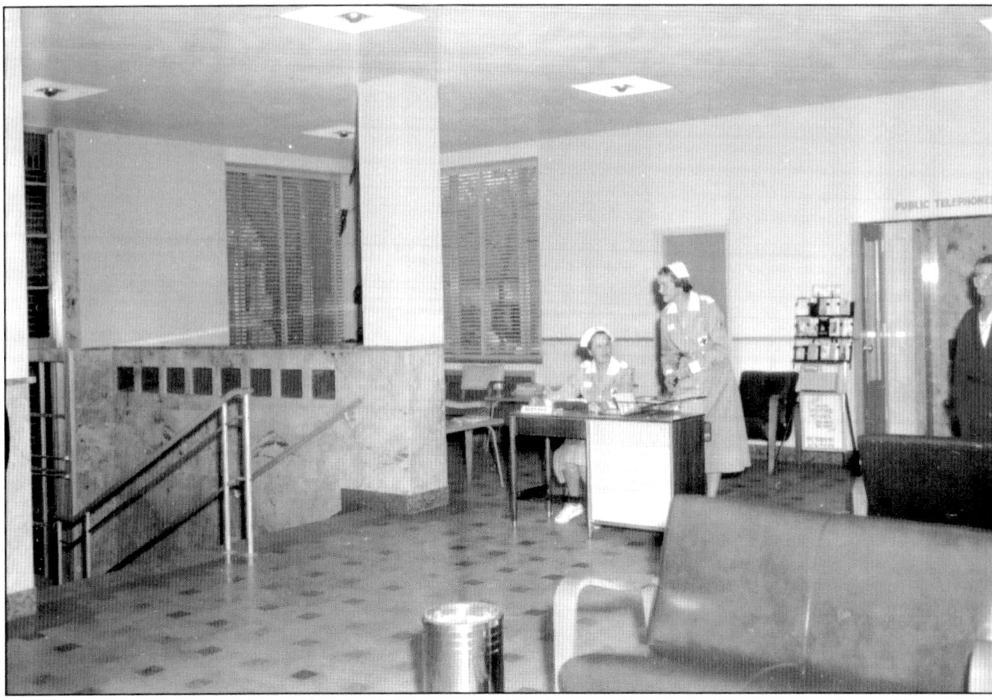

This is the new lobby of St. Elizabeth Hospital. The hospital's new addition was formally opened to the public on November 19, 1956. Both St. Elizabeth and Levering Hospitals built new wings and additions in the 1950s and '60s.

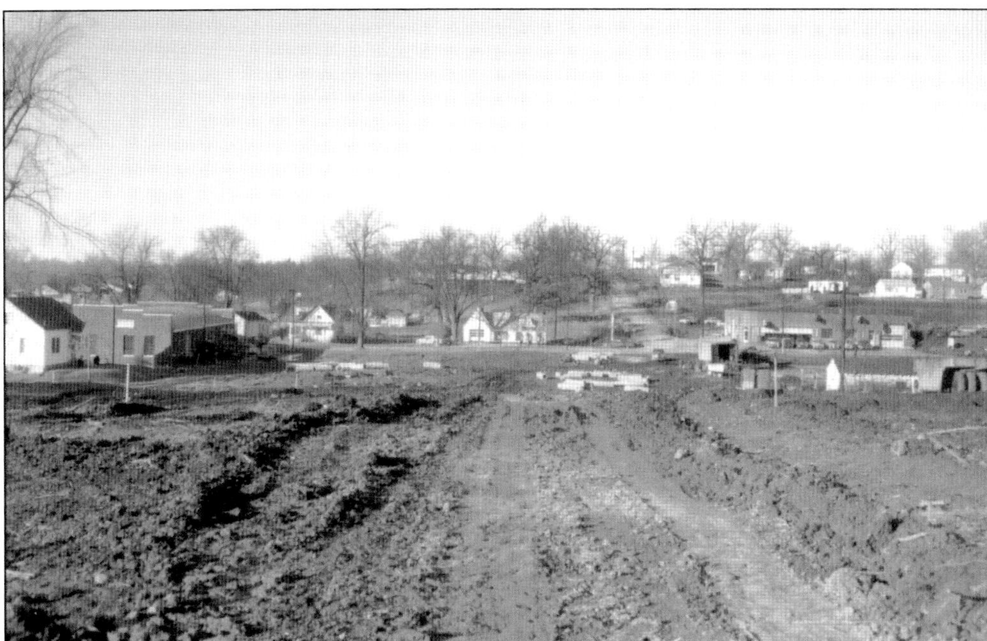

The site of the future overpass of U.S. 36 and U.S. 61 is shown in this November 1956 photo. Otis took this photo standing along the U.S. 36 corridor looking east. The Rol–Arena skating rink is visible at left.

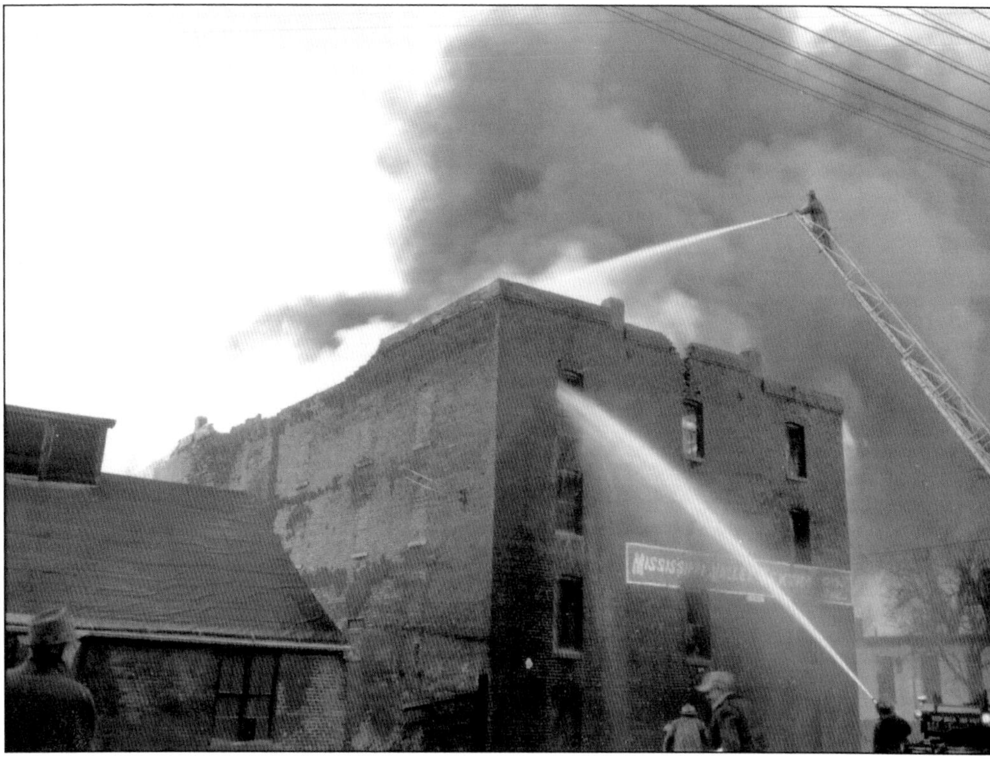

Firemen fight a blaze that destroyed the Mississippi Valley Textile Company building at the southeast corner of Ninth and Lyon. Mississippi Valley Textile made products such as towels and wash cloths. (February 1957)

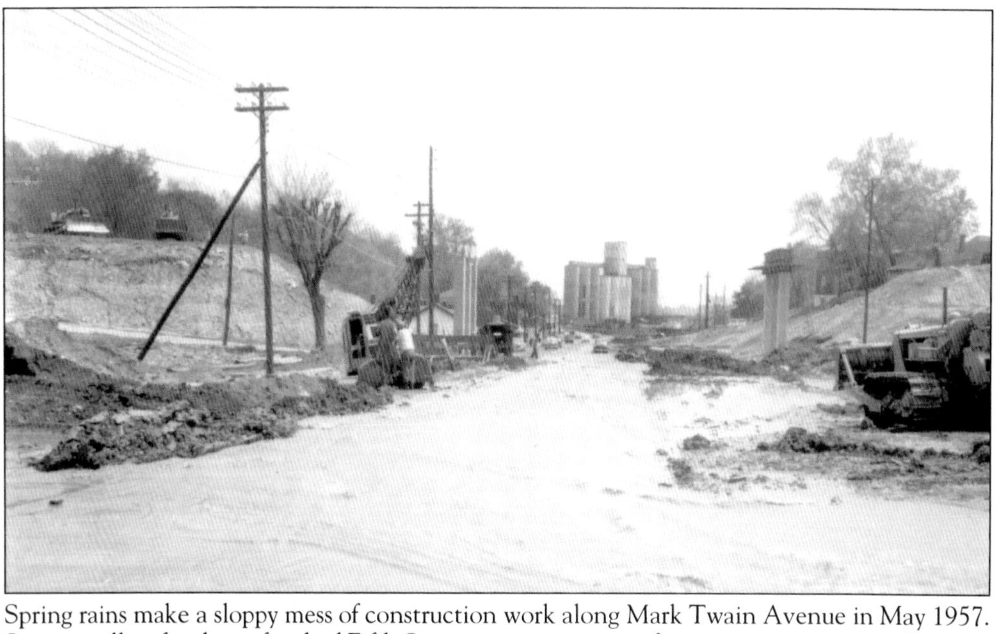

Spring rains make a sloppy mess of construction work along Mark Twain Avenue in May 1957. Support pillars for the unfinished Fifth Street overpass seem to form a giant gateway to the grain terminal in the distance.

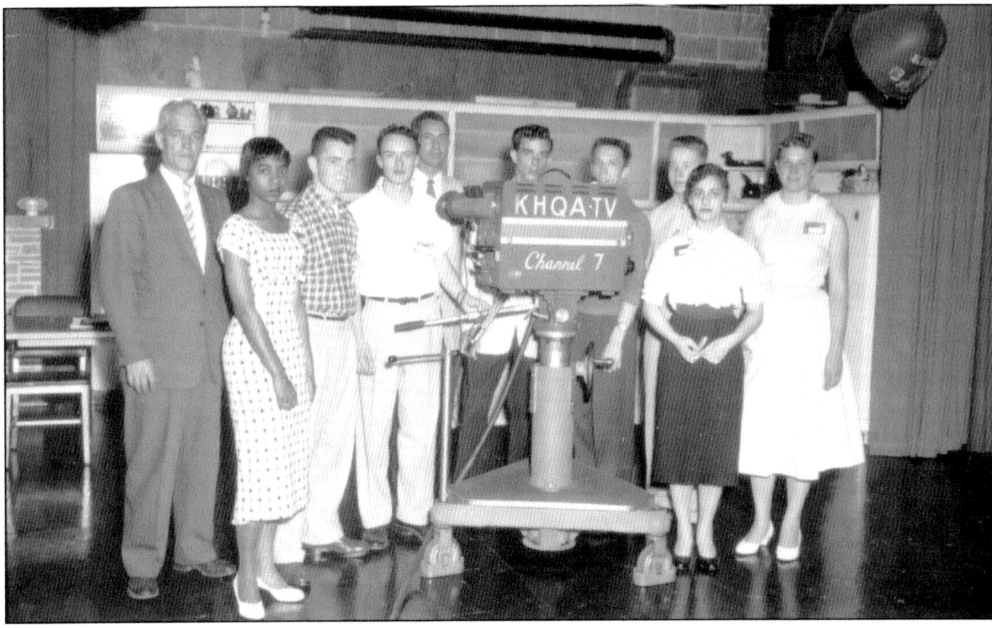

This photo documents a visit of Hannibal High School students to the KHQA studio. Pictured left to right are Paul McClelland (broadcaster), Priscilla Forte, Heine Schwartz, Jim Boling, Lloyd Estes (teacher), Bill Underhill, Gary Daniel, Pat Tharp, Judy Basford, and Marilyn Muehring. (May 1957)

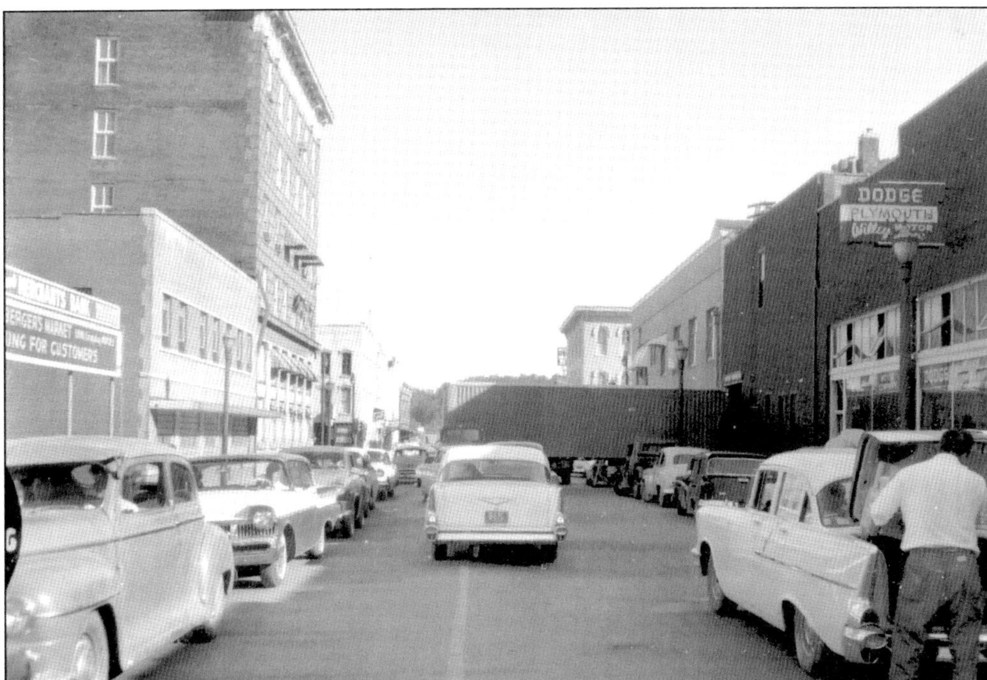

This photo looks south on Third Street from the Center Street intersection. Wiley Motors is at right. The tractor trailer is coming out of Breeding Transfer and Storage. At left is Heiberger's parking lot, the Rendlen Building, and the B&L Building. (August 1957)

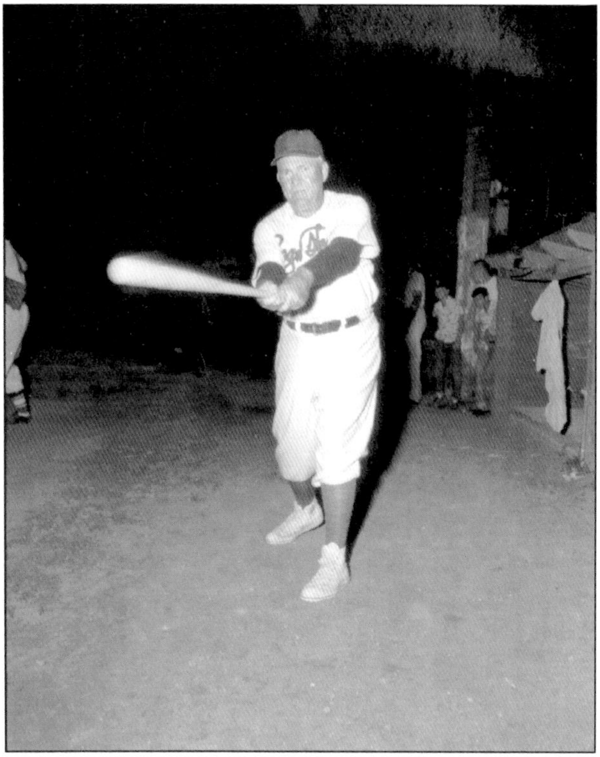

Otis Howell was a baseball fan, and a Cardinals fan in particular. One can only imagine the thrill he must have felt photographing Hall-of-Famer and Cardinals great Rogers Hornsby when he made an appearance in Hannibal on August 16, 1957.

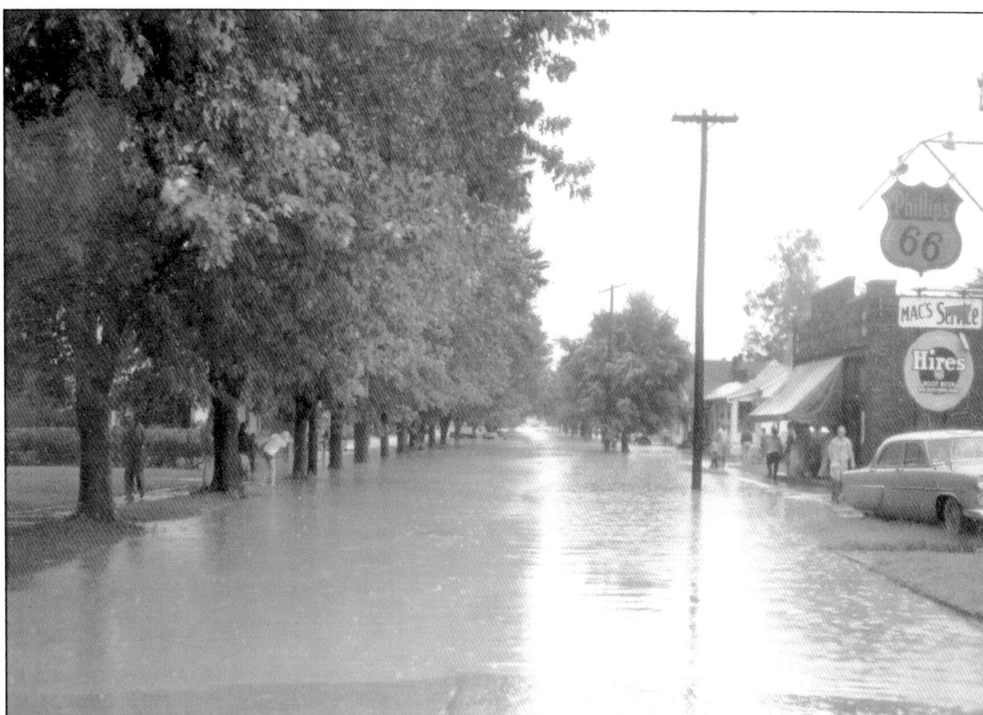

Heavy summer rains caused flash flooding as Bear Creek spilled over its banks onto Lindell Avenue. (August 1957)

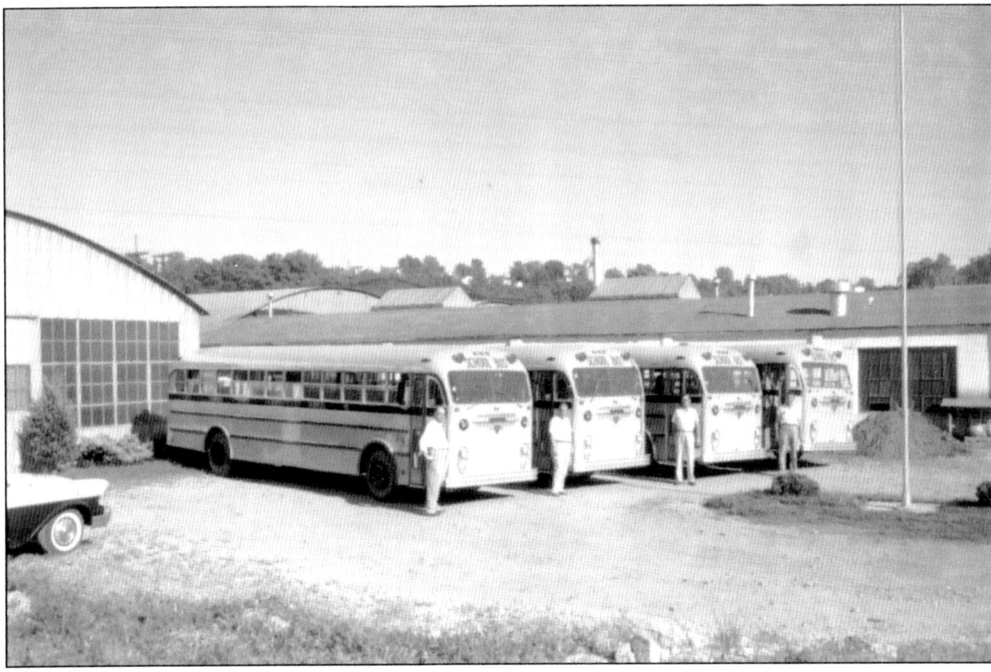

Here is the new fleet of school buses for the Hannibal public schools. Posed beside each of these 73-passenger, rear-engine buses are drivers, left to right, L.L. Fuqua, Leo Walker, John C. Hall, and John Oltman. Prior to school buses students walked or rode the city buses. (August 1957)

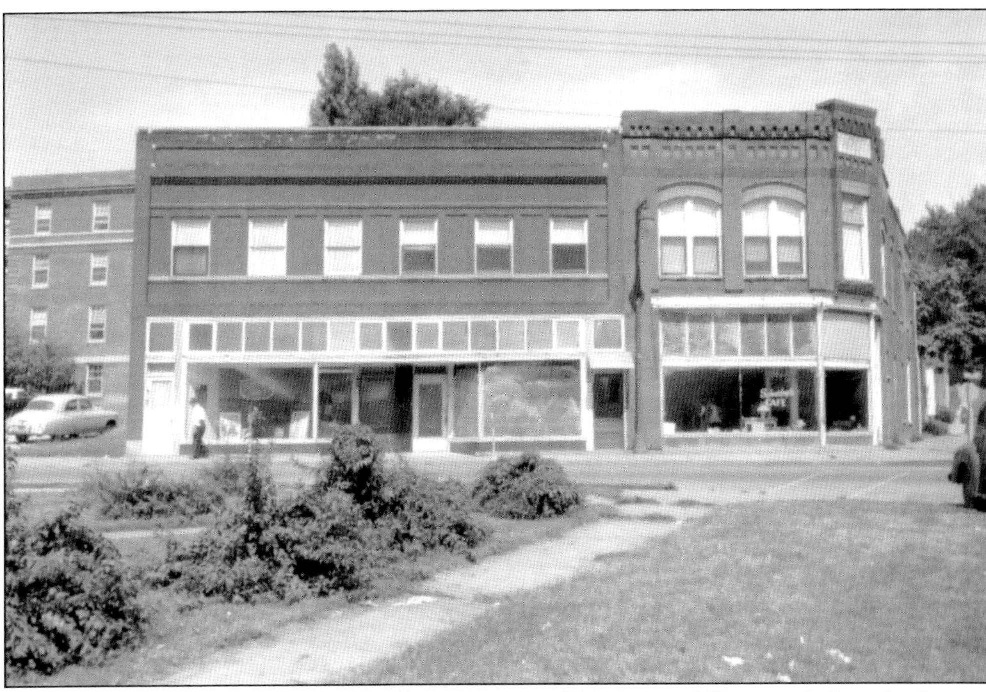

This is the business block at the northwest corner of Market and Houston before the lot was cleared for a parking area. Schadey's Café and West End Cleaners occupied the building at the time of the photo. (October 1957)

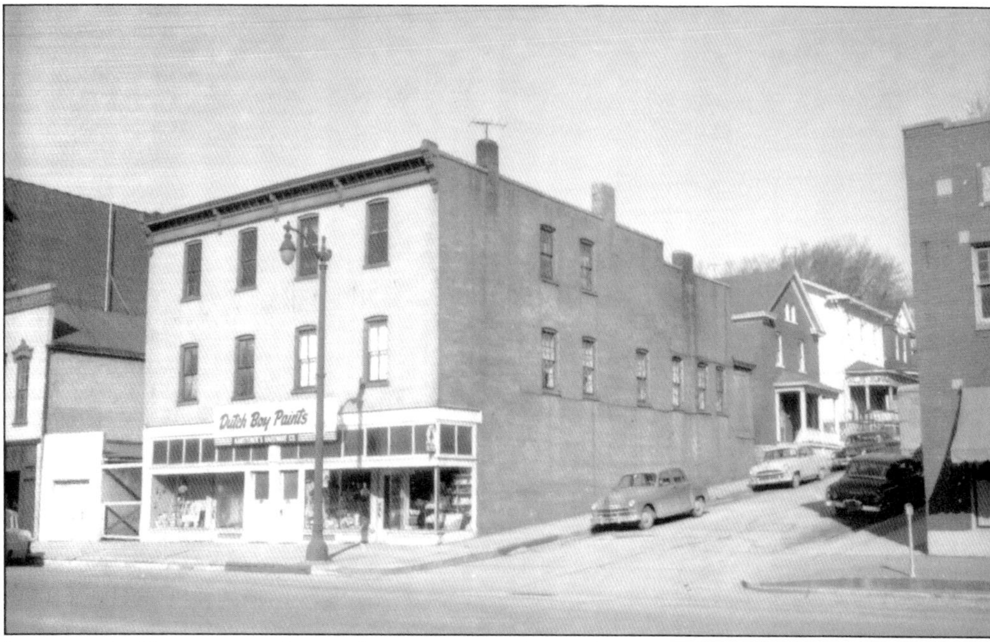

Kansteiner's Hardware at the northwest corner of Broadway and Eighth had been part of the Hannibal business community since after the Civil War. The store closed in 1957, and the building was demolished the following year for expansion of the Bell Telephone building. October 1957.

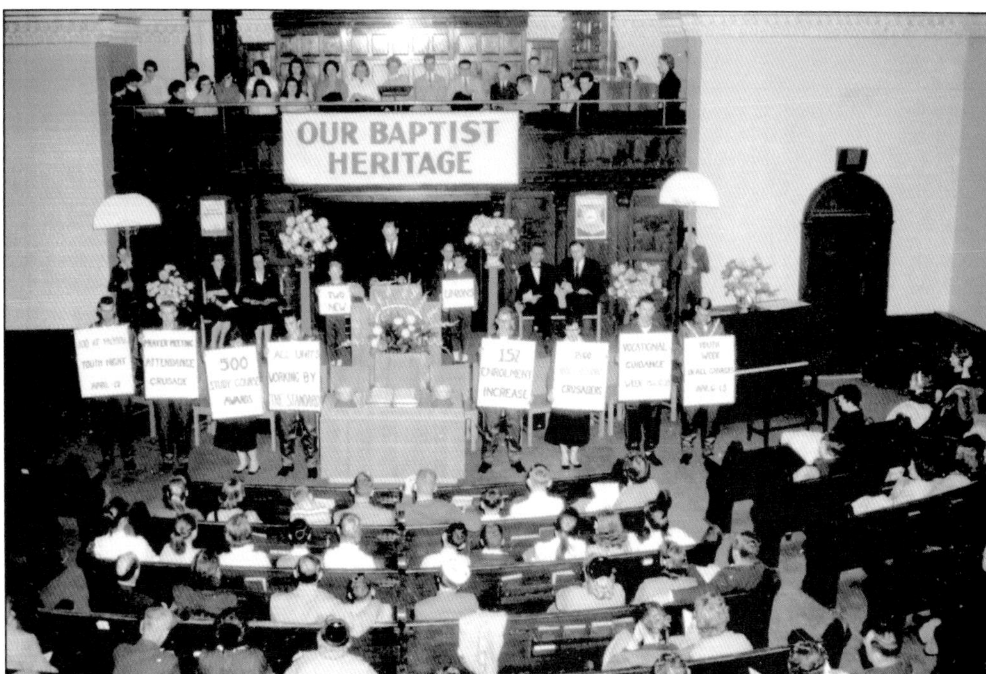

Students from Hannibal LaGrange College hold placards showing goals of the Bethel Baptist Association during "M" Night Associational Training Union Meeting held at the Fifth Street Baptist Church on December 2, 1957.

This was the kick-off for the Salvation Army's Tree of Lights campaign. Harry G. Shaffner of the American Trust Company screws in the first light bulb on the Tree of Lights, which was located at the Ben Franklin store at 1300 Market Street. Each light bulb represented a $10 donation to the campaign. (December 3, 1957)

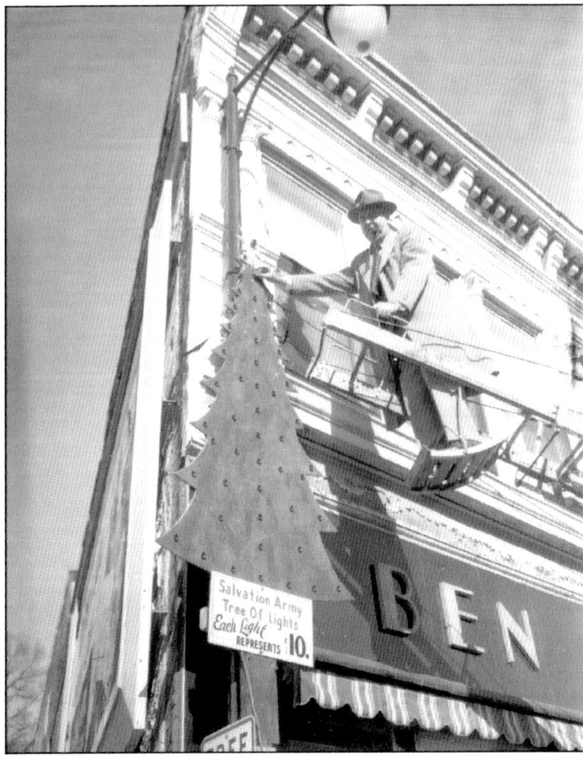

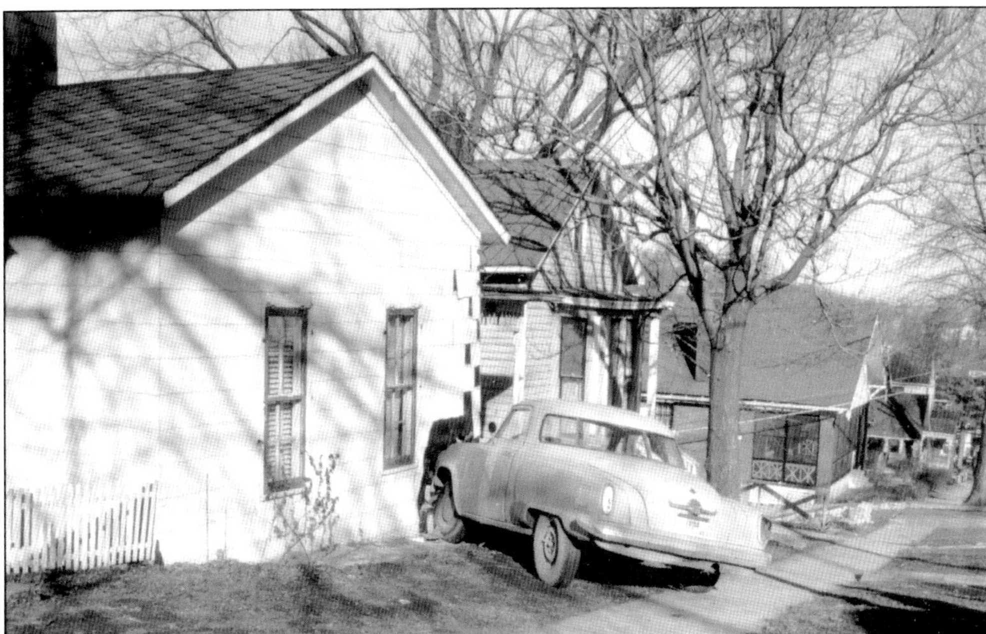

For Heaven's sake, set that brake! This photo shows a Studebaker with its nose buried in the corner of Paul Shumm's house at 602 Rock Street near Denkler's Alley. As many of Hannibal's residential streets are built on hills, accidents such as these happened now and then. This house, as well as the home to its right, no longer exist.

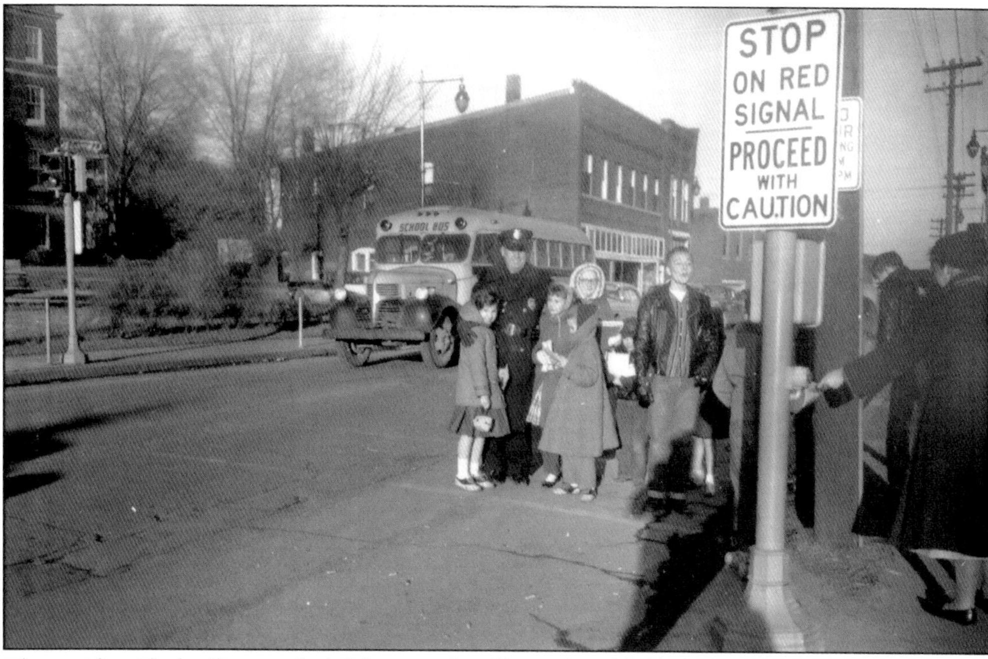

The unidentified officer and children in this December 1957 photo conjure up an image of small-town innocence. This photo was taken at the crosswalk in front of Eugene Field School on Market Street. Levering Hospital is partly visible at left.

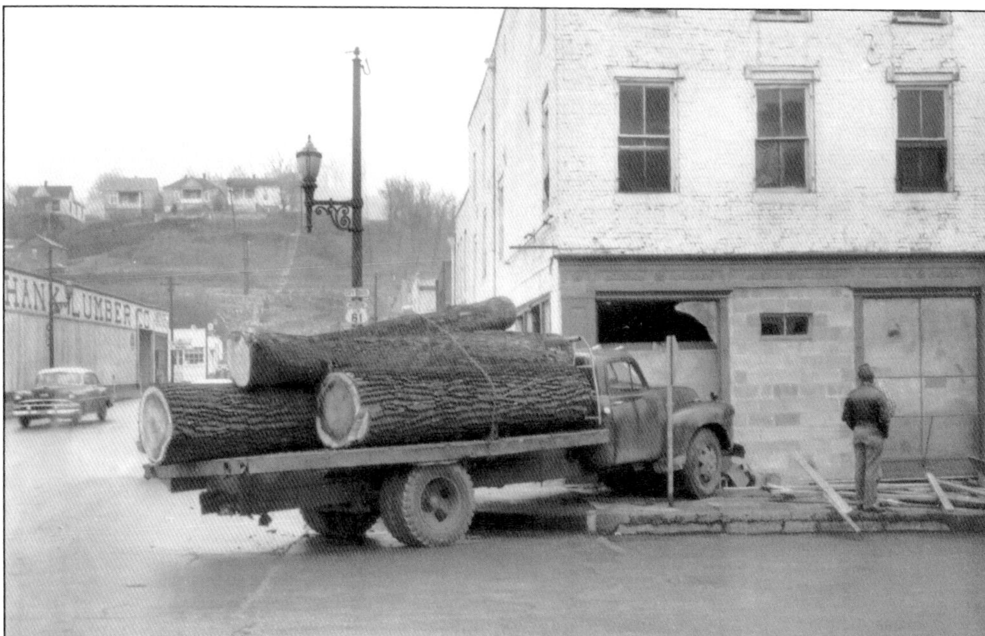

Here is still another vehicle mishap. The driver of this log truck stopped for lunch, and his unattended vehicle, loaded down with 20,000 lbs. of logs, rolled down Hill Street, across South Main, and into the Selmes Building. At the time, an aquarium attraction was located there. And how times have changed—damage from the collision was estimated at $300! (December 1957)

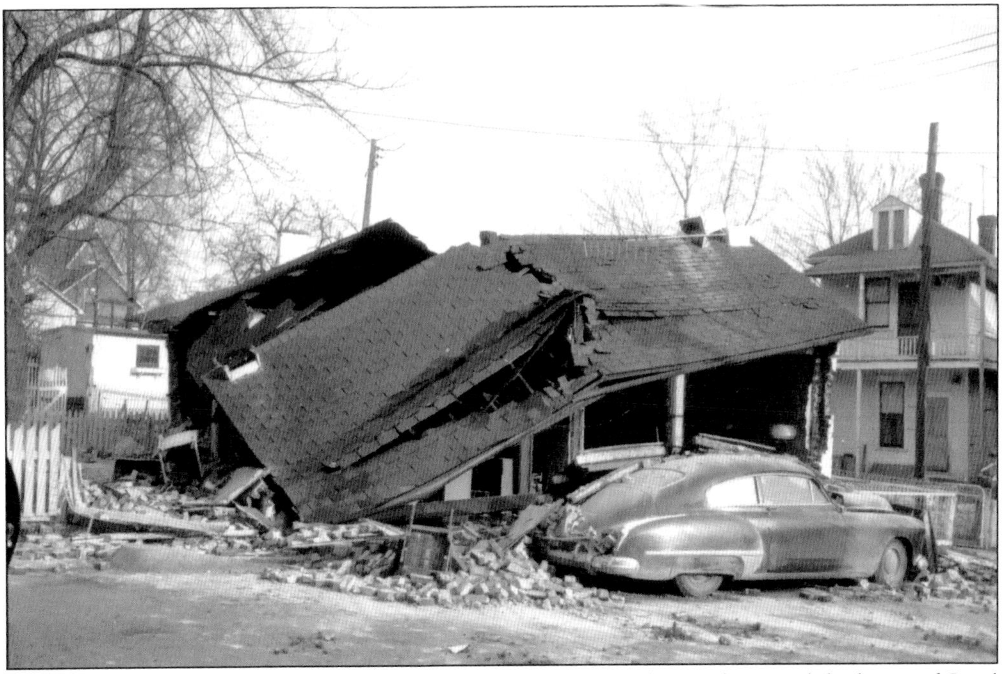

On February 14, 1958, tragedy struck in Hannibal when an explosion destroyed the home of Cecil Mallett at 110 Lemon Street. Mallett was mortally injured, and died later at Levering Hospital.

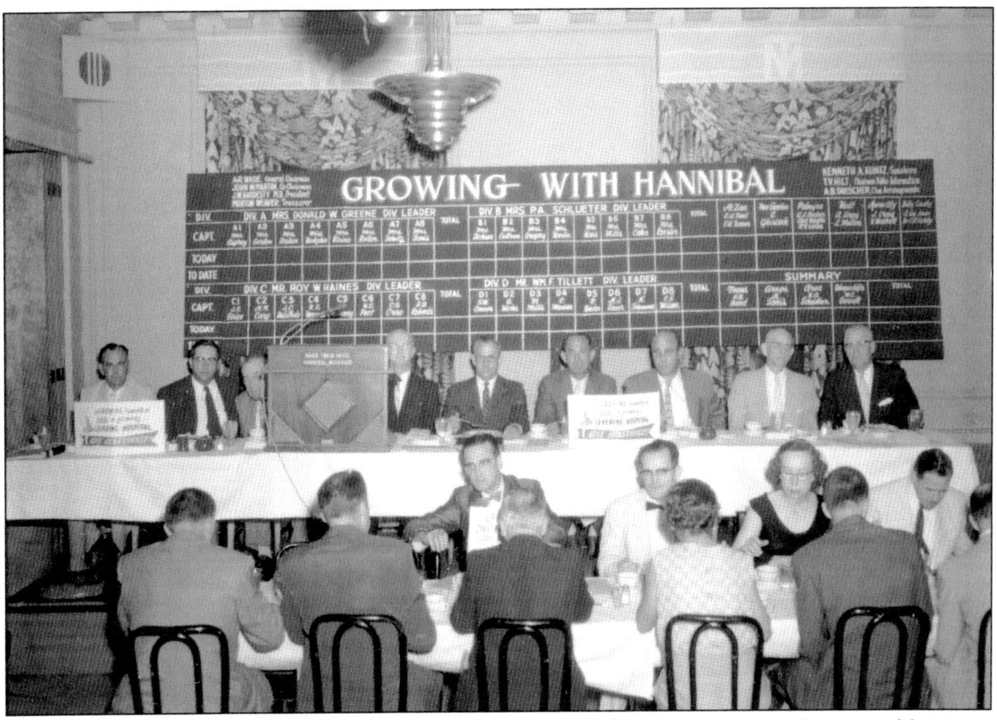

A fundraising dinner was held at the Mark Twain Hotel for construction of a new addition to Levering Hospital. "A growing Hannibal needs a growing Levering Hospital," their campaign proclaimed. The dinner was held in April 1958.

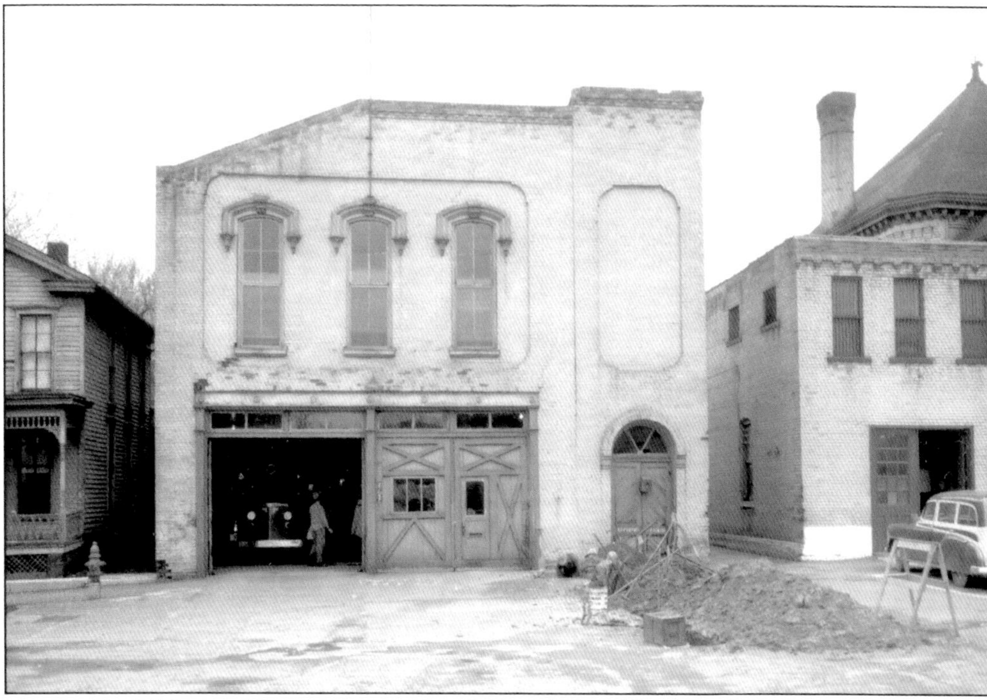

Hannibal's old Central Fire Station on South Fourth dated back to the 1870s. In this photo a gas line is being laid, which would supply a new heating system. Up to this time heat had been supplied by an antiquated wood stove. (April 1958)

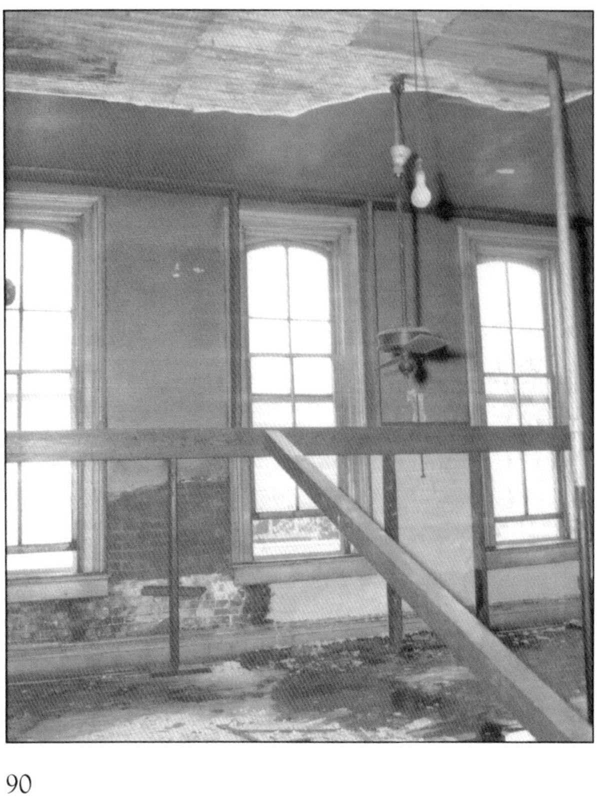

This is the second story of the old Central Fire Station showing the deteriorated condition of the building. Timber bracing is in place to shore up the outside wall and the roof was leaking, which caused part of the ceiling to collapse. This was the area where the firemen slept. This old station would be replaced with the current one in 1966. The photo is also from April 1958.

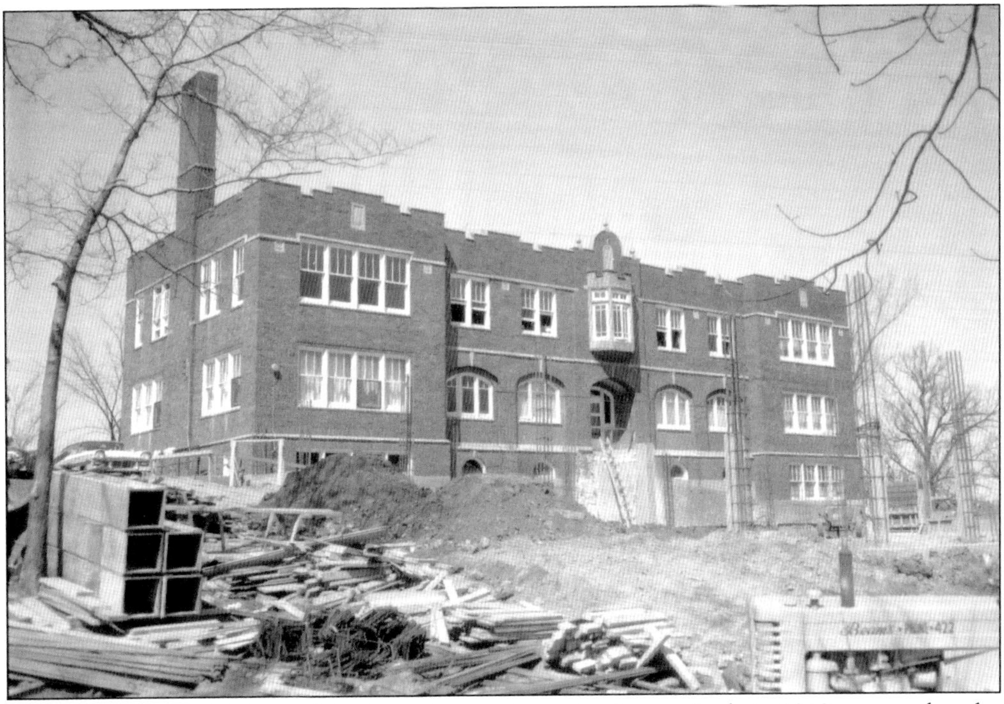

This was Hannibal's Home of the Friendless on Levering Street. Built in 1919, it served as the city's orphanage. As government agencies eliminated the need for the home, it closed in 1956. Two years later the building was sold to a Catholic order. It would be extensively remodeled and later open as St. Thomas Aquinas Seminary. (April 1958)

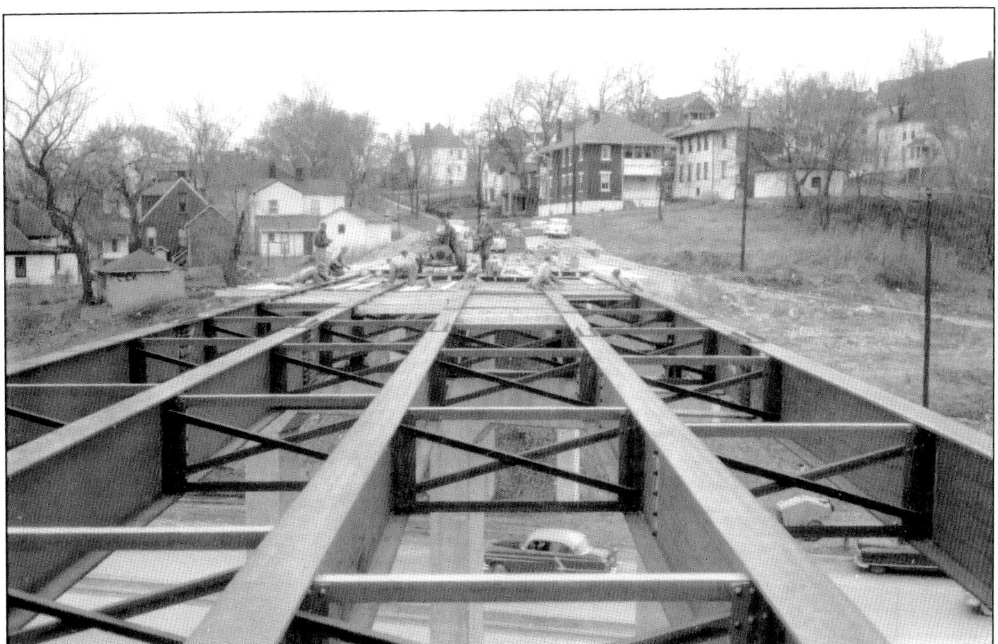

Construction workers lay decking on the Fifth Street overpass crossing Mark Twain Avenue. This view is from the north end looking south. (April 1958)

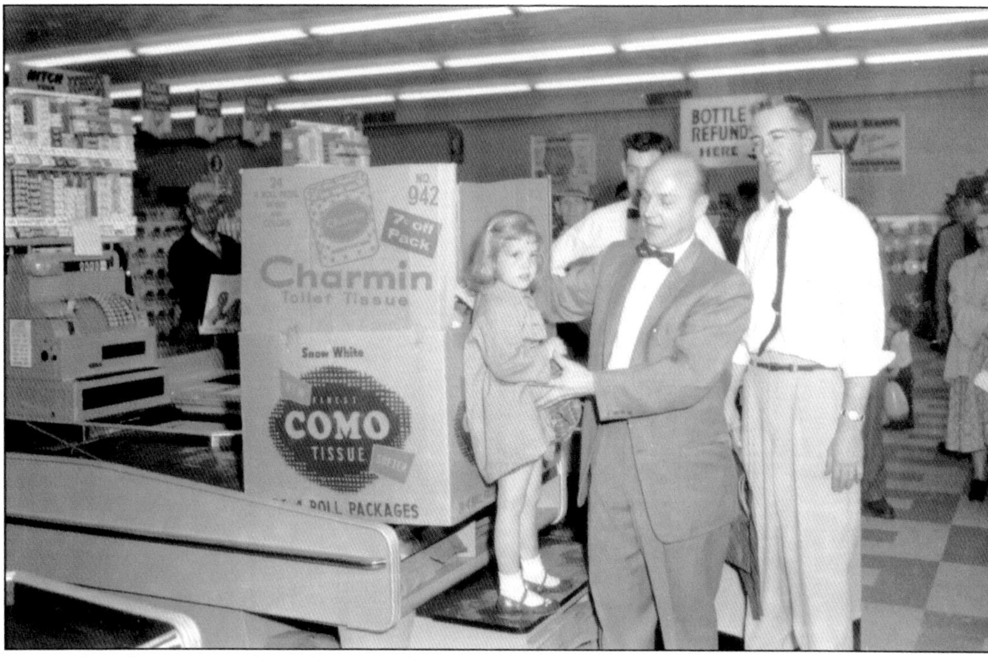

In April 1958, National Foods opened their new supermarket at 309 South Third. As part of their opening, they had a drawing for a brand-new 1958 Ford Ranch Wagon from B&R Motors. The pictured girl, Mary Jane Glascock drew the winning entry. The store's manager, Bob Wehrenberg, stands beside her.

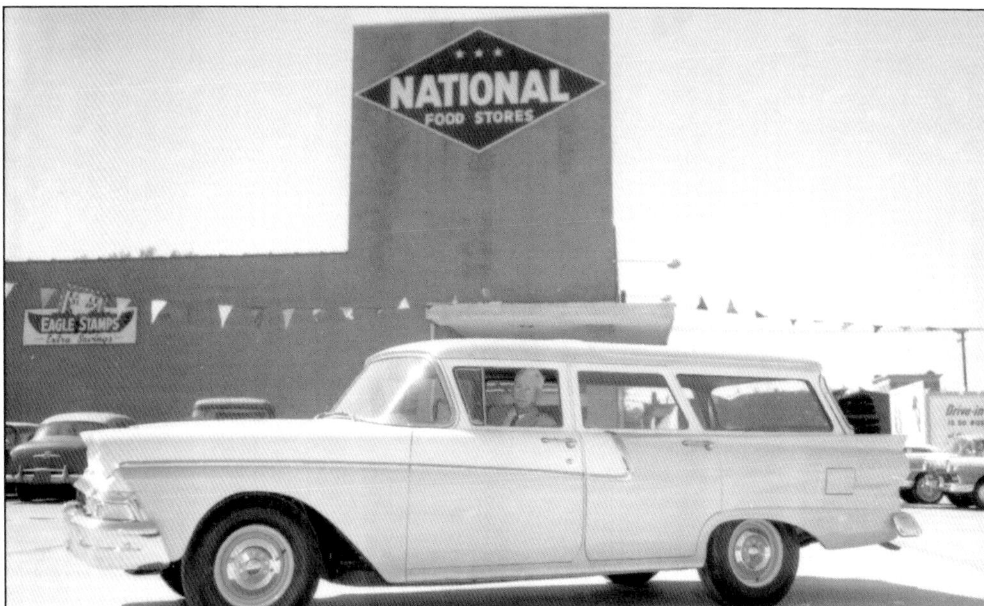

And here is the winner! The winner of the new Ford Ranch Wagon in the National Foods sweepstakes was Harry W. Watts. Though not present for the drawing, Mr. Watts arrived quickly to claim his prize. Here he is behind the wheel of his new car with National Foods in the background.

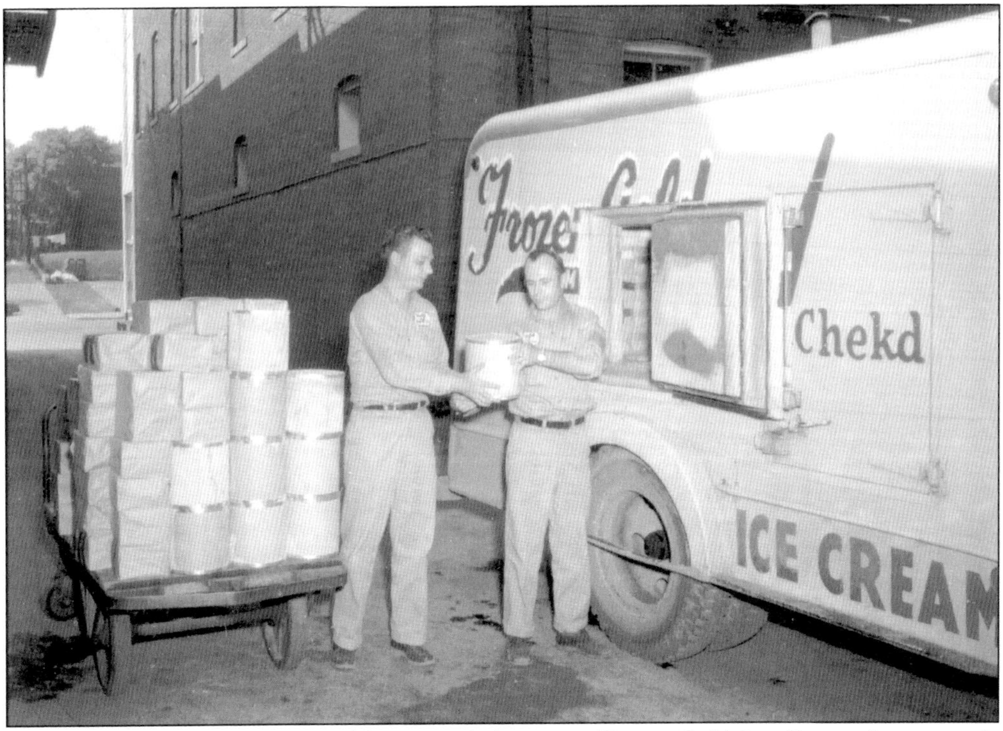

A treat remembered by many older Hannibalians was Frozen Gold Ice Cream. It was made locally by Menzel Ice Cream Co. at 117 South Seventh. Here, cartons of ice cream are being loaded into a refrigerated delivery truck in the alley behind the business. (June 1958)

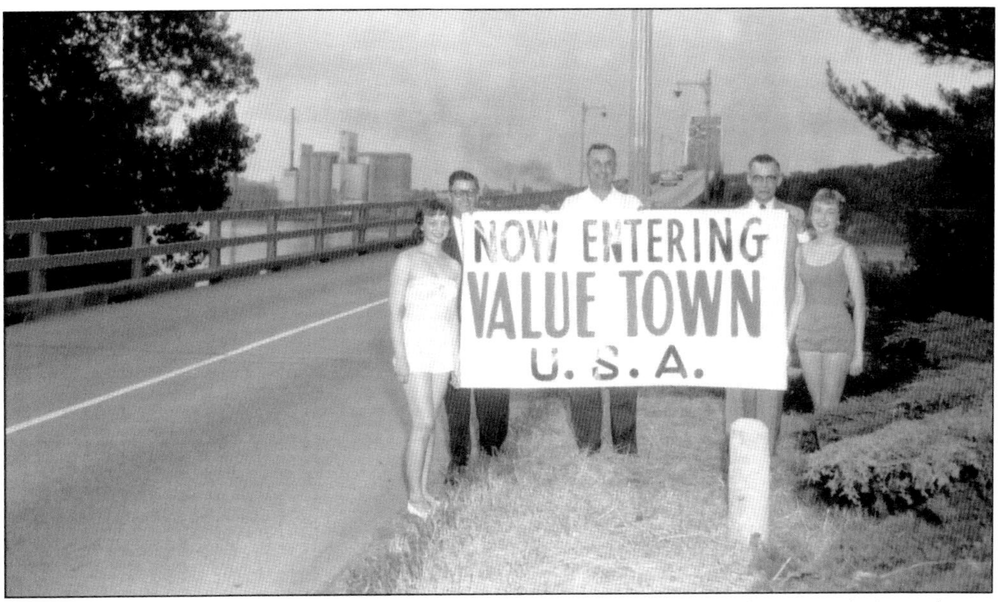

Shown here is a promotion for "Value Town U.S.A.", a campaign by the Hannibal merchants to promote shopping in Hannibal. Pictured holding the banner at the Illinois approach to the Mark Twain Bridge are (left to right) Miss Chesney Smith, H.J. Winning, Mayor Clyde Toalson, Milton Baker, and Mrs. Harlie Love. (June 1958)

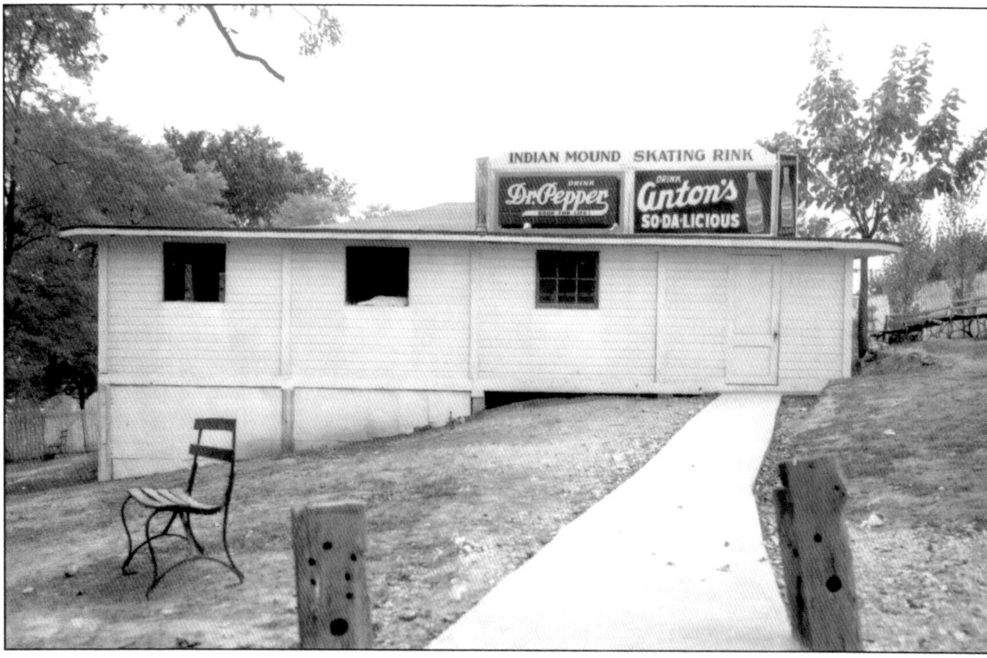

Old Indian Mound Skating Rink as it appeared in 1958, prior to demolition for construction of new U.S. 36 highway. This wooden structure was built in the 1920s as a dance pavilion, and later converted to a skating rink.

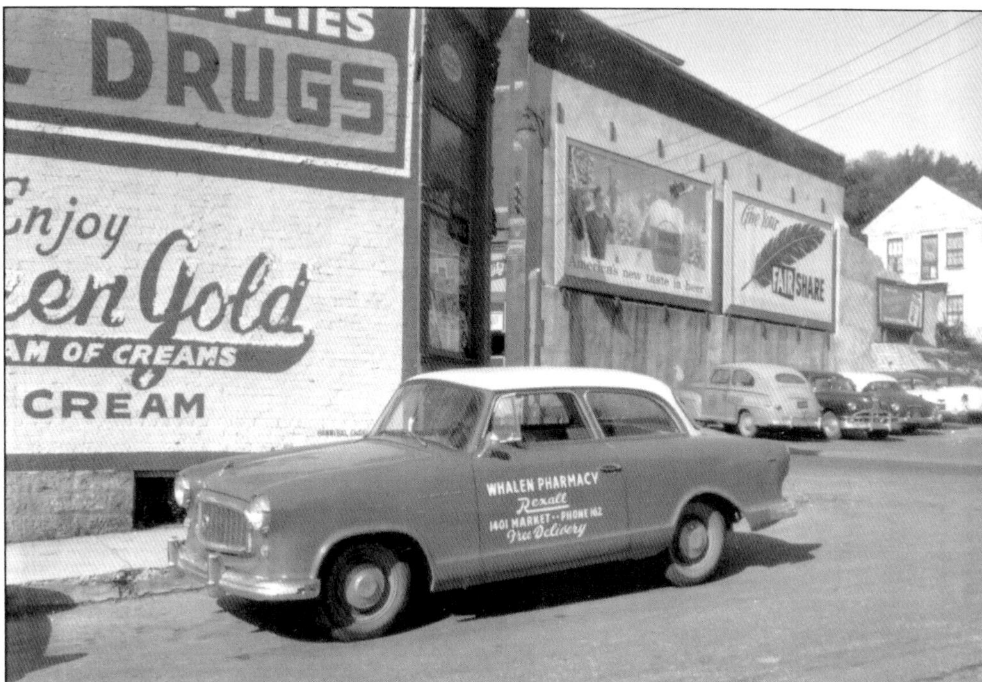

This was the delivery vehicle for Whalen Pharmacy, parked beside the business at 1401 Market Street. The car is a Nash Rambler. Whalen Pharmacy was the successor to the old Hoffbauer Drug Store, a business in the Wedge area that dated prior to 1900. (October 1958)

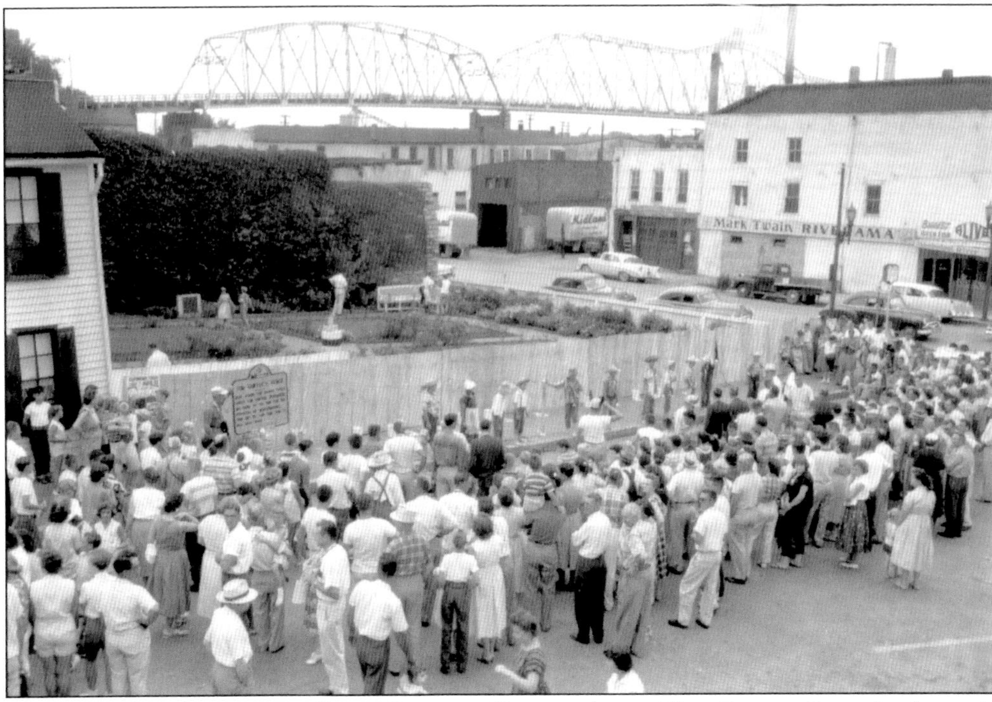

A Hannibal tradition is the Fence Painting Contest during Tom Sawyer Days. In the early years, the Hannibal Jaycees, sponsors of Tom Sawyer Days, held the annual event in August, but beginning in 1959 the event was moved to the week of July 4, when it is still held today. (August 1958)

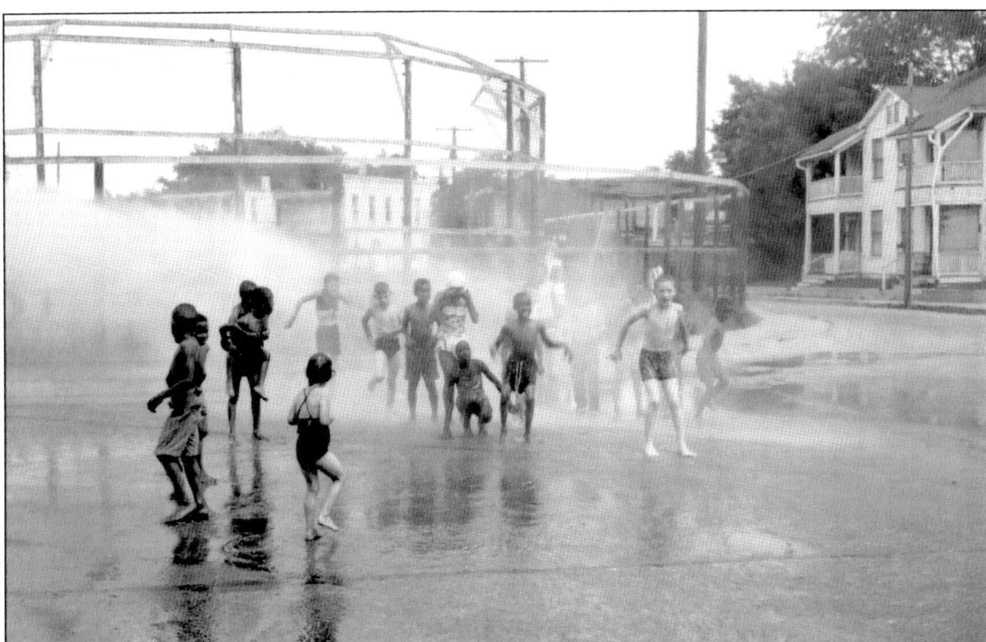

Children find refuge from summer heat in the spray of an opened fire hydrant near Douglass School. (August 1958)

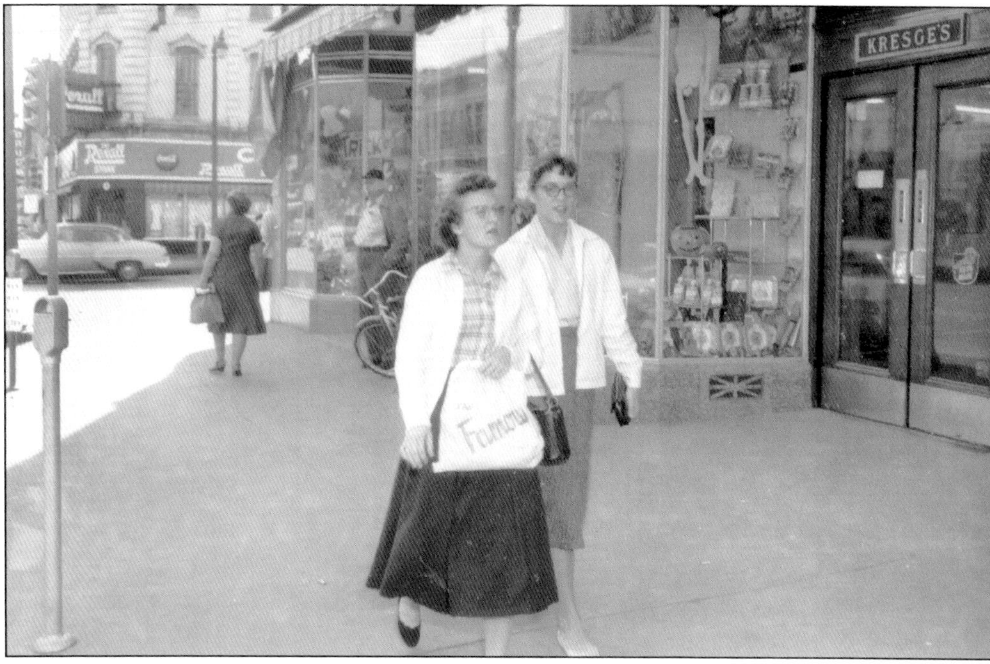

This photo recalls the days when most, if not all, shopping was done downtown. From clothing and shoes to furnishings, household, and automobiles, it was all to be found downtown. This was taken on North Main, just past the Broadway intersection, as two unidentified women shoppers pass by the store windows of Kresges. Notice all the Halloween merchandise on display. The young lady at left is Dorothy Sims. (October 1958)

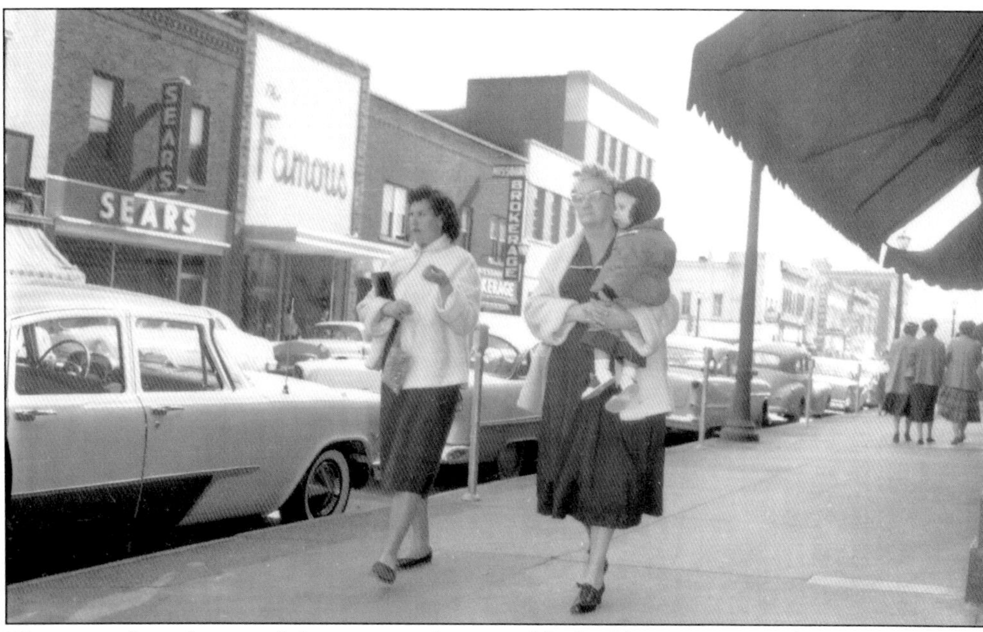

This is another glimpse of shoppers in the same block. Glancing across the street, one can make out signs for Sears, the Famous, and Missouri Brokerage. Of those three only the Famous remains downtown today. (October 1958)

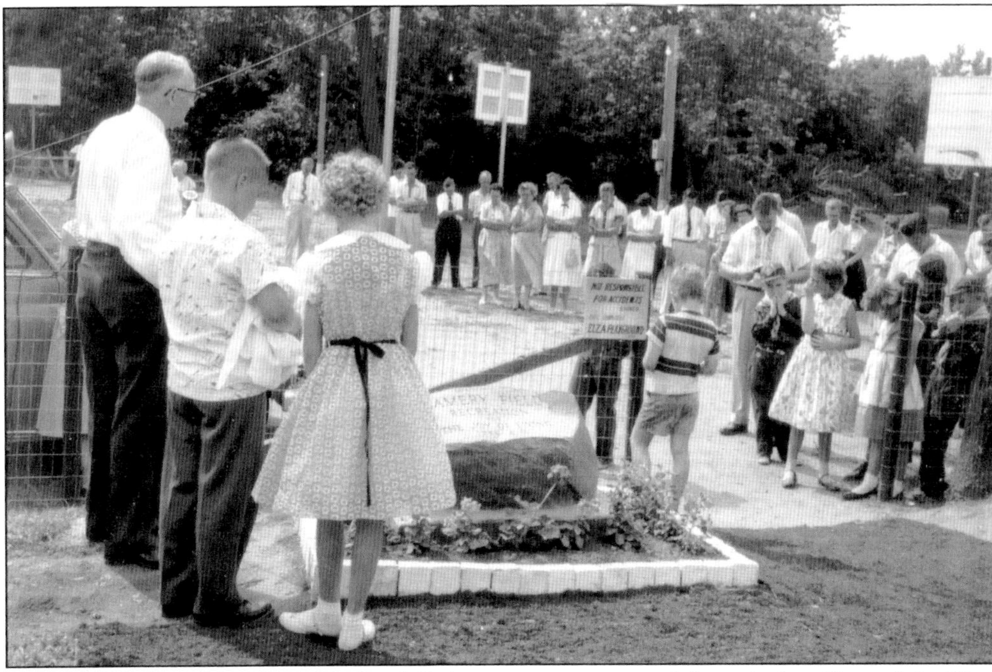

Camery Field was located at 1501 Lindell Avenue, it was created through the efforts of the Elzea Playground Association to give the neighborhood children a place to play. The park included a ball field, playground equipment, a shelter house, and an old 1923 fire truck, which the city had provided. This photo shows the park's opening in June 1956. The park was used until 1972.

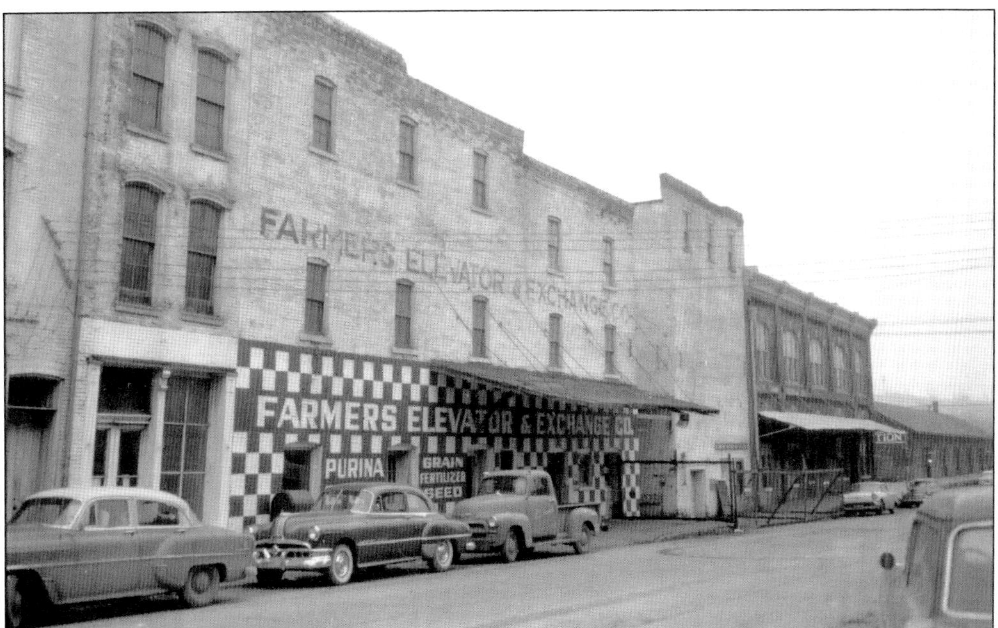

Here is the Farmers Elevator and Exchange building in the 100 block of South Third, prior to demolition for parking lot. This had once been the old Eagle Mills, which began operation in the 1860s. (February 1959)

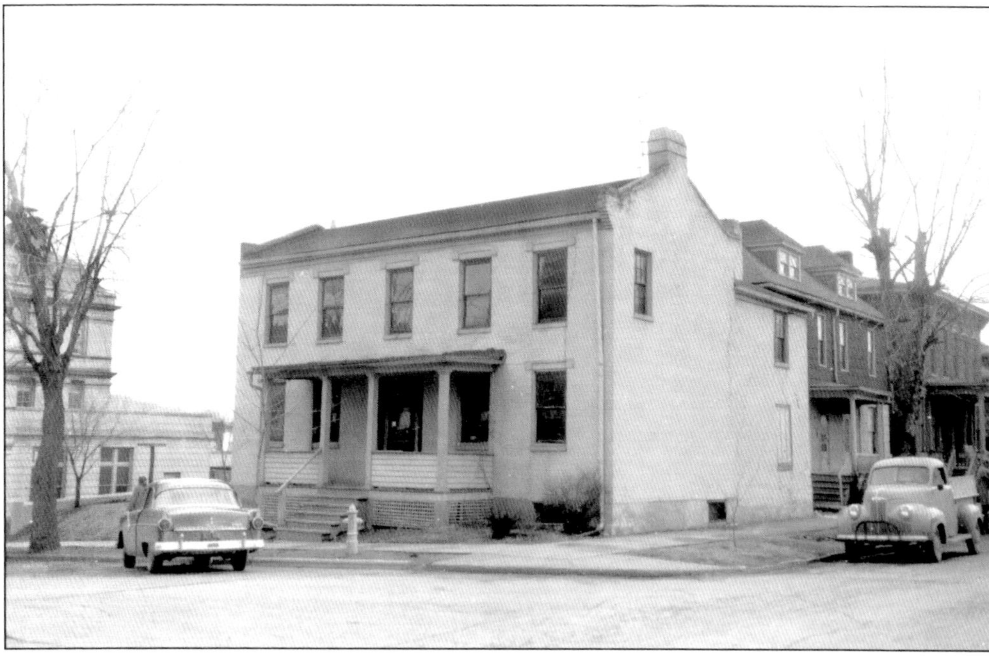

This is the SW corner of Center and Sixth, as the residence which sat on its lot was about to be demolished. Part of the old Federal building is visible at left. (March 1959)

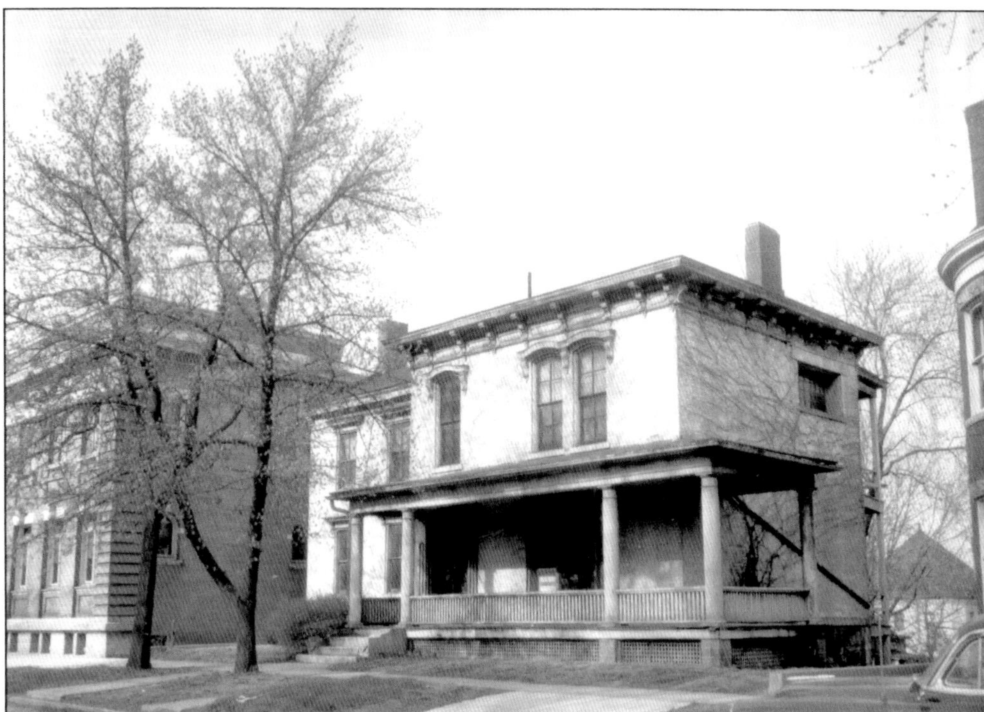

Another old house about to be torn down was Dr. H.L. Banks' home at 208 South Fifth. It was being removed for a parking lot for the library. (April 1959)

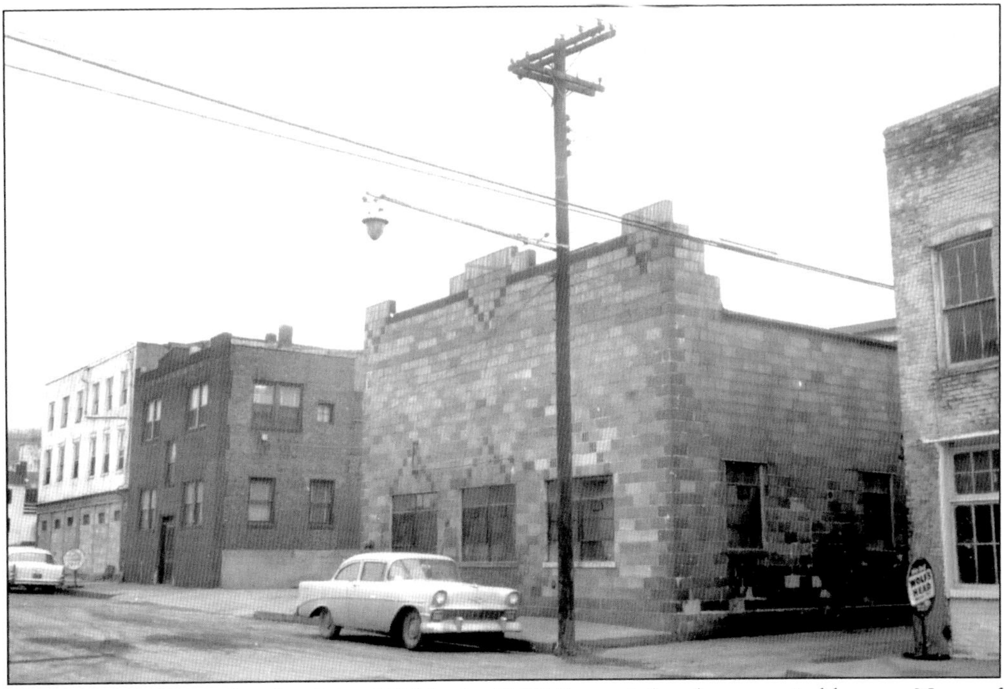

This view of the north side of the 100 block of Hill Street is barely recognizable now. None of these buildings remain today. (March 1959)

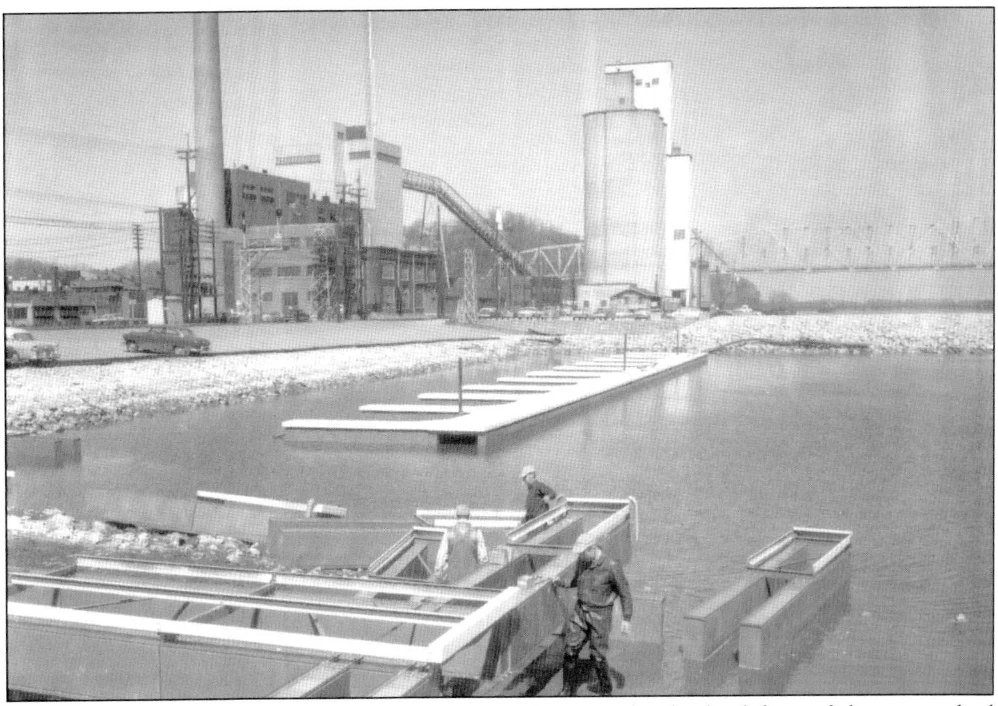

Hannibal's new marina is pieced together by workers amidst the backdrop of three vanished giants—the Municipal Power Plant, the grain terminal, and the old Mark Twain Memorial Bridge. (April 1959)

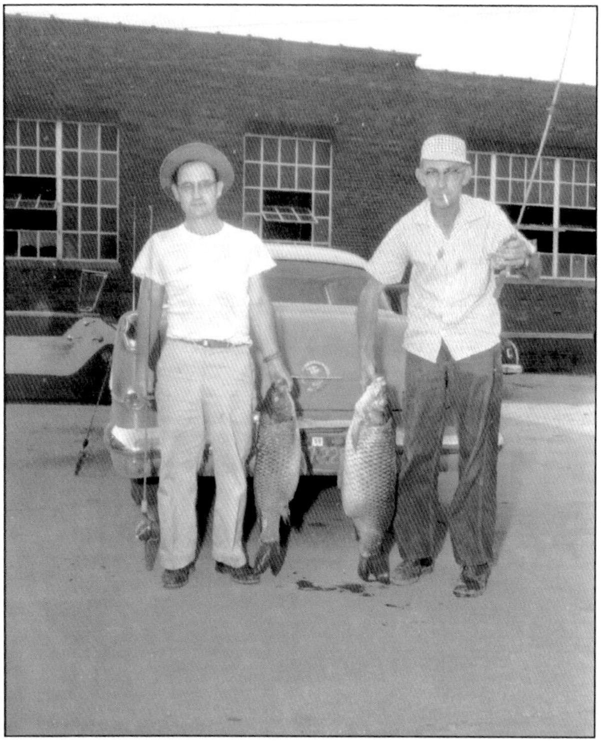

There is no telling how many local residents Otis photographed who had grown the biggest this or caught the biggest that. People loved to see their accomplishments in print. Here, are Donald McIntyre, of 1635 Broadway, and Virgil White, of Palmyra, show off their catch of fish in the parking lot of the *Hannibal Courier-Post*. (May 1959)

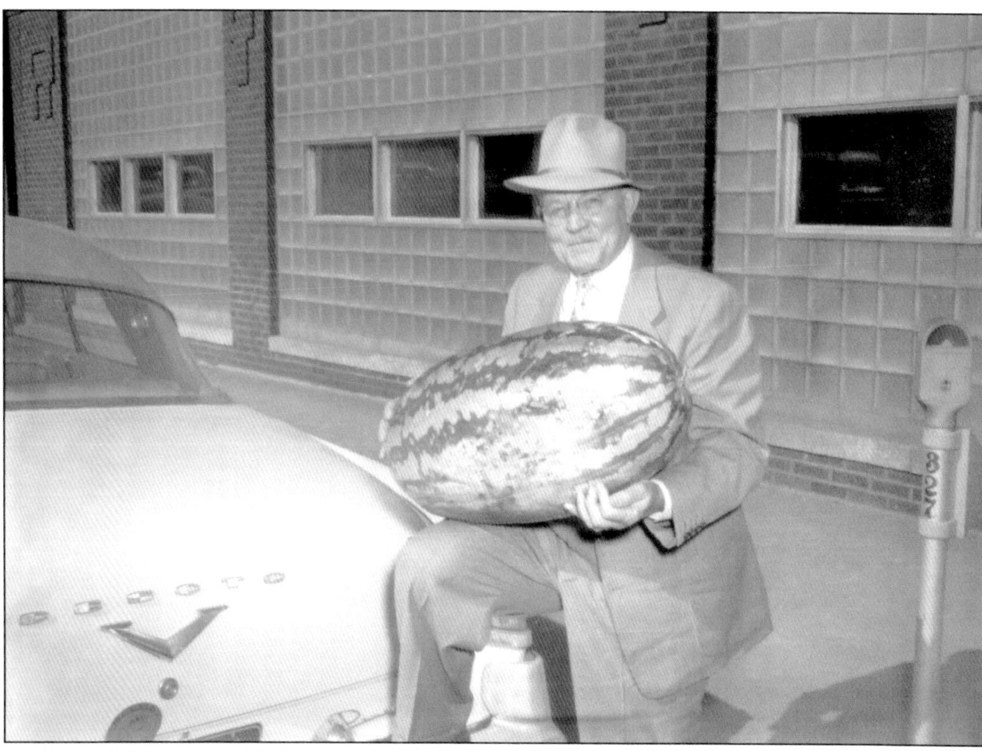

And here E.C. Frank of Palmyra poses in front of the *Courier-Post* with an 35-lb. watermelon, which was grown by a friend in Hillsboro, Missouri. (September 1959)

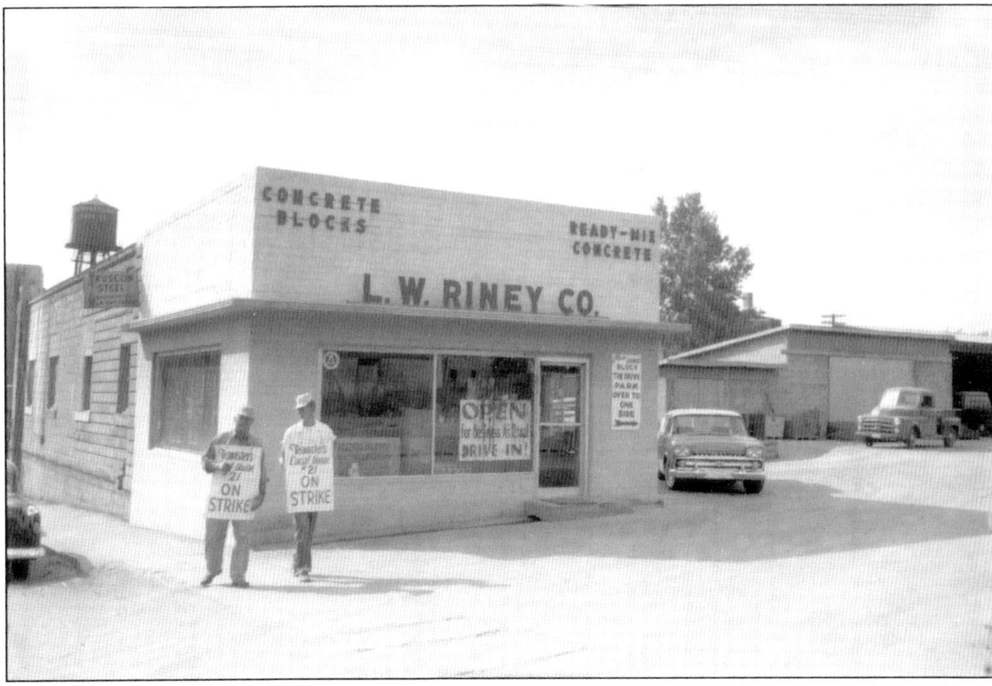

Strikers picket in front of the L.W. Riney company at 323 South Maple in September 1959.

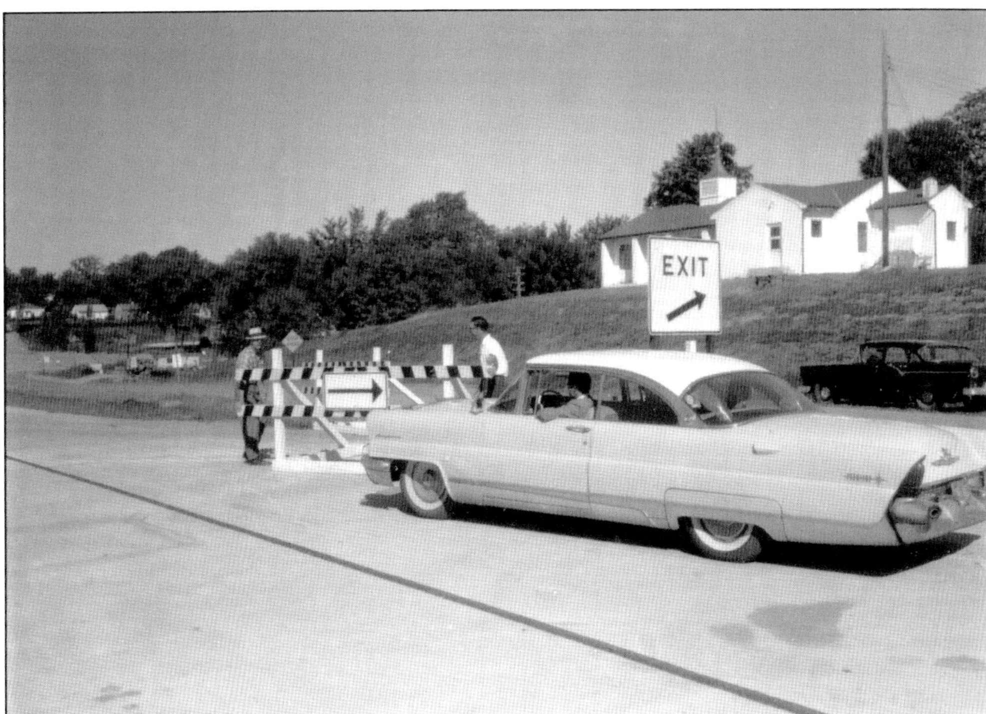

This is the first car to pass over the new stretch of U.S. 36, west from Hannibal. The car, a Lincoln driven by Dr. James A. Shaw of Quincy, crossed the new U.S. 36 overpass over McMasters at 9:03 a.m., Friday, September 4, 1959. Dr. Shaw and his party were en route to Chillicothe, Missouri.

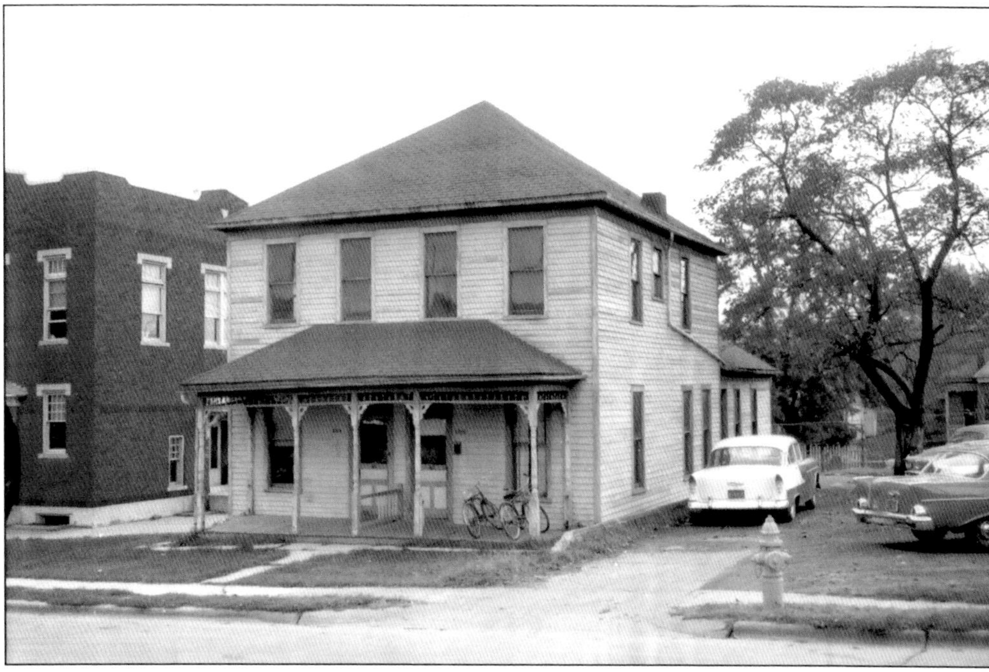

Here is a duplex which stood at 1321–1323 Lyon Street. St. John's Lutheran School is partly visible at the far left. This duplex would soon be demolished for expansion of the school. (October 1959)

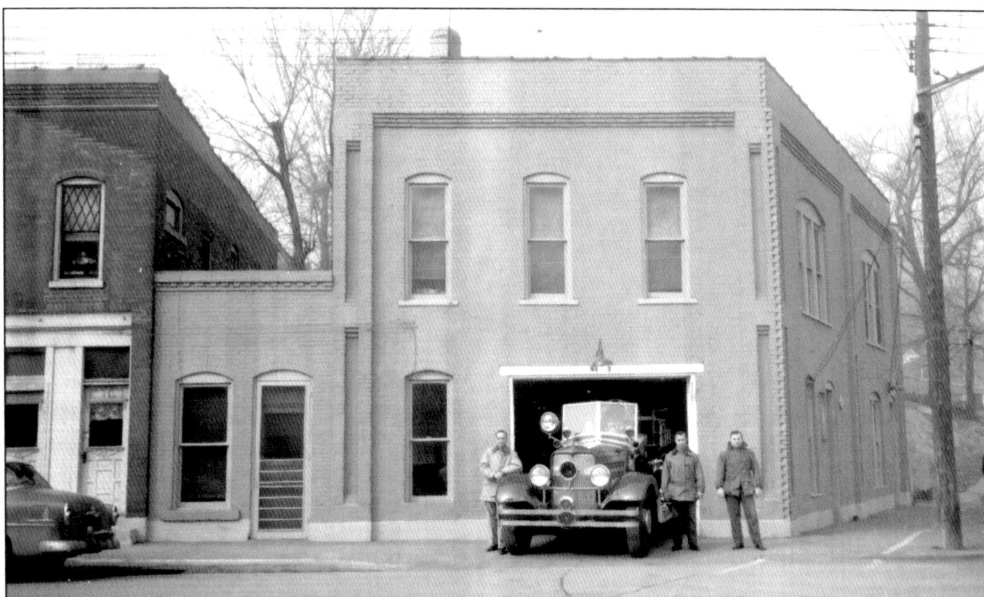

Hannibal fire station #3 (Southside fire station) at 501 Union Street. This station was necessary for protection of the south side because trains often blocked access from the central fire station, as did flooding along Bear Creek. It became obsolete with the opening of the Third Street Viaduct in 1967. The 1966 bond issue provided for the closing of the Southside station and construction of a new fire station on McMasters in 1968. The Southside fire station was torn down in the 1970s. (November 1959)

Three

New Frontiers in Hannibal *1960–1967*

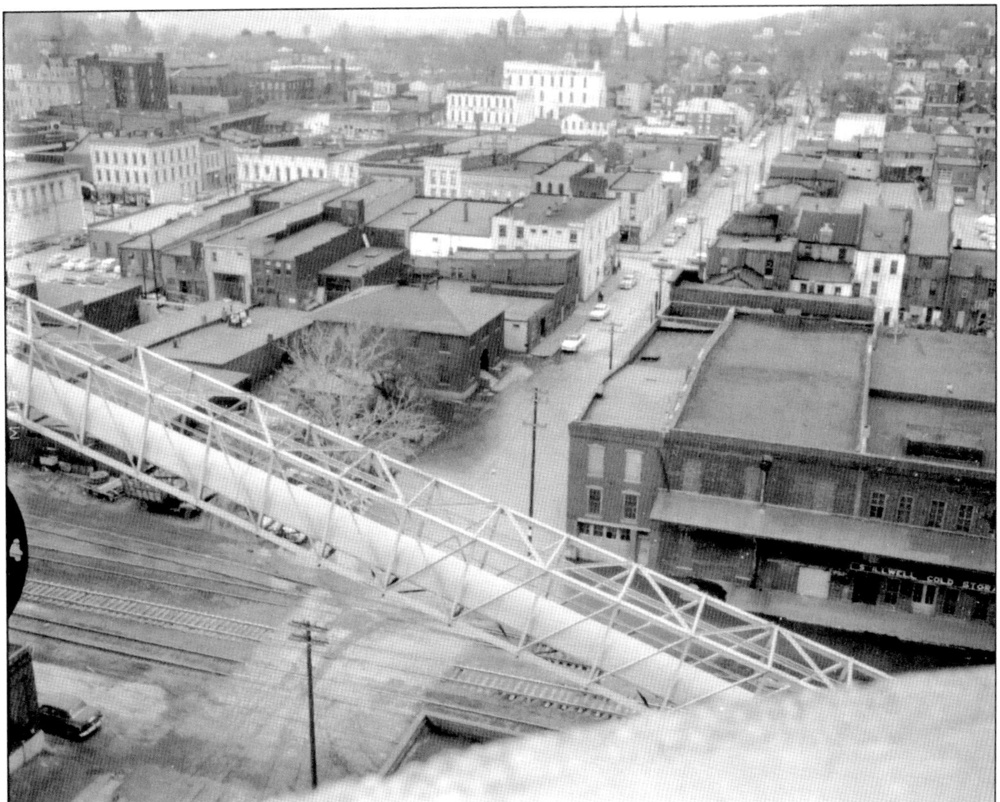

This panorama of downtown Hannibal was taken from atop one of the tall silos of the grain terminal, during the flood of April 1960. Water covering the 100 block of Bird is visible in the foreground.

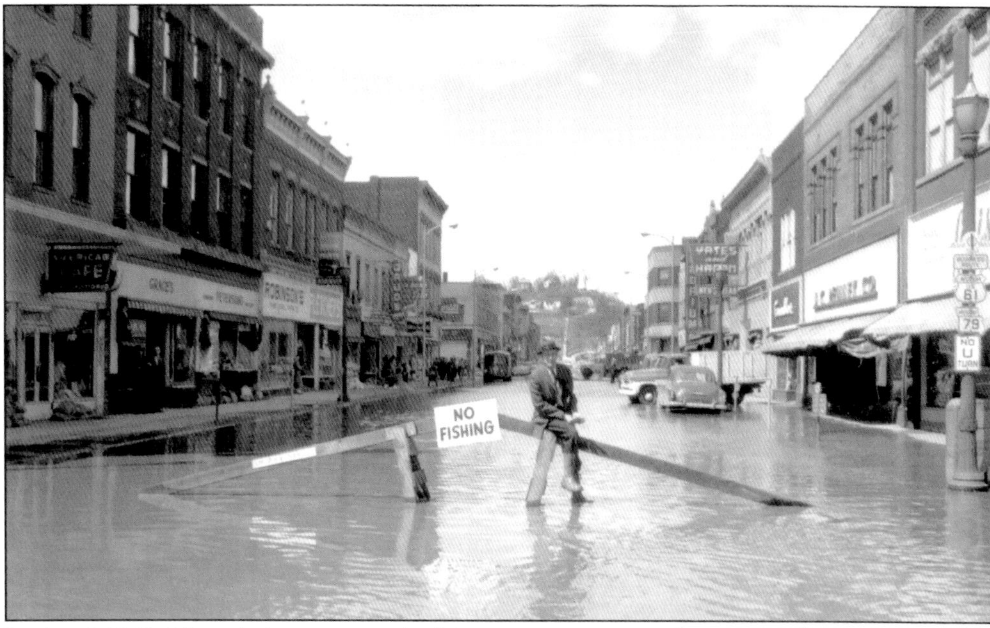

In April 1960, Hannibal again saw the Mississippi rise onto downtown doorsteps and into businesses and homes. There were those, however, who refused to let floodwaters dampen their sense of humor. Here the former president of Hannibal's Chamber of Commerce, Kenneth Abrams, clowns around, pretending to fish from a barricade with a "No Fishing" sign at the intersection of Church and South Main. In the background a truck evacuates merchandise from the Gambles store.

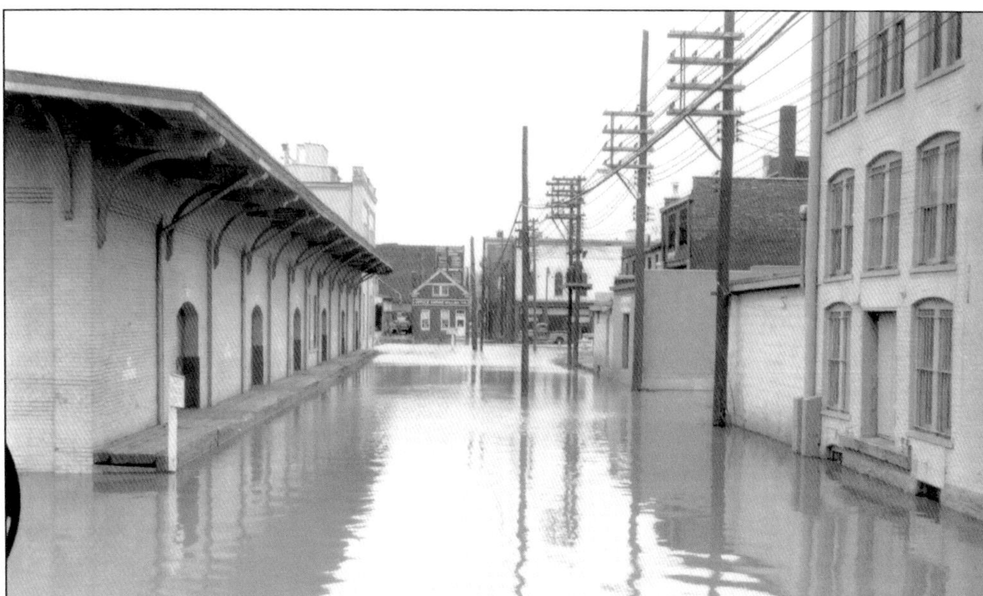

This photo looks south down the alley between East Broadway and Center, and behind the Sonnenberg building during the flood. To the left is part of the Wabash Freight House, which would be demolished in 1962 for parking. Visible also at the end of the alley on East Broadway is the Empire Mills office. (April 1960)

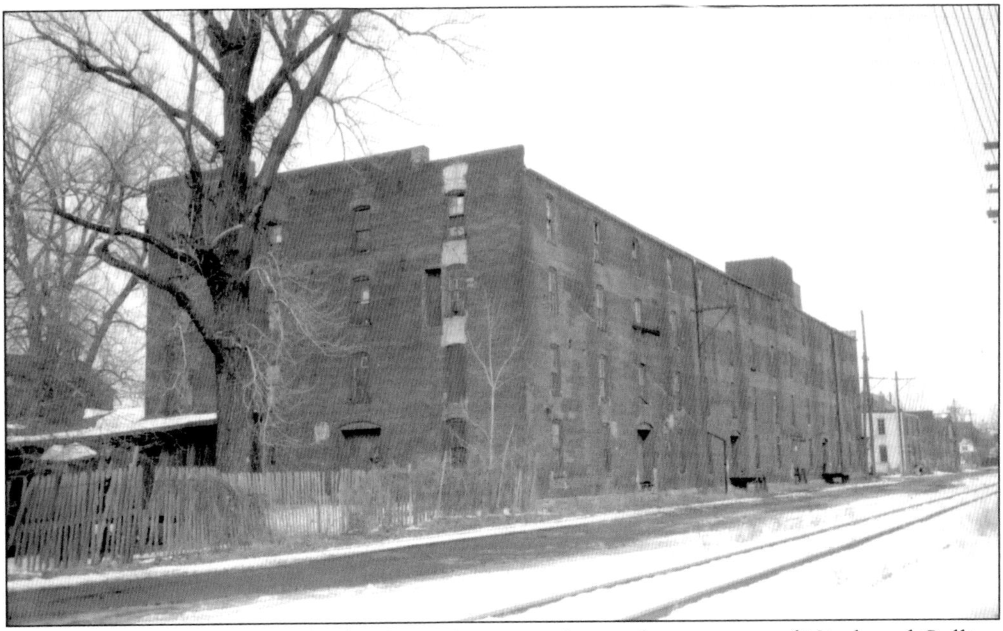

This was the old Duffy-Trowbridge Stove factory at the southeast corner of Ninth and Collier, which closed in the early 1900s. In the years since that time it had seen a number of tenants. The blast furnaces were dismantled in 1951. This is how the old factory looked in March of 1960. In four years it would be destroyed by fire.

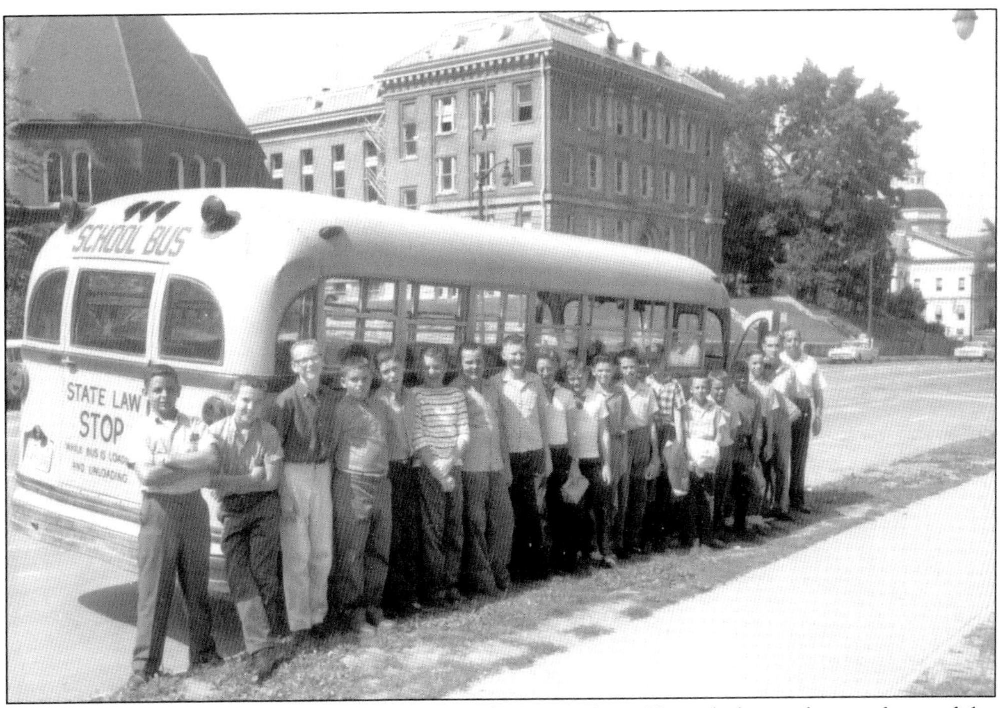

Headed out to the Boys' State Convention is the group from Hannibal, standing in front of the bus on Broadway. The old Hannibal High School, at that time the home of the Naval Reserve Training Center, is visible in the background. (June 1960)

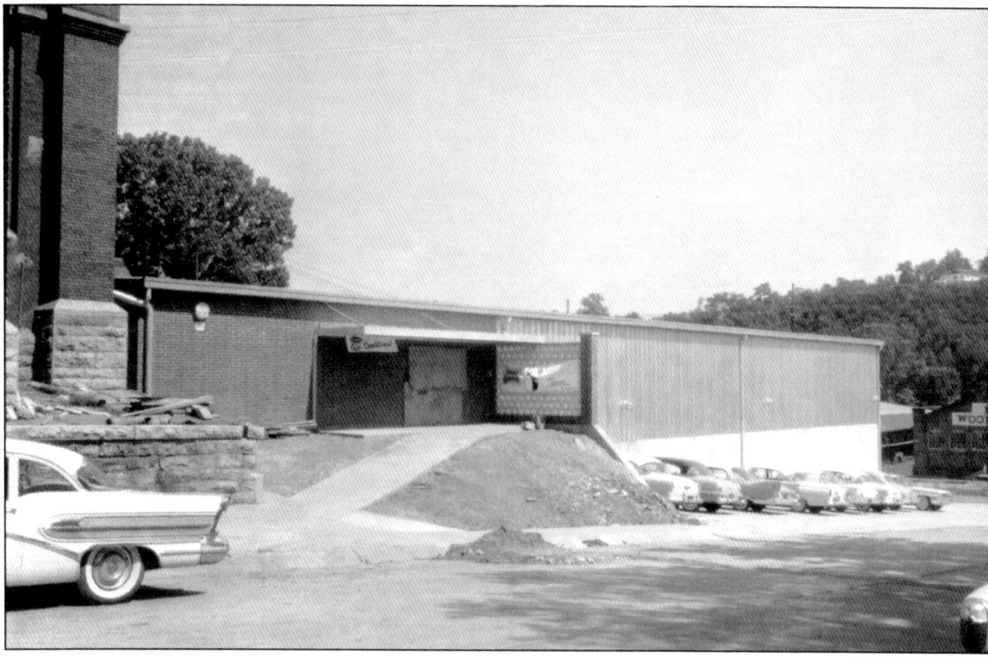

In 1954, the American Legion acquired the old Immaculate Conception Catholic Church. Six years later they built a bowling alley on the south side of the old church. This photo shows Legion Lanes during its grand opening in August 1960.

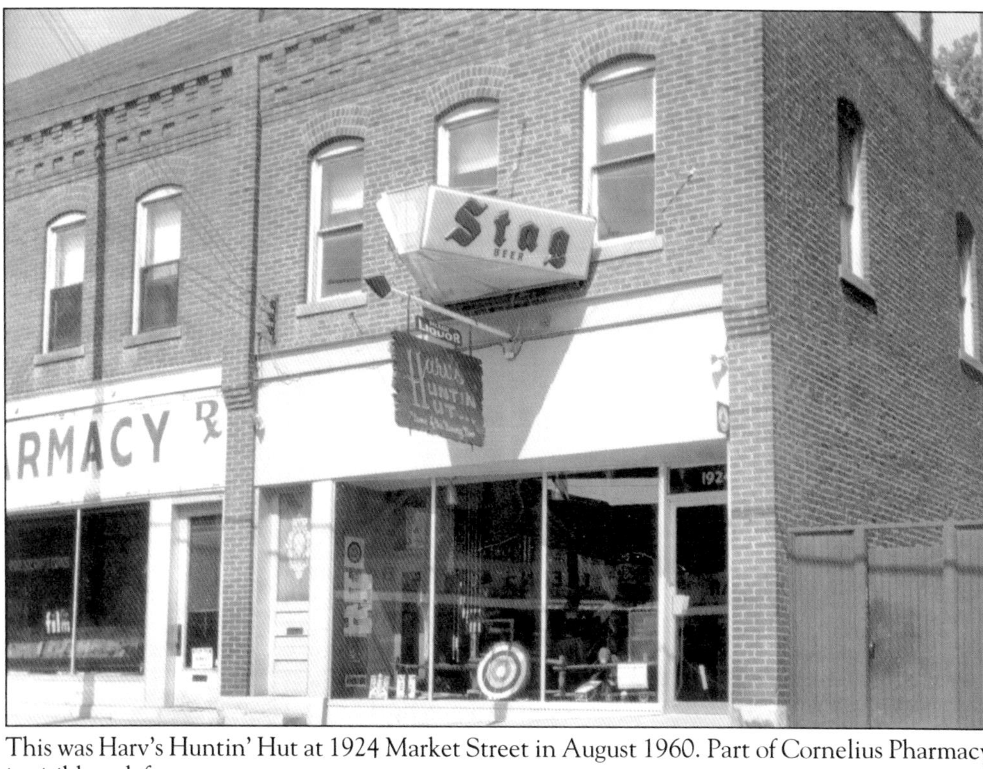

This was Harv's Huntin' Hut at 1924 Market Street in August 1960. Part of Cornelius Pharmacy is visible at left.

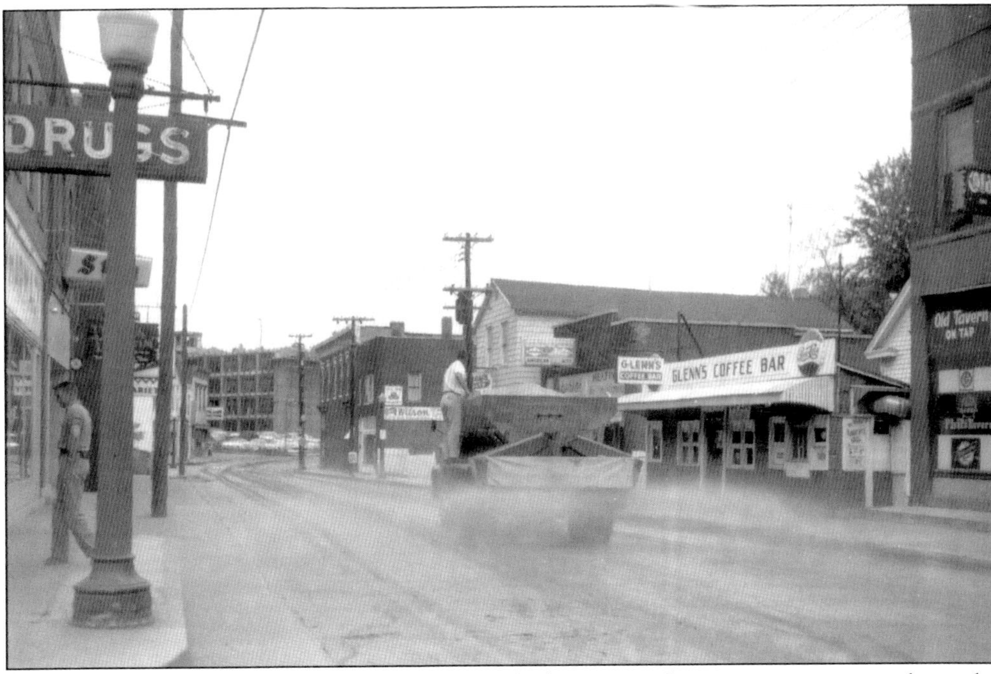

This view of the 1900 block of Market Street, looking east, shows construction work on the new wing of Levering Hospital in the distance. (September 1960)

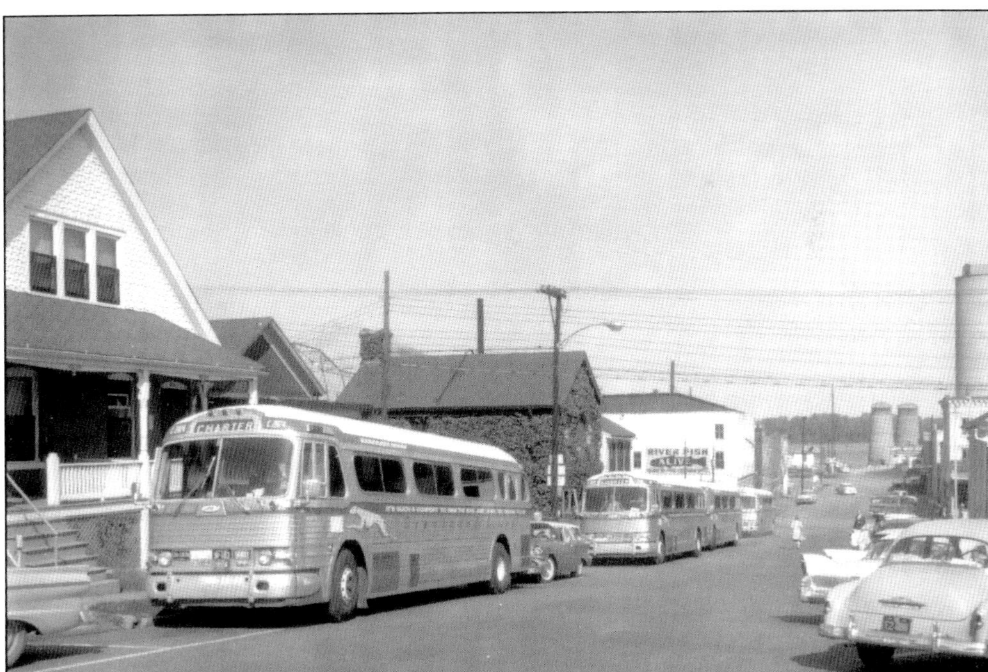

This October 1960 shot of Hannibal's tourist mecca shows the section of Hill Street in front of the Mark Twain Boyhood Home prior to its being closed to traffic. Note the tour buses lined up in front of the museum and home. Both the house at the far left, and the partly visible home to the right were removed and are part of the Mark Twain Dinette property.

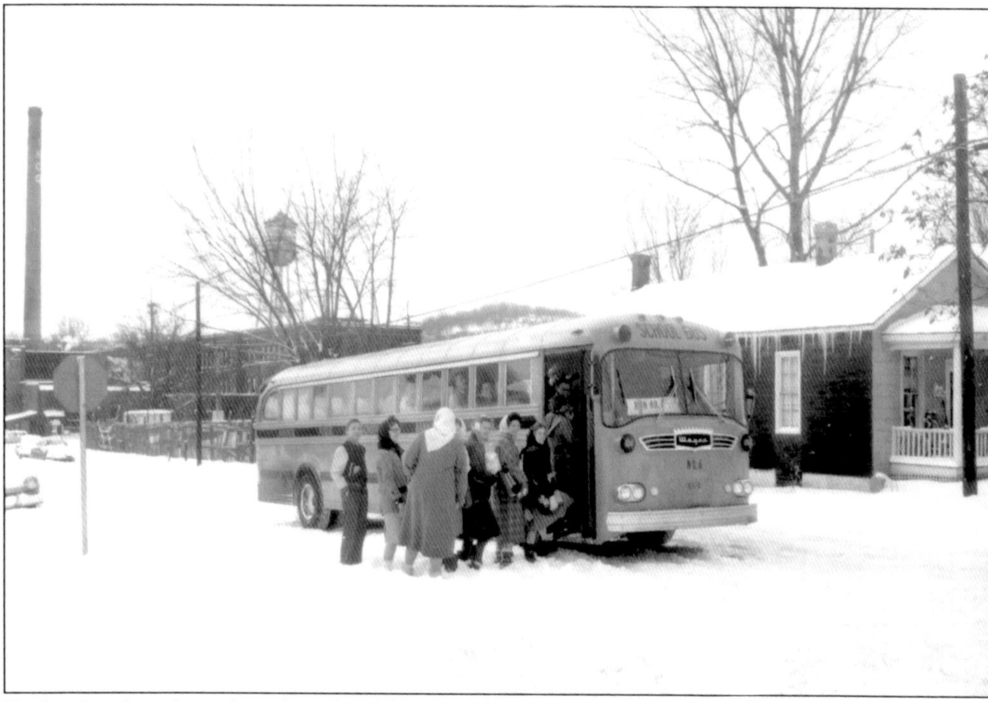

High school students board a school bus at Seventh and Lyon Streets during a snowy morning in February 1961. Notice the shoe factory visible in background.

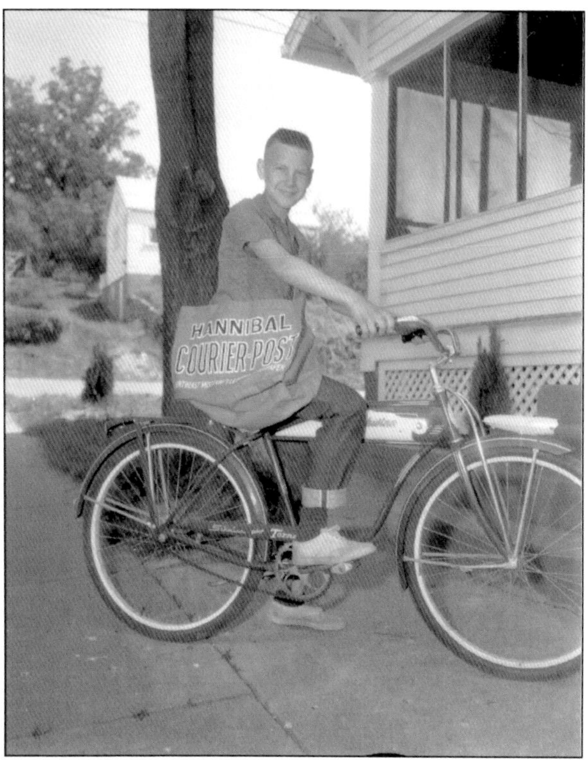

This *Courier-Post* paperboy is Gary Ronimous, son of Mr. and Mrs. C.W. Ronimous, Jr. He was one of the winners of a nine-day trip to Buckhorn Mountain Guest Ranch in Colorado. Otis himself had once delivered papers for the *Courier-Post*. Today the bicycle paper routes are all but a thing of the past . (June 1961)

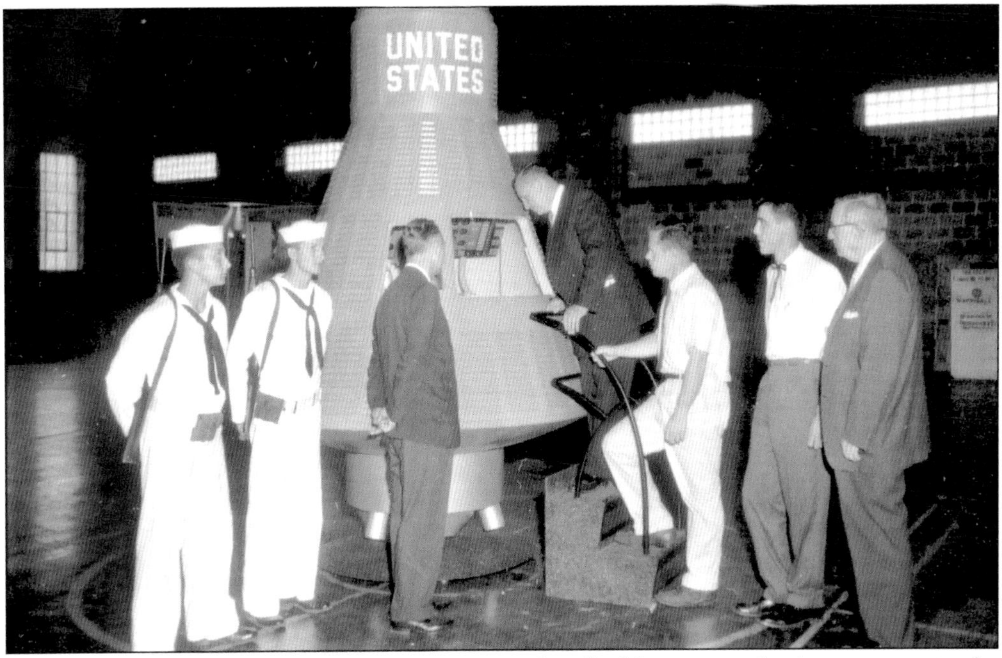

When Alan Shepard rode into space in January 1961, all of America took a keen interest in the space program. Through the efforts of Hannibal's Chamber of Commerce secretary Frank Russell and congressman Clarence Cannon, NASA provided a Mercury space capsule for display in Hannibal during Tom Sawyer Days. Here is the capsule exhibited in the Admiral Coontz Armory, with Mayor Clyde Toalson peering inside. At left are two volunteer guards from the United States Naval Reserve. Beside them is Lt. Comdr. James T. Ball. To the right of Mayor Toalson, waiting to view the capsule are Bob Carroll, Chamber of Commerce president; Dave Lacy, Tom Sawyer Days Chairman; Frank Russell, Chamber of Commerce secretary. (June 30, 1961)

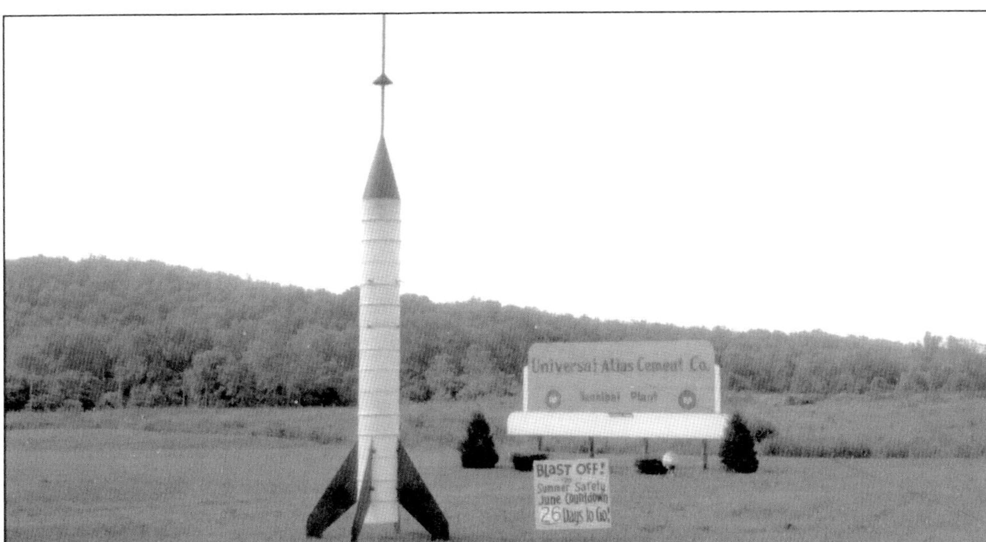

Rocket travel and space were popular themes in the early 1960s. Here, the Universal Atlas Cement Plant erected a rocket mock-up near their front entrance to promote their current safety program. (June 1961)

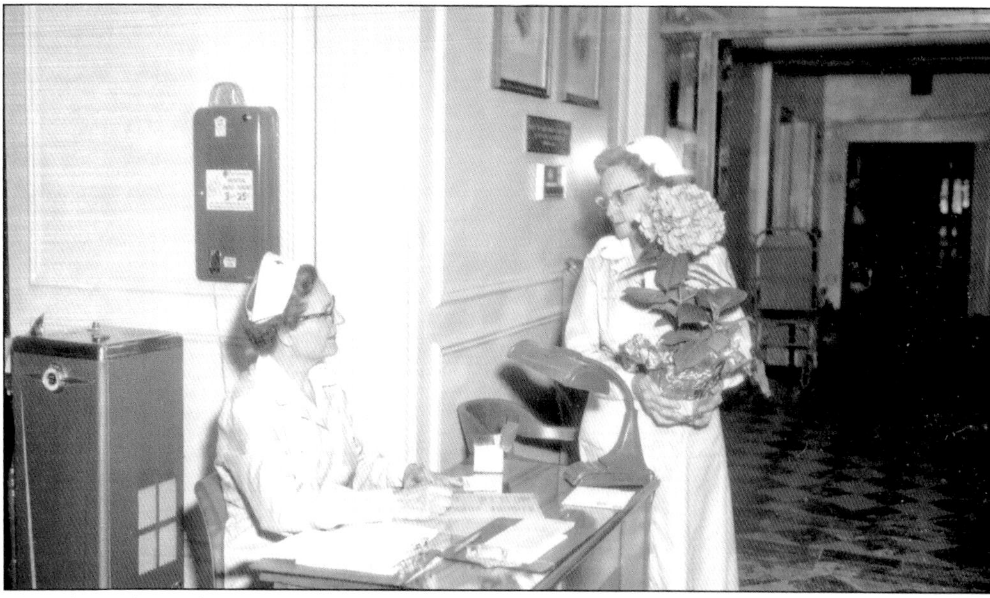

This photo shows the "Grey Ladies" on duty at Levering Hospital. Seated at the information desk is Mrs. Robert Dryden, and standing at right with flowers is Mrs. Eric James. The Grey Ladies were a volunteer unit of the American Red Cross. This was part of a series of photos Otis took for a special feature in the paper that highlighted the opening of the new addition. (June 1961)

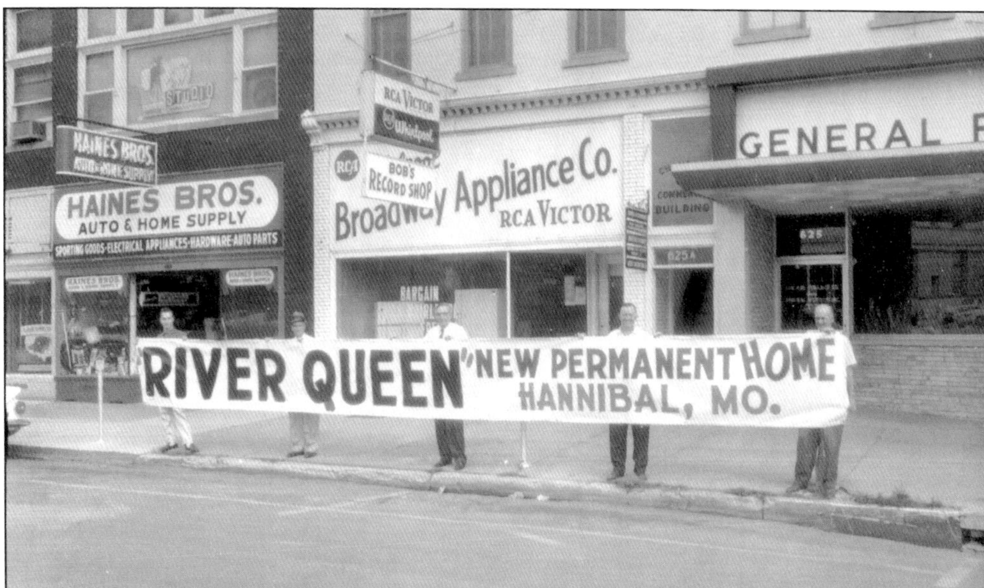

Chamber of Commerce members hold the banner for the River Queen riverboat advertising Hannibal as its new permanent home. There was much fanfare for the boat, which was berthed just across the river on the Illinois side. The River Queen was in Hannibal from 1961 through 1964 when it was moved to St. Louis. It sank on the St. Louis riverfront several years later and was scrapped. Photo taken in front of the Chamber of Commerce Building at 625 Broadway in July 1961.

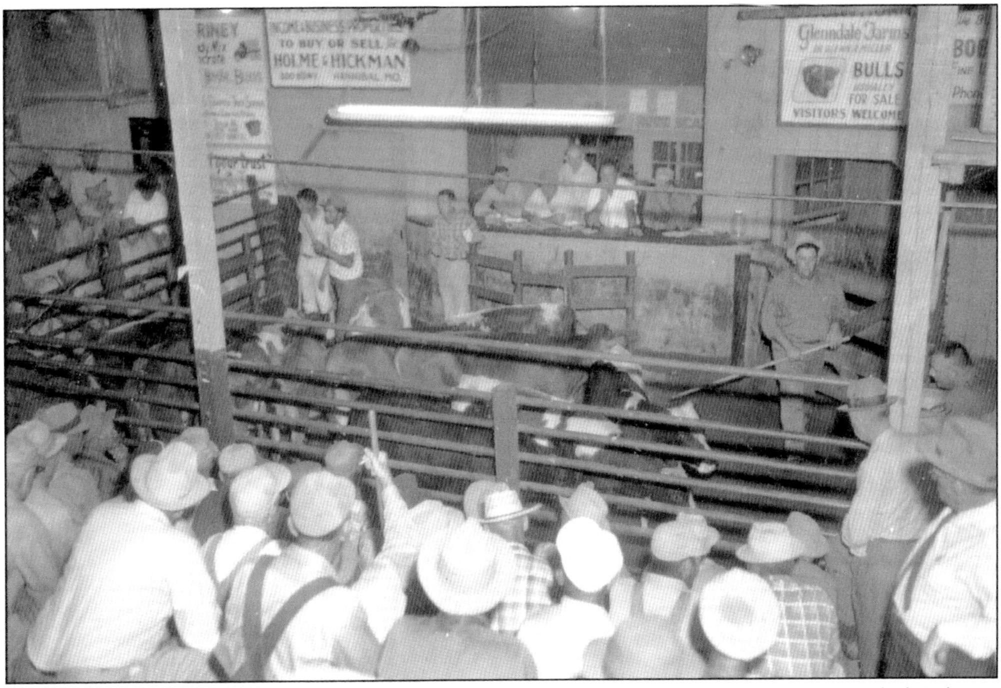

This picture shows an auction in progress at the Hannibal Sales Company. Hannibal Sales, a livestock auction service, was located on U.S. 61 at West Ely, where Steamboat Bend Shopping Center now stands. It was owned by the Scoville family. (October 1961)

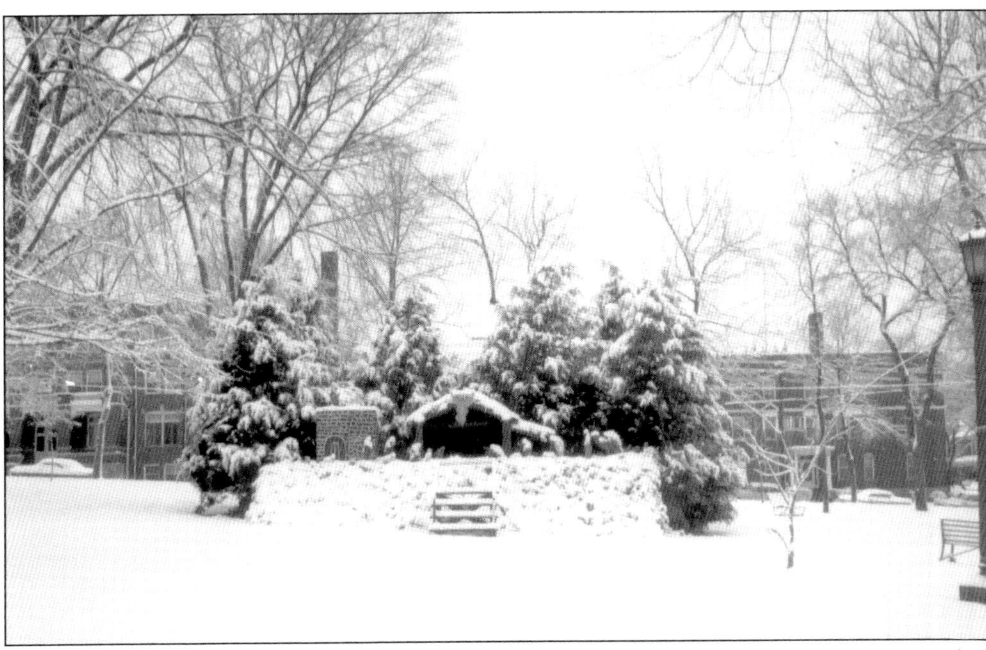

In a simpler day, before people worried about "political correctness," many communities had Nativity scenes as part of their Christmas decorations. This photo shows Hannibal's Nativity scene set atop the old fountain in the middle of Central Park. A blanket of snow completes the scene—one can almost hear a faint chord of "Silent Night" in the background. (December 1961)

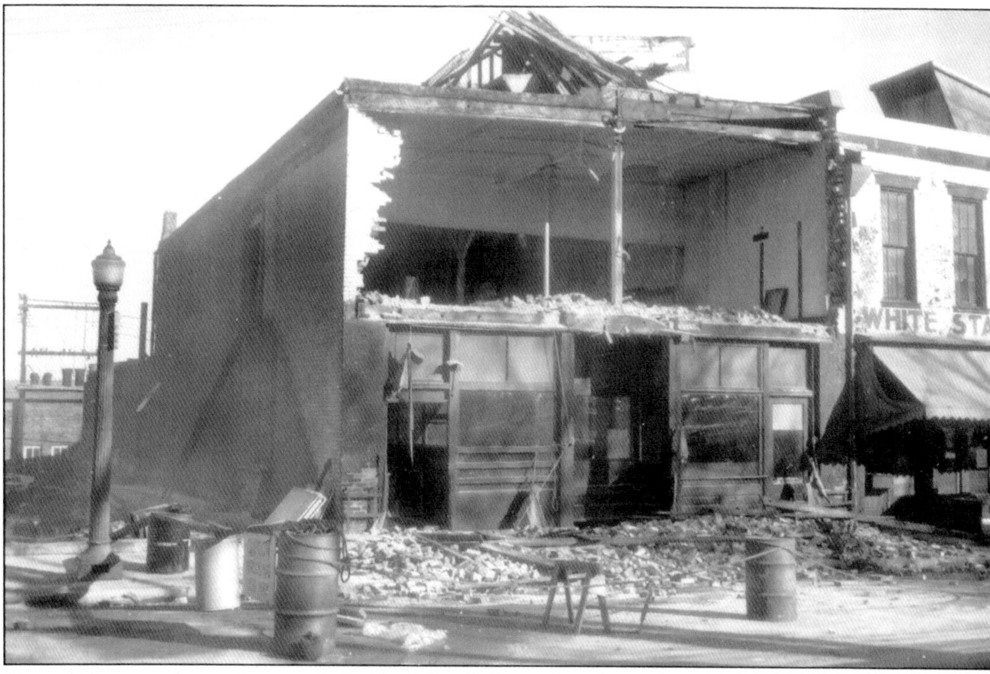

Demolition work on the north half of the White Star Laundry plant, at 106 North Fourth. This old structure was to be cleared to make way for a new building. Work was being done by the Hagerty Construction Company. This demolition would turn tragic when a worker was killed when the structure collapsed on top of him just nine days after this photo was taken. (January 4, 1962)

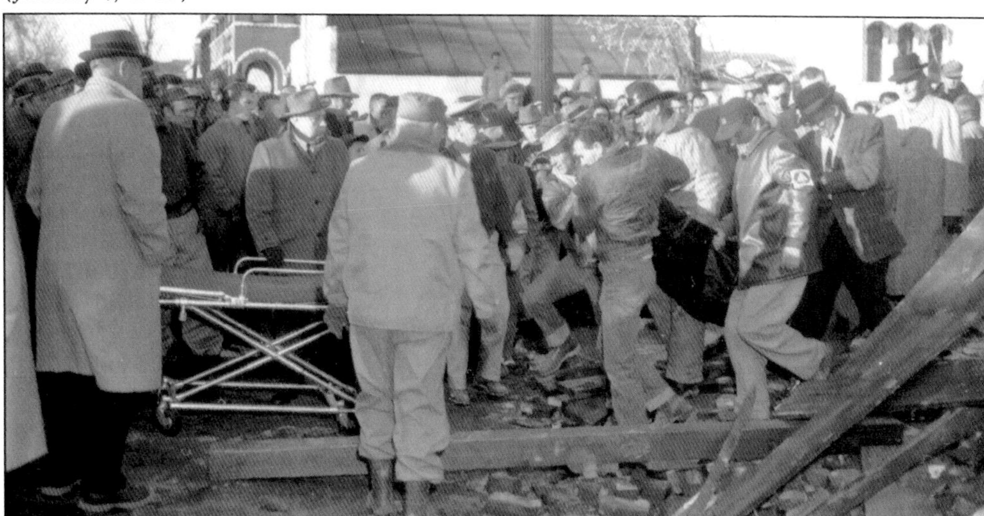

This photo shows the evacuation of the young man killed in the building collapse at 106 North Fourth, which he had been tearing down. The victim, 18-year-old James Maple, was one of three workers in the building when it collapsed. The other two workers, Clark Johnston and Allen Hagerty, were both injured but survived. The trio had just entered the building's second floor to do some inside work, as it had been too cold to work outside. It collapsed shortly afterward. The first two men were rescued fairly quickly, however, it took some time to locate and extricate Maple. This photo shows rescuers removing Maple's body from the wreckage. (January 13, 1962)

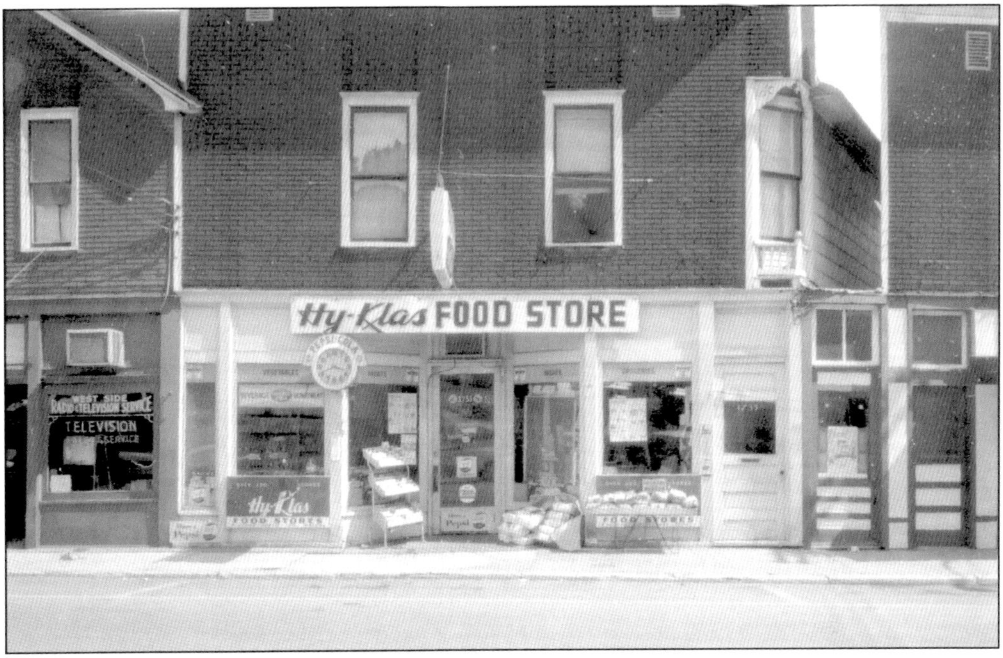

These photos show two of Hannibal's Hy-Klas food markets. The store pictured at top was located at 1735 Market, next to West Side Radio and Television Service. This row of buildings burned in the 1990s. The bottom photo shows the store at 400 Mark Twain Avenue. This building would also meet its demise in the 1990s. (May 1962)

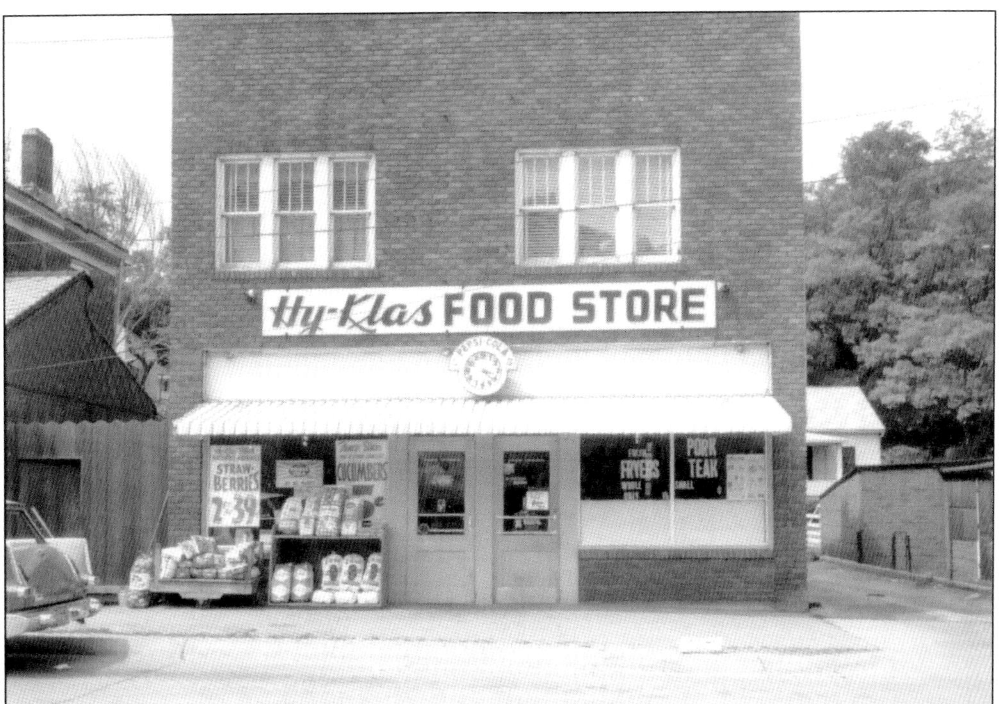

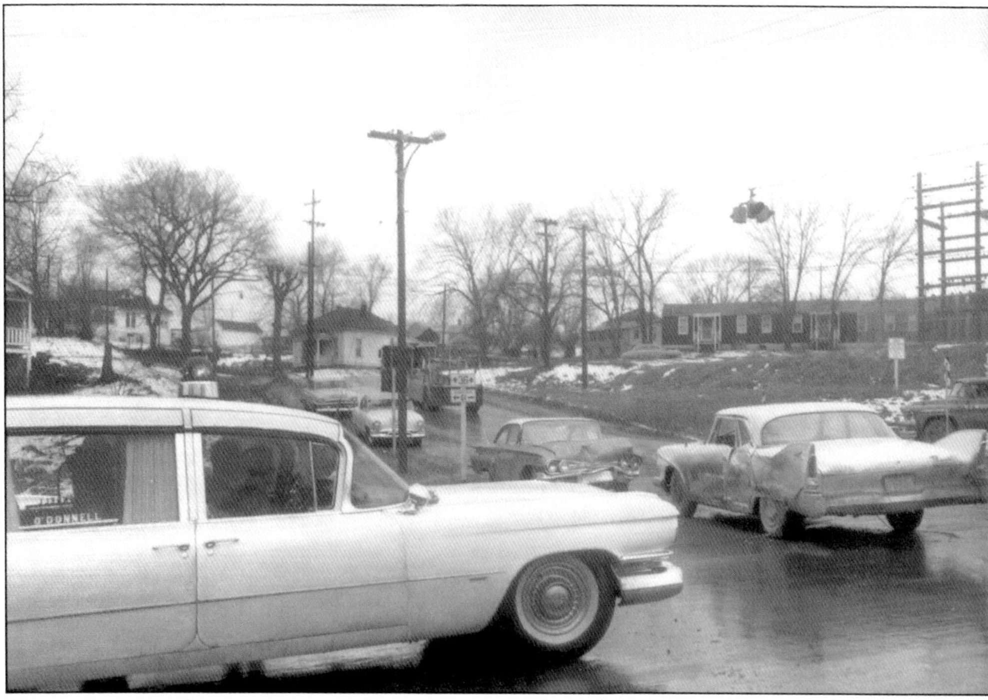

This collision at the intersection of Hazel Street and Mark Twain Avenue gives the appearance that the two cars are facing each other in some sort of a standoff. The interesting detail in this photo is the barracks-type housing in the background. These units would later be removed for construction of the municipal swimming pool. (January 1962)

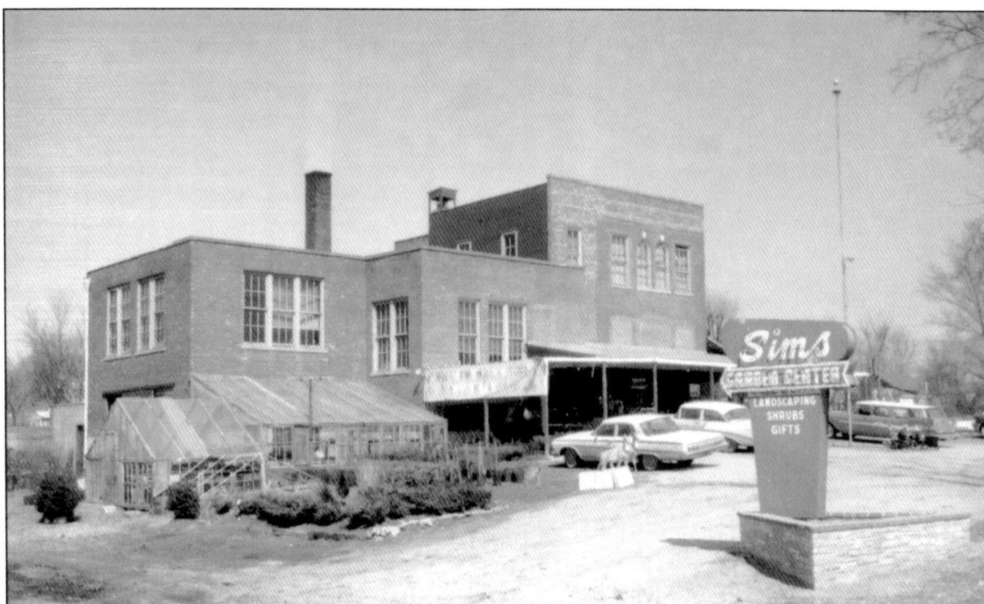

This is the Sims Garden Center, which was located in the old Tilden School building at 4001 Market Street. The old school building would be torn down some time after this photo was taken. (May 1962)

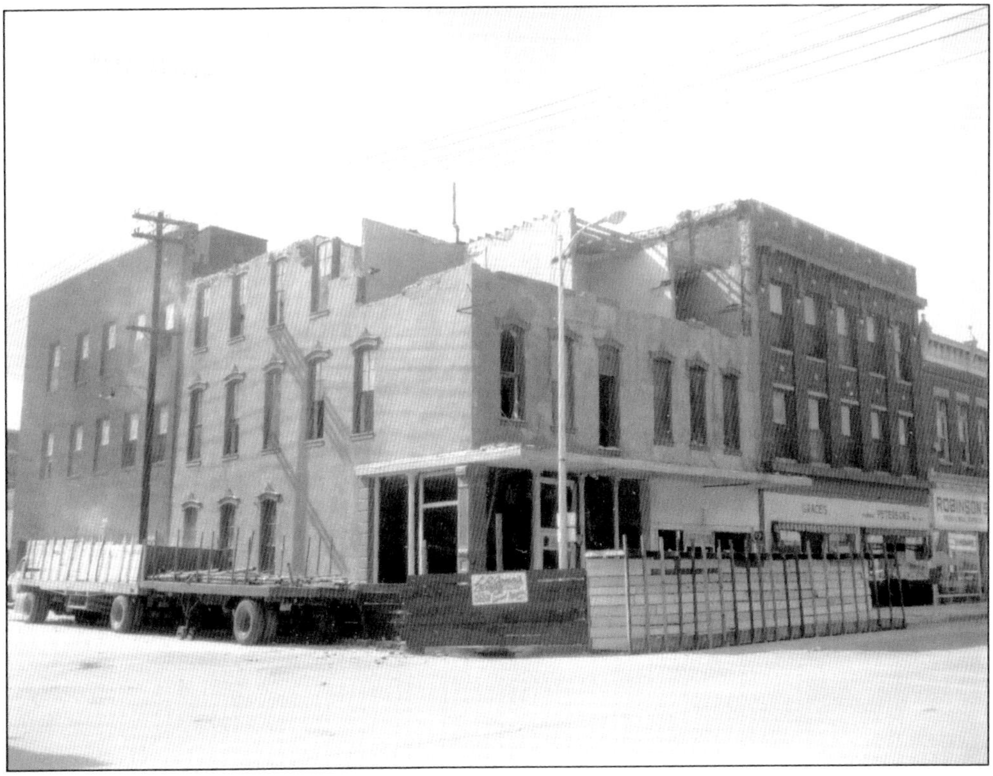

One of Hannibal's historic old hotels had a date with the wrecking ball in late 1962. The Hotel Windsor, which stood at the northwest corner of Church and Main, was the hotel where Mark Twain stayed in 1902 during his last return to Hannibal. The demolition was plagued with mishaps—on October 2 half of the remaining front toppled out onto the sidewalk and street (luckily no injuries). In December, the ruins caught fire, and the blaze spread to the adjoining building which housed Grace's Sporting Goods and Peterson Jewelry (*right*). Both of these businesses were a total loss.

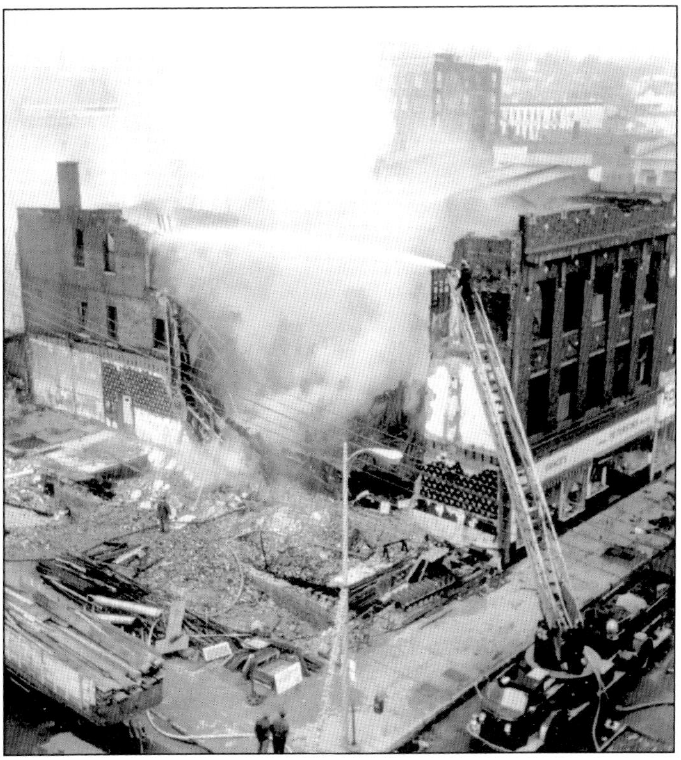

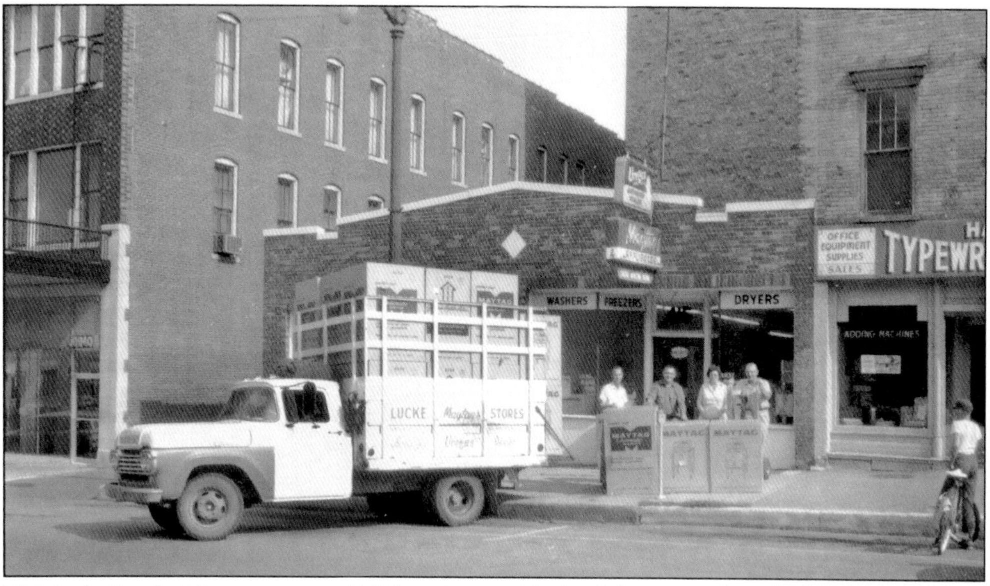

This is the Lucke Maytag store at 415 Broadway, with the delivery truck parked in front. Herbert Lucke was the proprietor. (August 1962)

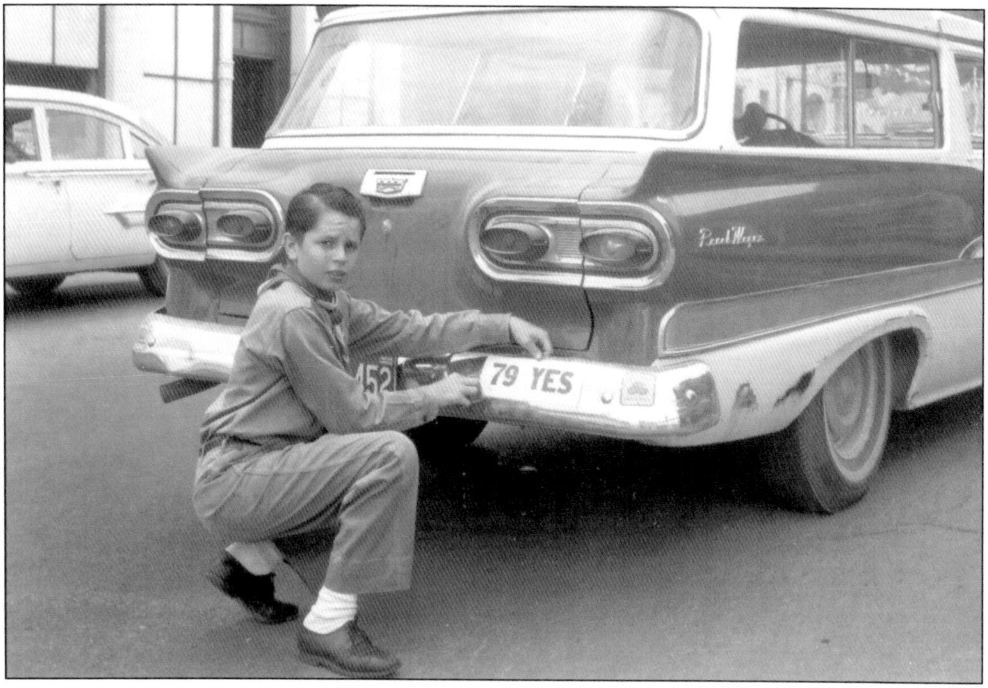

Boy scout Forrest Mickels, of troop 105, affixes a bumper sticker on a station wagon, campaigning for the $175,000 bond issue for an I-79 construction project. The bond issue was for general obligation bonds to fund the city's portion of right-of-way acquisition costs for property from Third and Broadway south to the city limits. A new viaduct would cross Bear Creek and help provide a faster link between Hannibal and St. Louis. The boy scouts helped to promote the September 10, 1963 election by putting bumper stickers on cars. Photo taken in 200 block of North Third. (August 1963)

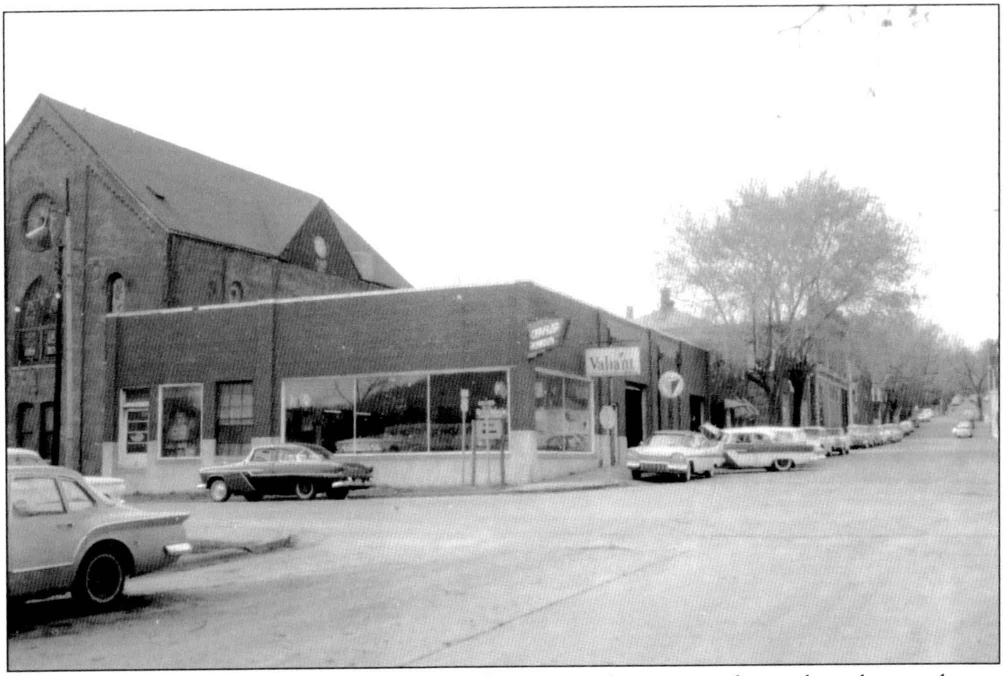

This is a photo of the old Murphy Motor Company when it was located at the northwest corner of Eighth and Church Streets. The church adjacent to the dealership is the Allen AME Chapel, which dated back to 1869. Both of these buildings would be razed for the construction of Hannibal's new Federal building. (April 1963)

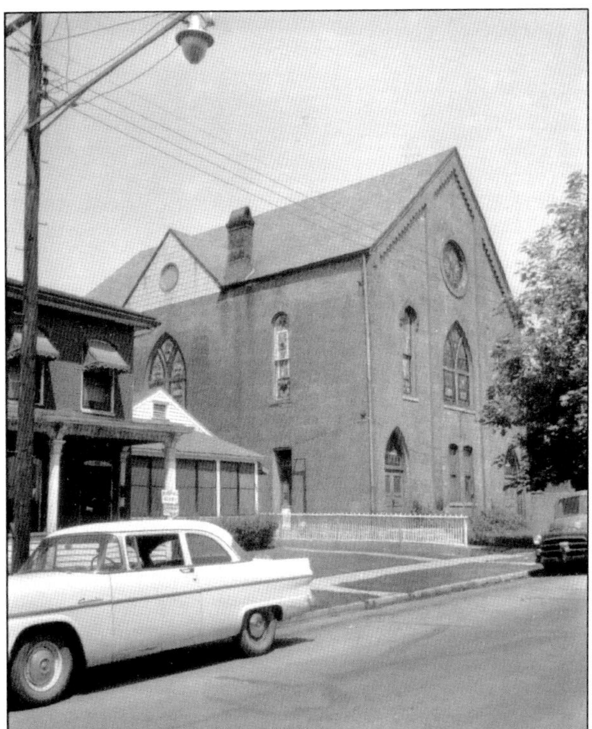

Here is another view of the Allen AME Chapel, which stood at 804 Church Street. Rev. Jos. Moseley was the pastor. (April 1963)

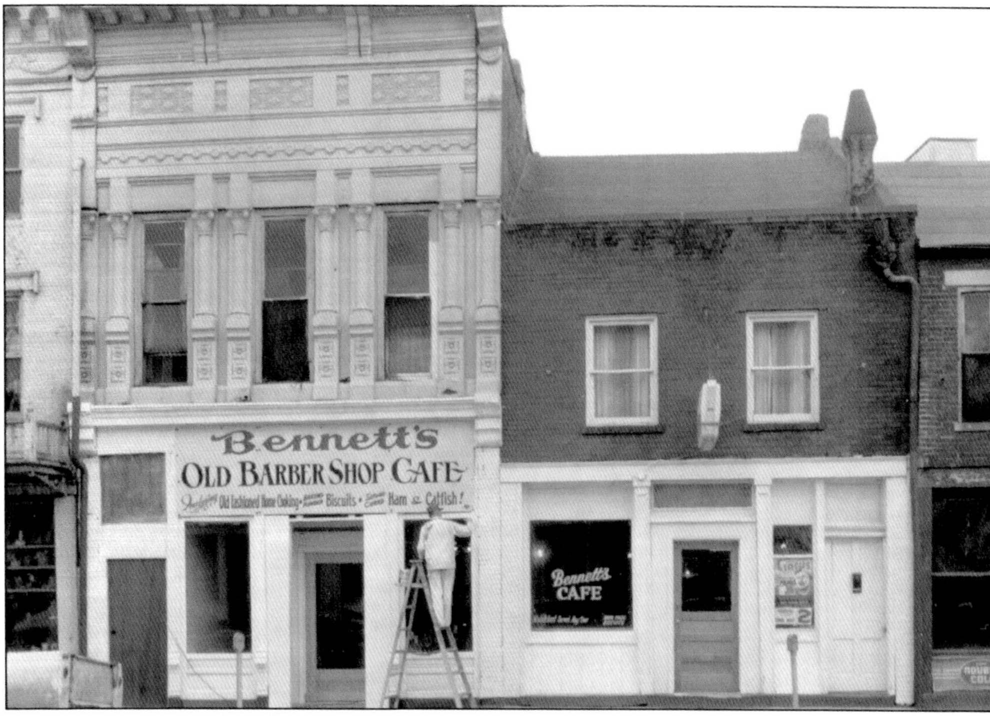

This is Bennett's Old Barbershop Café at 322–324 North Main. Business was good—they had just added an additional dining room. The eatery was owned and operated by Mr. and Mrs. Martin Bennett. (April 1963)

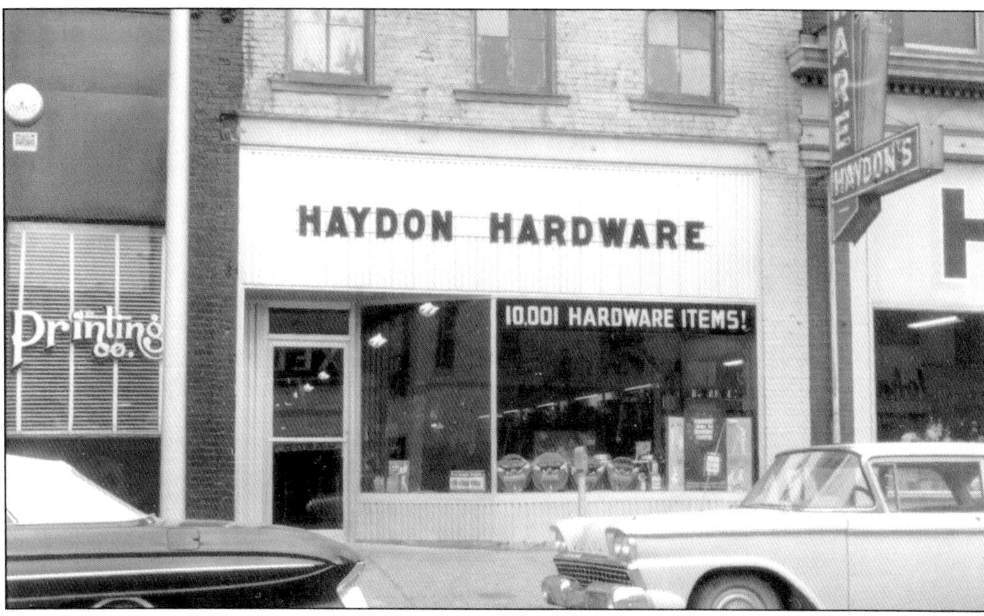

Haydon Hardware had just remodeled their exterior and installed this aluminum and glass storefront. There was a campaign to clean up and beautify the downtown area at the time, and this was one of the modifications that was made and noted by the newspaper at the time. Haydon Hardware was located at 207 North Main. (April 1963)

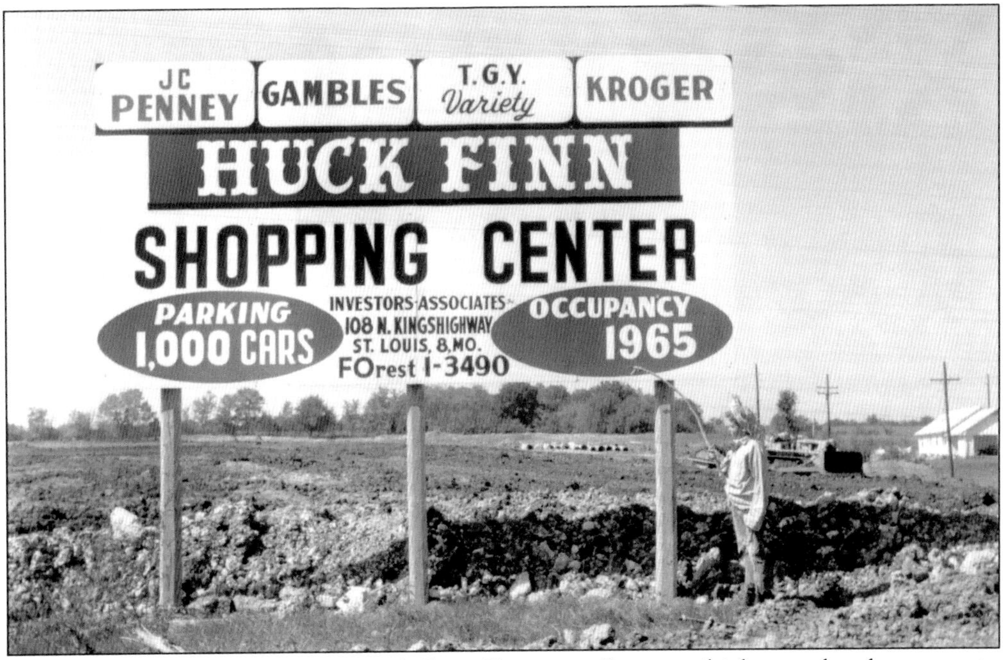

Work is underway on the new Huck Finn Shopping Center, which was slated to open in 1965. Here, a little Huck Finn model poses in front of the sign for the new shopping center. (August 1964)

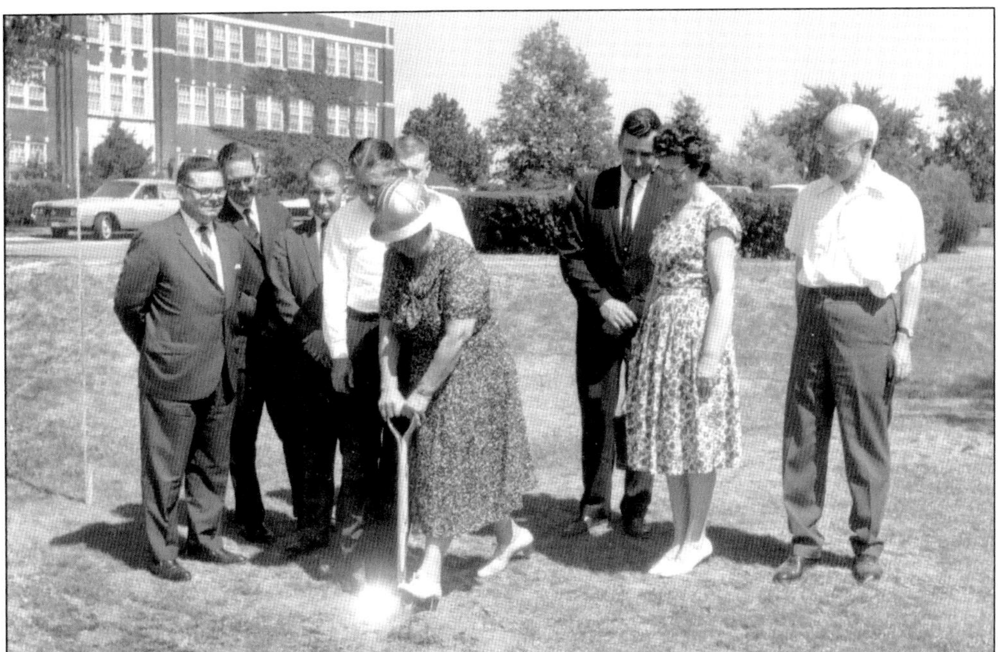

Also in 1964, a neighbor of the new shopping center had a groundbreaking of their own. Hannibal LaGrange College was constructing a new library and science center. On August 18, the ceremonial shovel broke the first clump of sod. Martin Construction Company estimated fifteen months to complete the job. The individuals in the photo are not identified.

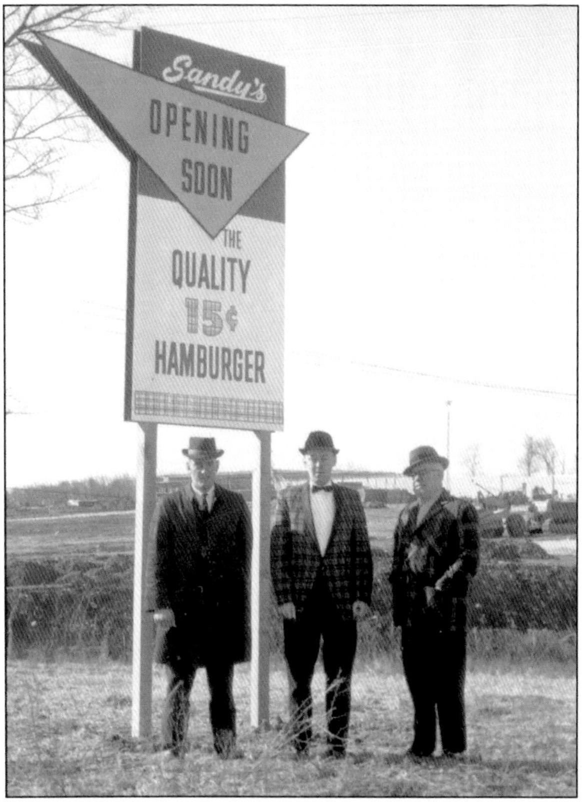

Anticipation. Representatives from Sandy's restaurant chain came to Hannibal to place the sign announcing the restaurant's construction. Pictured from left to right are Alvin Earhardt, Thomas Daly, and Bernard Willer. The Hannibal Sandy's, which featured 15¢ hamburgers, was to be one of about a hundred restaurants in twenty-five states. Two were located in Quincy. The Sandy's chain was purchased by Hardees in 1975. Construction work on the new Huck Finn Shopping Center is visible in the background. (February 1965)

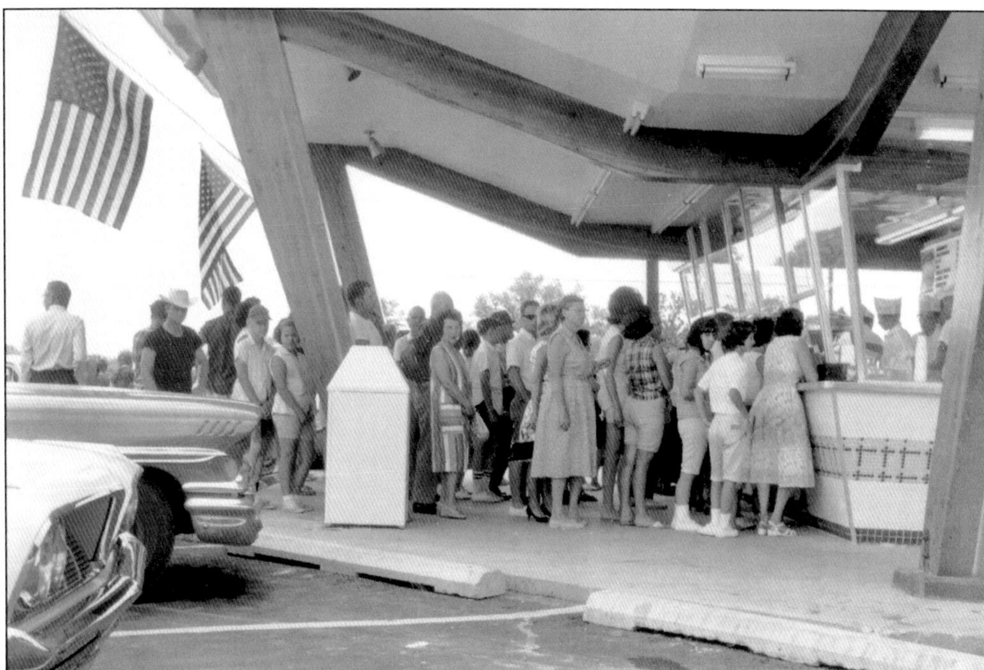

Realization! Crowds gather at the new fast food restaurant on the opening day in July 1965. Drive-up windows, with their annoying speakers, were still some years in the future.

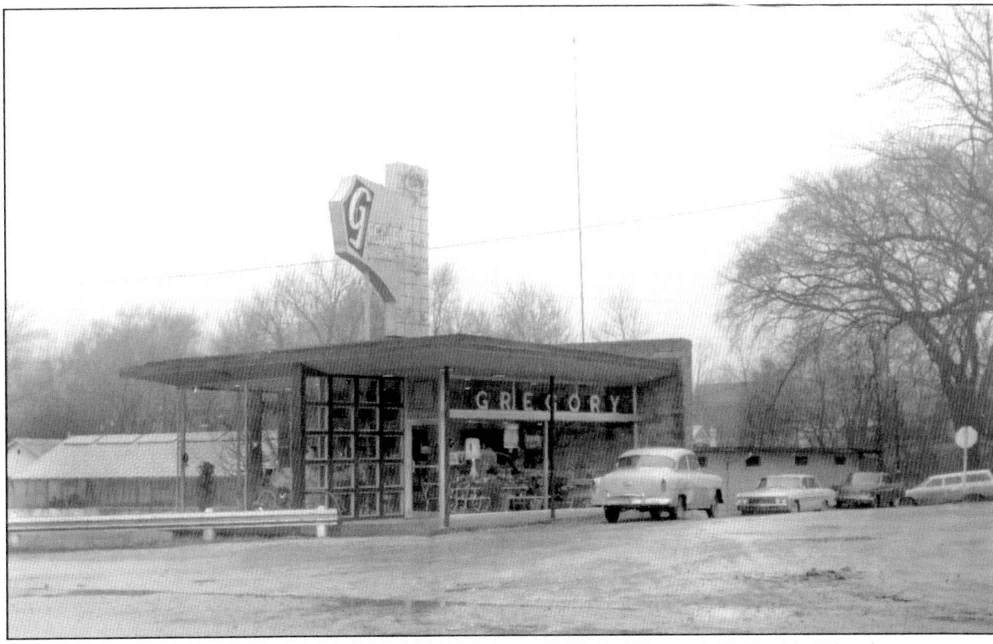

Gregory Floral Company sat at the intersection of West Ely and U.S. 61. The business was owned by Ruth and Homer Gregory. It was demolished in the 1990s, and as of 2004 it is the site of a Walgreens store. (February 1965)

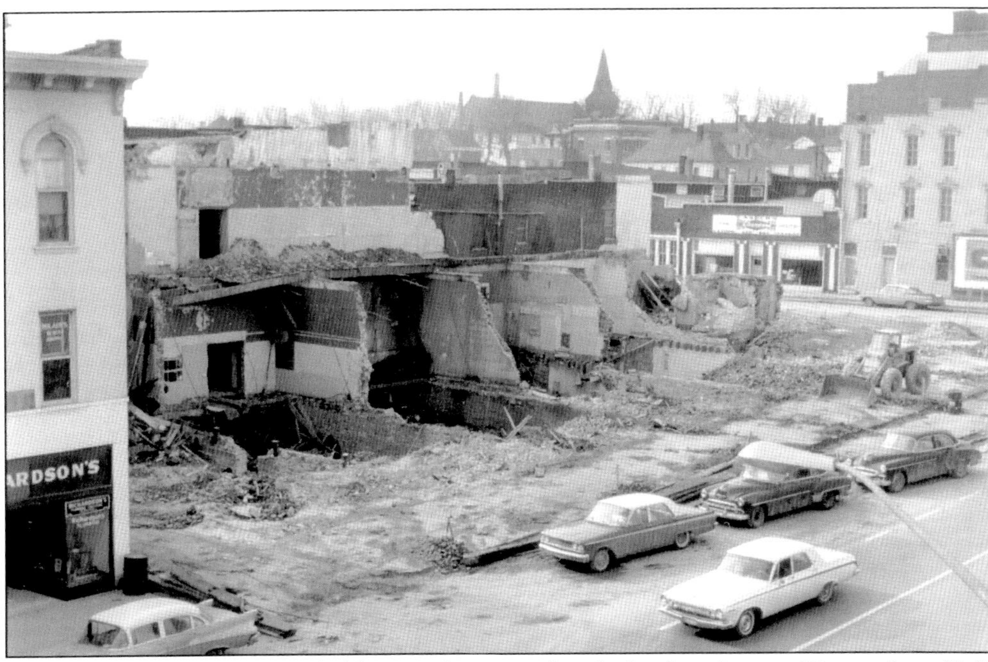

A tremendous piece of Hannibal history disappeared with the demolition of Brittingham Hall. Built in 1859, it was reputed to have served as a hospital and a prison during the Civil War. Better known as the Avery Burch building, it stood on the south side of the 300 block of Broadway. Demolition work began in November 1964 and when this photo was taken in February 1965 the job was about halfway complete. A Wareco filling station would be built on the site.

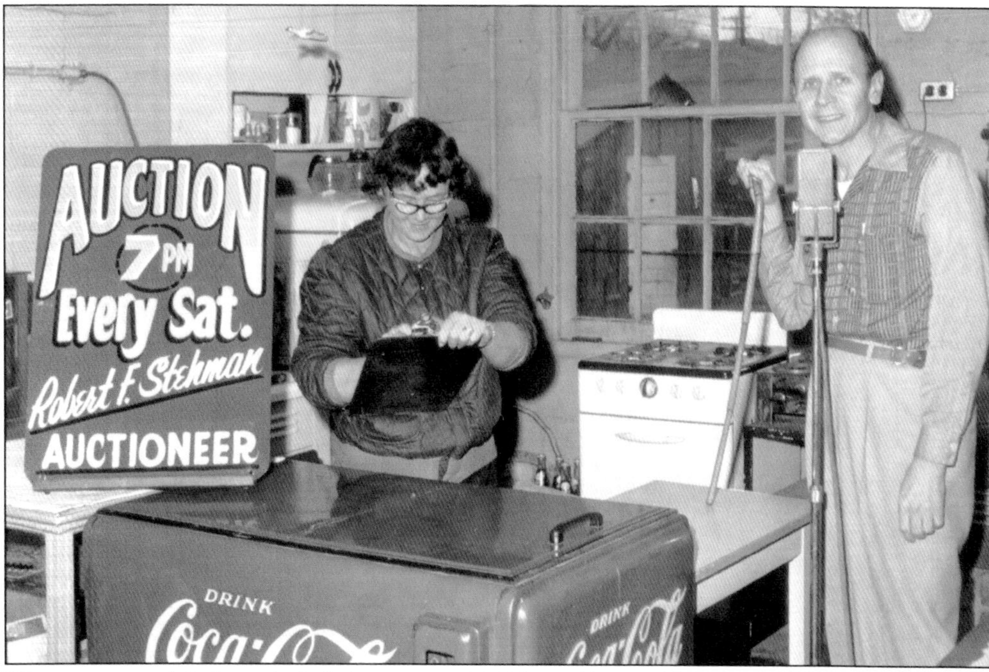

This is a view of Stehman's A-1 Auction at 1248 Lyon Street. (February 1965)

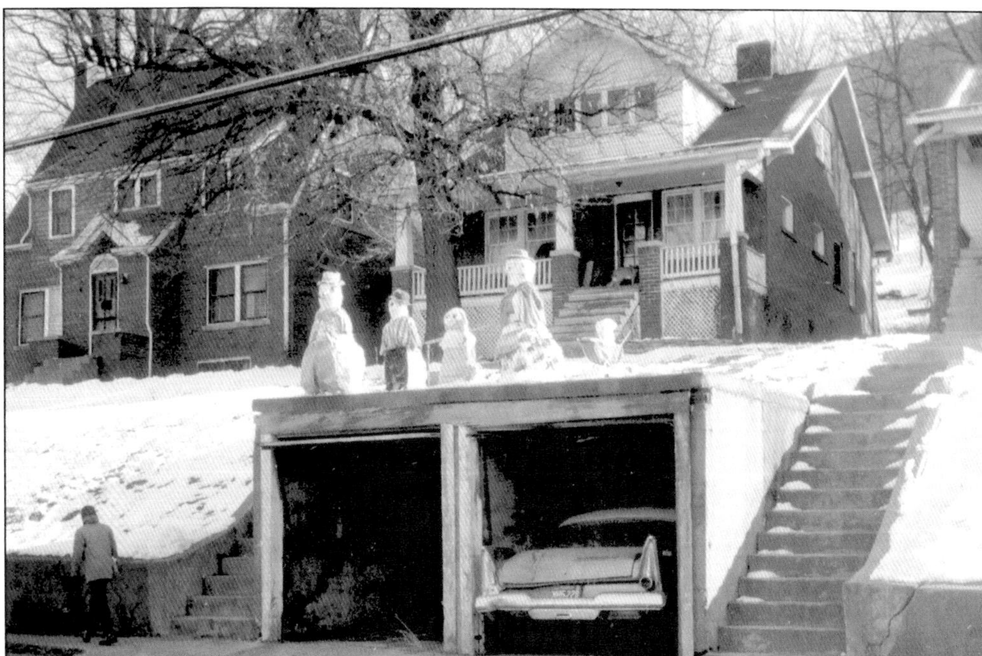
This photo captures a scene that probably caught Otis' eye as he was driving by. The snowman family built atop a garage at 3629 St. Mary's Avenue was built by owner Robert Faulkner and his daughters, Gigi, age 6, and Jenny, age 3. Mrs. Faulkner and 18-month-old Kevin provided moral support. The garage has since been removed, and judging from the tight fit of their car and the location on a busy avenue, one can guess why. (March 1965)

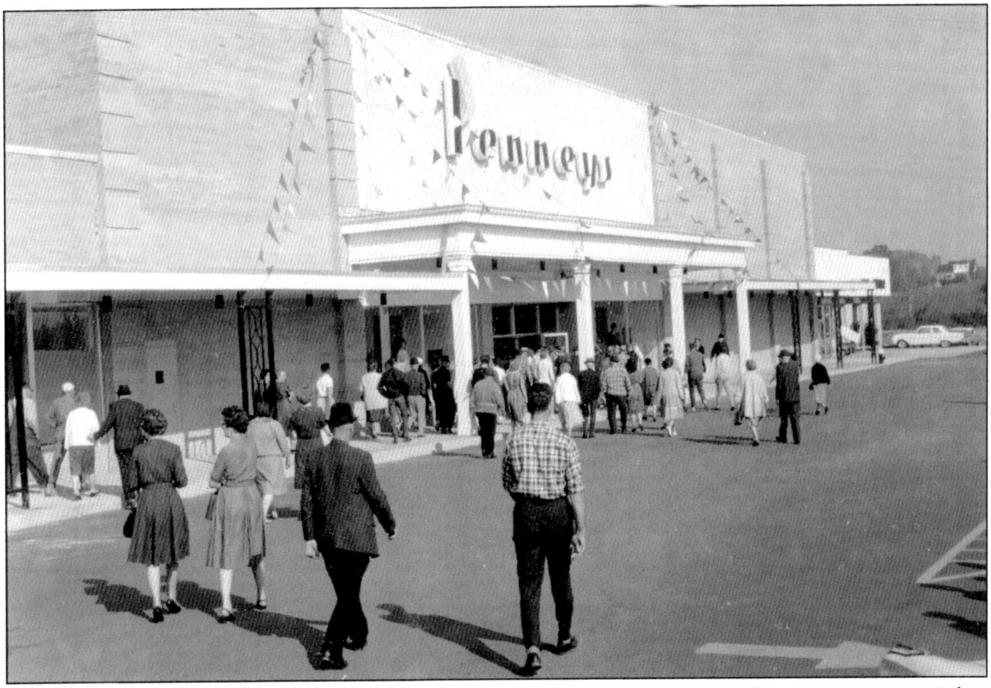

This is the grand opening of J.C. Penney's new store at the Huck Finn Shopping Center. After having been located on South Main Street for years, J.C. Penney moved into the modern era of shopping. (October 1965)

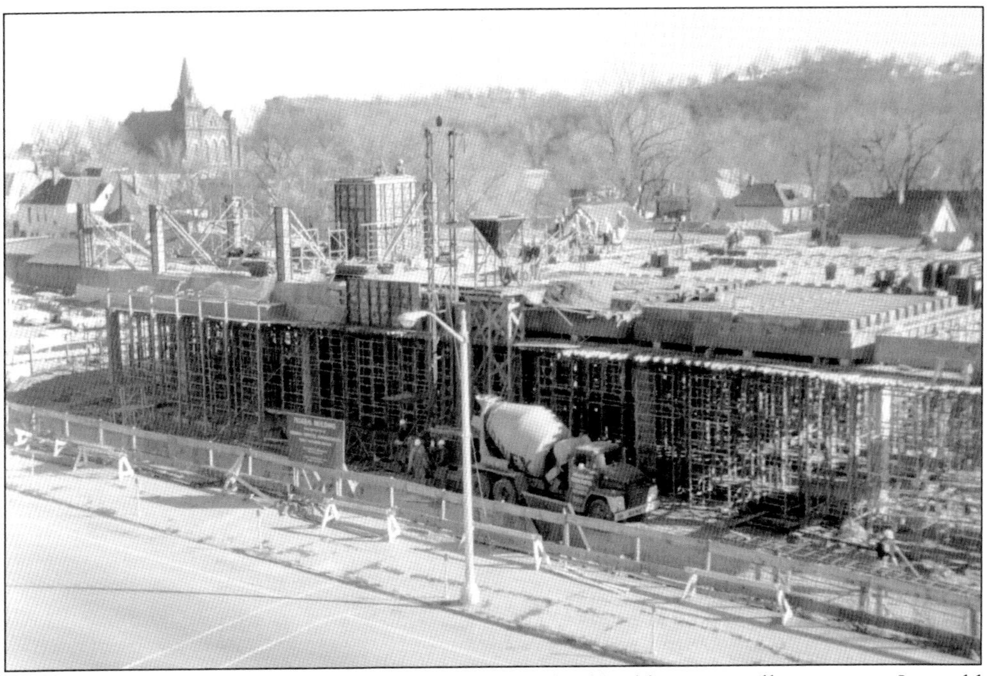

In November 1965, construction work on the new Federal building was well on its way. It would formally open to the public in 1967. Notice the Immaculate Conception Church standing tall in the background. The old steeple would be removed in 1970.

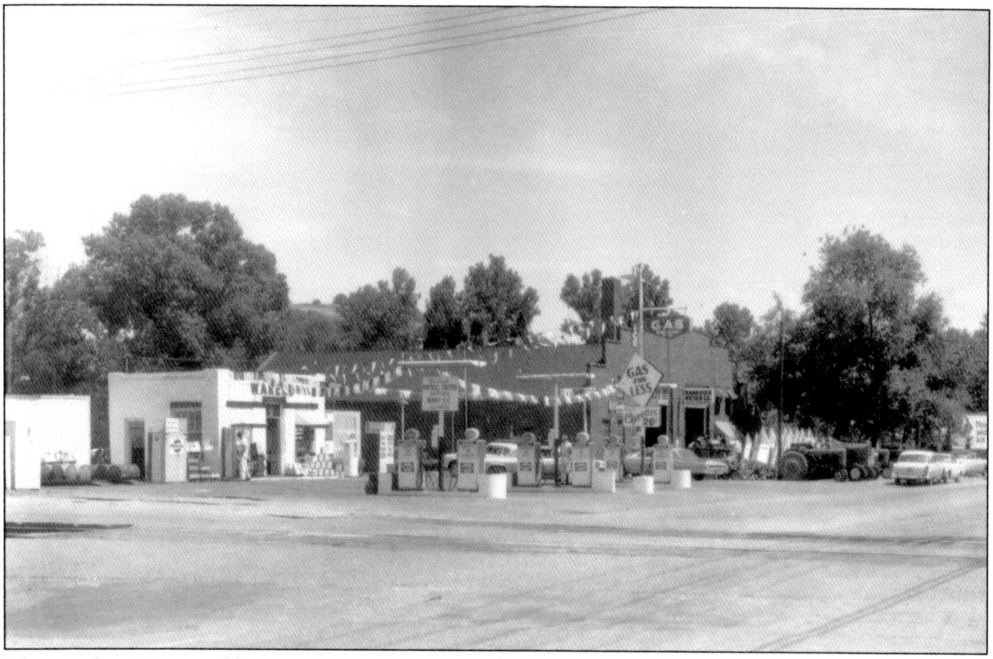

This is the Wareco filling station at 406 South Third, as it appeared in July 1966. Harrison Motors is visible just beyond.

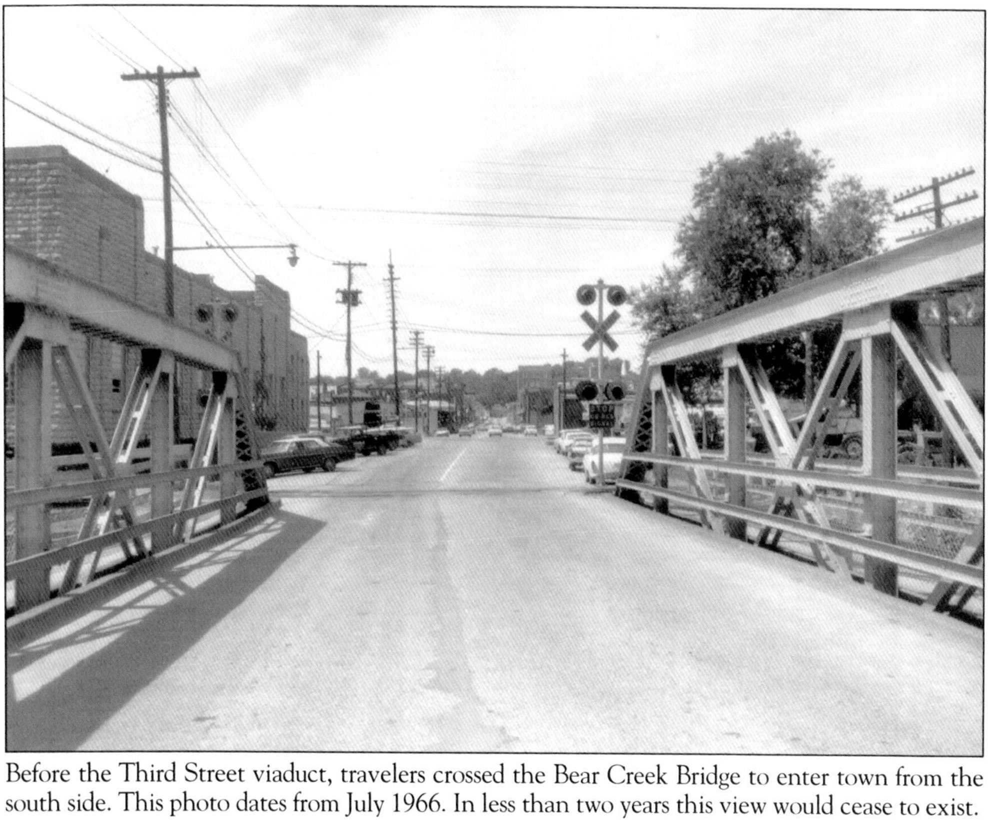

Before the Third Street viaduct, travelers crossed the Bear Creek Bridge to enter town from the south side. This photo dates from July 1966. In less than two years this view would cease to exist.

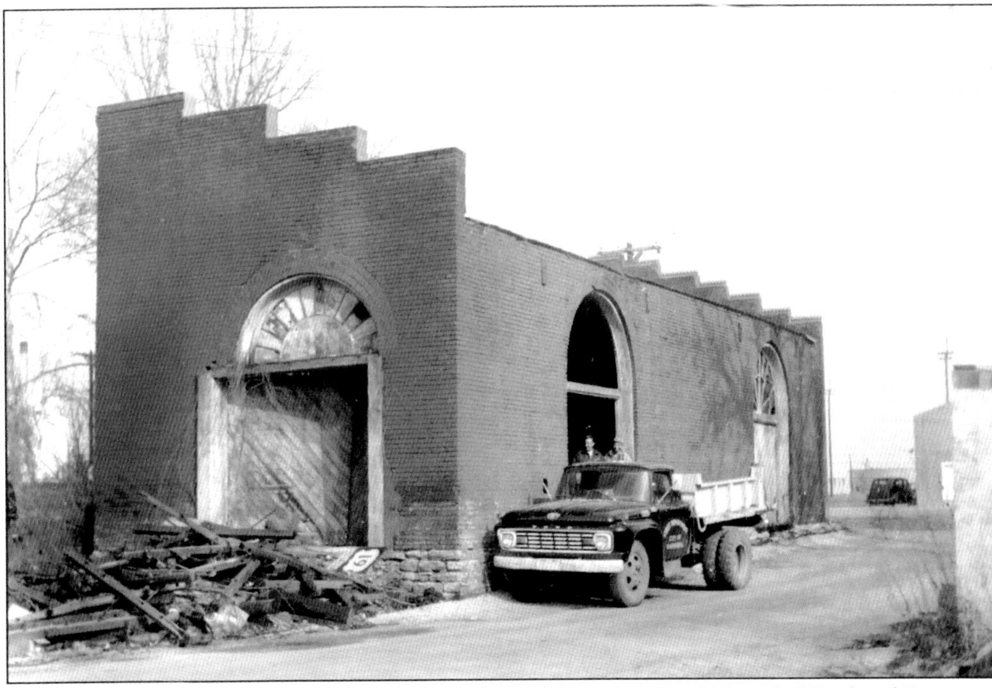

In 1967, workers demolished what remained of the old St. Louis and Hannibal Railroad Depot on the 500 block of South Main. Built in the 1870s, its primary functionality ended when the St. Louis & Hannibal Railroad folded in 1944. Most recently, the building had been used for storage.

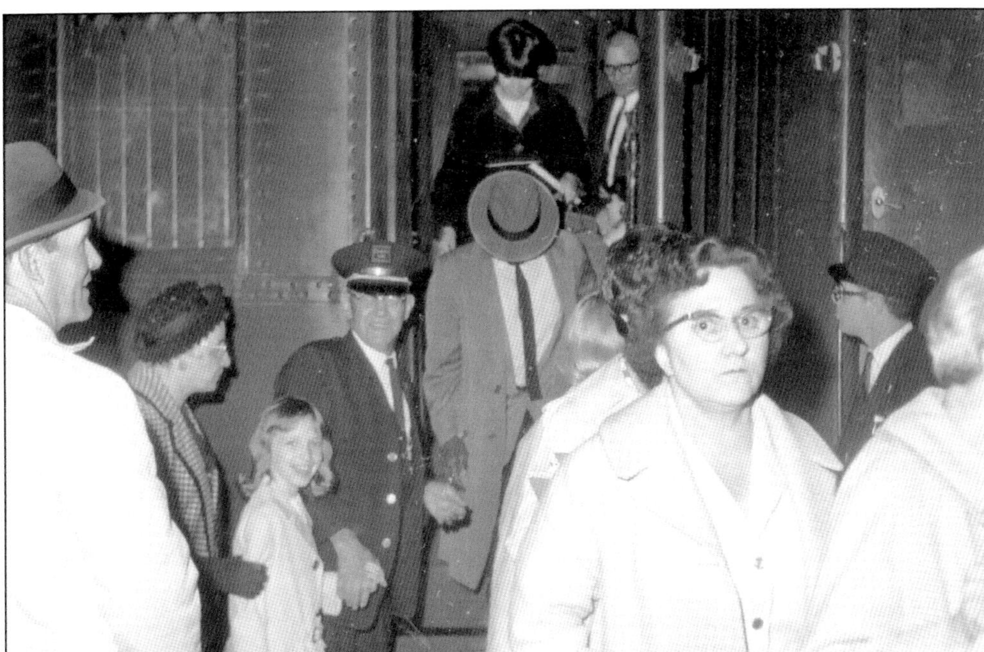

Another major footnote in railroad history occurred in 1967. On April 8, the last run of passenger rail service left the Burlington Depot. As people began to travel by bus and automobile more and more following World War II, it became difficult to make passenger runs paying propositions.

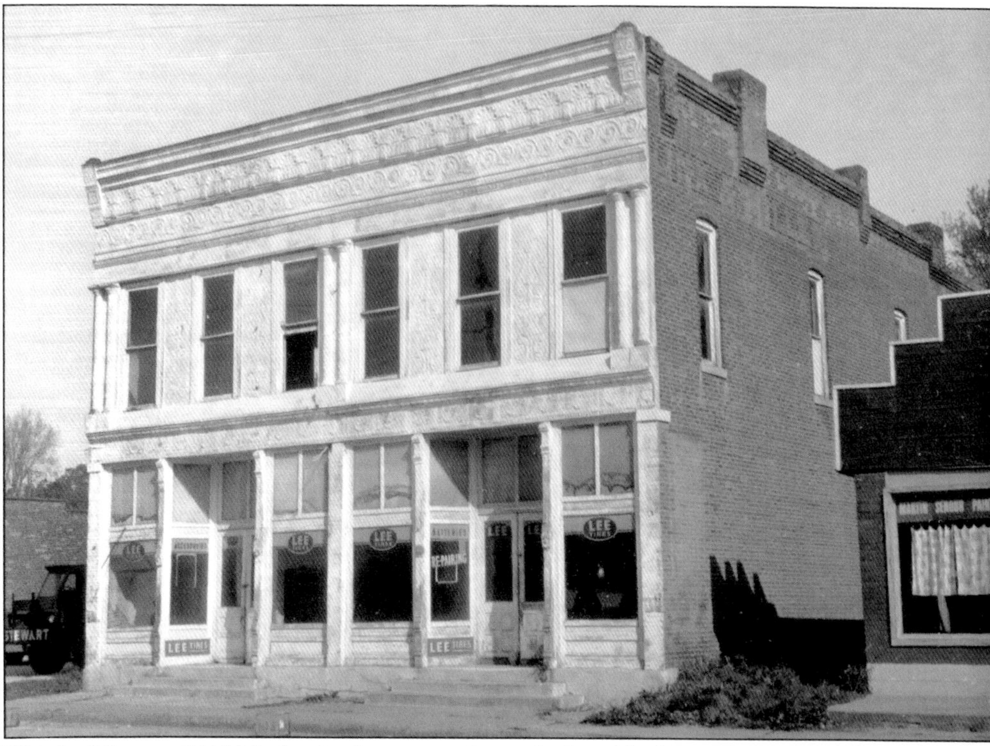

This building at 3414 Market had come to the end of its life. It was being torn down in order to construct a parking lot for Link's Market. What made this noteworthy was the fact that this building had been erected in 1884 by Link's grandfather for a grocery. As of 2004, this is the parking lot of Oakwood Market. (May 1967)

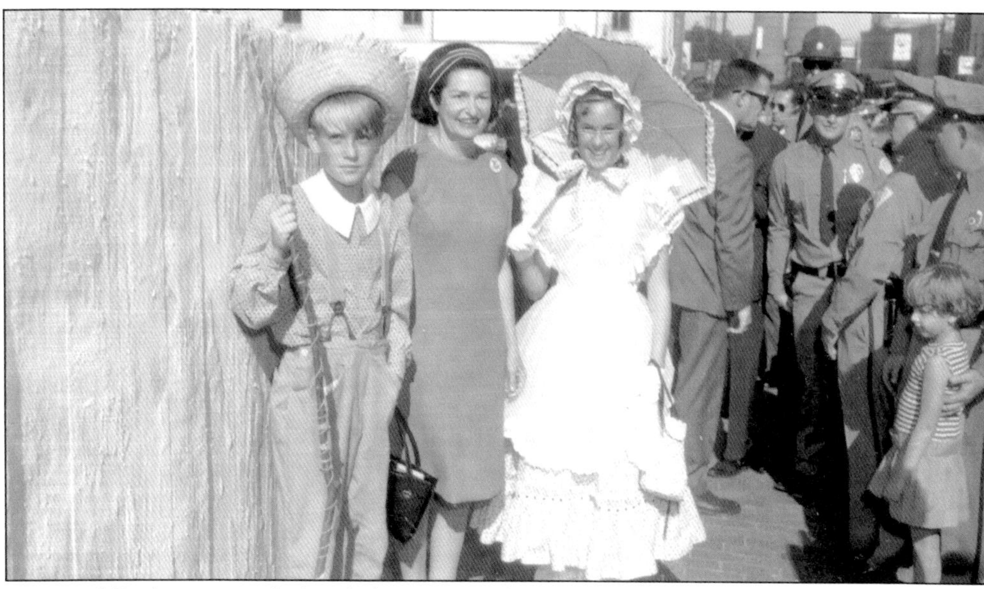

Tom and Becky pose with first lady Mrs. Lyndon B. Johnson during her visit to Hannibal. The photo was taken in front of fence at the Mark Twain Home. Tom was portrayed by John Webdell, and Becky by Mary Beth Orscheln. (September 1967)

INDEX